DEALING WITH DIFFICULT SITUATIONS

AT WORK AND AT HOME

ROBERTA CAVA

Copyright © 2013 by Roberta Cava

All rights reserved. No part of this work covered by the copyrights hereon may be reproduced or used in any form or by any means - graphic, electronic or mechanical, including photocopying, recording, taping or information storage and retrieval systems - without the prior written permission of the publisher.

Dealing with Difficult Situations

At Work and at Home

Roberta Cava

Published by Cava Consulting

105 / 3 Township Drive,

Burleigh Heads, 4220, Queensland, Australia

info@dealingwithdifficultpeople.info

Discover other titles by Roberta Cava at
www.dealingwithdifficultpeople.info

National Library of Australia

Cataloguing-in-publication data:

ISBN 978-09872594-6-2

BOOKS BY ROBERTA CAVA

Dealing with Difficult People;
(22 publishers – in 16 languages);
Dealing with Difficult Situations; at Work and at Home;
Dealing with Difficult Spouses and Children;
Dealing with Difficult Relatives and In-Laws;
Dealing with School Bullying;
Dealing with Workplace Bullying;
What am I going to do with the rest of my life?
Before tying the knot; Questions couples Must ask each other
Before they marry!
How Women can advance in business;
Survival Skills for Supervisors and Managers;
Human Resources at its Best!
Human Resources Policies and Procedures;
Employee Handbook;
Easy Come; Hard to go; The Art of Hiring,
Disciplining and Firing Employees;
Time and Stress; Today's Silent Killers;
Take Command of your Future; Make things Happen
Belly Laughs for All! Volumes 1 to 4
Wisdom of the World – The happy, sad and wise things in life

Dealing with Difficult Situations

At Work and At Home
Table of Contents

Introduction   *11*

Part 1 – At Work

Chapter 1 – Difficult Situations – The Boss   *15*

Supervisors from Hell!
Disciplines in public
Process of feedback
The bullying boss - tantrums
Sexual harassment
Are moody- have unpredictable behaviour
Boss labels me - doesn't value or respect others' opinions
Won't back up staff
Lack of proper job description
Employee development and training
Performance appraisals
Leadership style of supervisor/manager
Do as I say - not do as I do
Lacking company policies and procedures
Poor work ethic
No development - low interest in job
Supervisor not available
Won't listen to my ideas
Boss is a perfectionist
Workaholic Boss
Supervising former peers
Manager lets staff by- pass me
Authoritarian Style of Management - Abuse of Power
Won't discipline staff
Personality clashes
Favouritism and Bias
Poor Role Model
Can't manage time

Nepotism
Won't keep promises
Immature Supervisor

Chapter 2 – Difficult Situations - Subordinates   43

I hate being a supervisor!
What is a supervisor?
Supervisor has tantrums
Helping your employees accept change
Young female supervisor
Women supervising men
Hired the wrong person
Reference checking
Aggressive worker
Low Productivity
Staff motivators
I lead - but they won't follow!
Coffee and smoke break abuses
The overlong lunch hour
Personal phone calls
Ethnic problems
Buck-passing employees
Work avoidance
Interrupters
The 'Silent Treatment'
Difficult counselling interviews
Sick leave abusers
The alcoholic employee
Error-prone employees
Employee daydreaming
Show offs
Won't answer phone calls and emails

Chapter 3 – Difficult Situations – Colleagues and Others   87

Answering phone messages
Dysfunctional childhood
Serviceman gets uncivil treatment
Customer service
Colleague has tantrums
What a chauvinist!

Sarcasm
Power trips
Problem meeting participants
Why do assertive women intimidate some men?
Staff object to my style of management
Dating colleagues and clients
Dating mentors
Saboteur - or I'll go through the motions - but will fight you every step of the way!
Personality clashes
Always slow
Procrastinator
Lateness
Know-it-alls
Class clowns
Gossip
Sticky-iffies (backhanded compliments)
Held back from a promotion
Freezes under pressure
Bashful
Self-beraters
Uninvolved
Sham assertive
Bootlickers
Over-committers – renegers
Stalking co-worker
Email abuses

Chapter 4 – Difficult Situations – Unhappy at Work   123

I hate my job!
Anger expressed at work
Mid-life crisis
Reasons for choosing the wrong career
Career decisions
The rewards of choosing the right career
Overlooked for a promotion

Dealing with Difficult Situations

Part 2 – At Home

Chapter 5 – Difficult Situations - Couples **141**

Confused messages
Male/female friendships
Emotional abuse and sniping
Equality
Breadwinner/child and home care roles
The two-career couple - can their marriage survive?
Getting help at home
Home time management
Guilt giving

Chapter 6 – Difficult Situations - Wives **157**

Moody
Unwarranted fears
Everyone must love me!
Guilt
Stealing from work
Wife sexually harassed at work
Want some peace and quiet!
Battle of the sexes
Wife wants more intimacy
She mumbles
Has high-pitched voice
Misunderstandings
Can't read maps
I need solutions - not emotional support
I never get my way!
My wife is a nag!
Indecisive
Worrier
Dependent

Chapter 7 – Difficult Situations - Husbands **179**

The 'Silent Treatment'
Use of humour
Non-verbal communication

Rush hour traffic
Can't say 'No'
Workaholic husband
Forgetful or neglect
Blasted from our bedroom
Husband is a poor listener
Explosive issues
We're lost!
My husband - the expert
Disinterested husband
Husband won't discuss his work
Unresolved conflicts
Won't argue
Controlling husband
No will
Makes all the decisions
Jealous husband

Chapter 8 – Difficult Situations - Children   *199*

Children in control
Using feedback
Can't you do anything right?
Not as smart as your brother
Destructive criticism
Compulsive behaviour
Low self-esteem
Neglected children
Lying
Tattle Tale
Pretends he's sick
Falling behind at schooling
Dealing with tantrums
The 'Terrible Two's'
Battling children
Dealing with bullies
Monkey see - monkey do
Stay together for the children
Divorce
Summer vacation blues
Mother/daughter relationships

Daughter's dating
Sloppiness
Spends too much on clothes
Boy crazy
Daughter wants contraceptives
Double standard
Secretive
Jealousy and envy

Chapter 9 – Difficult Situations - Seniors 235

I want to stay in my home!
Alzheimer's Disease
After all I've done for you!
Dealing with retirement
Building security
Dangerous inaccessibility
Heart problems
English as a second language
Not important any more
Handling grief
We're taking away your driver's licence!
Step children
Undisciplined grandchildren
Clinging to son
Whiners, whingers and complainers
Role reversal
I won't fight - but I won't give in either!
The sufferer - after all I've done for you!
Can't wake up
Always phoning
Allergies

Conclusion 261

Bibliography 263

INTRODUCTION

This book is a compilation of many of the newspaper and magazine articles I have written over the years to help others deal with difficult people and situations. If you have to deal with irate, rude, impatient, emotional, persistent or aggressive people in your business or family life - you'll likely find them in this book.

Have you started your morning feeling happy with the world, but find your day going rapidly downhill because of the difficult situations you encounter? Do you let other people or situations control what kind of day you have? Do you often feel as if you are not in control during difficult situations? It's the little annoyances that can ruin your day, so if you can handle them constructively, you're certainly ahead of the game. Learning to deal with difficult people involves learning how to manage your side of a two-way transaction. This gives the other person a chance to work with you to resolve whatever is making him or her difficult. Although you might make several attempts to change other's difficult behaviour - your chances of making a difference depend upon the receptiveness of your difficult people to change. What you do have full control over however - is your reaction to others' difficult behaviour.

Difficult people are the ones who try to:

- Make us loose our cool;
- Force us to do things we don't want to do;
- Prevent us from doing what we want or need to do; often use coercion, manipulation or other underhanded methods to get their way;
- Make us feel guilty if we don't go along with their wishes;
- Make us feel anxious, upset, frustrated, angry, depressed, jealous, inferior, defeated, sad or any other negative feeling;
- Make us do their share of the work.

People come in all shapes and sizes and they also display many kinds of behaviour. The five major kinds of behaviour are: passive, passive-resistant, assertive, indirect aggressive and aggressive.

Most people use rational tactics including logic and bargaining to show they're willing to comply or compromise to find the best solution to differences. They negotiate by giving up a little, if the other person agrees to do the same. Many find both positive and negative manipulation effective for influencing others to do what they want. Positive manipulation is good; because it helps others improve their lives. This manipulation includes giving praise, recognition and encouragement and is welcomed.

'Game players' however; use negative manipulation to acquire what they want by the use of passive resistant, indirect aggressive, aggressive or passive/aggressive behaviour. Their negative games are manipulative and dishonest and use indirect and unclear communication. Many playing games aren't even aware they're doing so and can't understand other's negative reactions. Although some may achieve a temporary sense of power, if they're caught playing games, others' trust in them vanishes.

What tactics do you use when trying to persuade someone to do something? Do you try to manipulate others by using negative manipulation? Could others object to this manipulation and result in many of the difficult situations you face? As you read the examples in this book ask yourself if you too could be guilty of any of the situations that cause such grief to others.

Throughout this book, I describe techniques that work. How do I know they work? Because over 54,000 participants world-wide have attended my ***Dealing with Difficult People*** seminars.

The contents of this book are not to be construed as being professional advice. In some instances I have quoted laws, but readers must always check their Federal and State laws to ensure that they are acting according to the laws in their areas. Any decision made by the reader as a result of reading this book, is the sole responsibility of the reader.

PART 1

AT WORK

Dealing with Difficult Situations

CHAPTER 1

DIFFICULT SITUATIONS - THE 'BOSS'

Supervisors from hell!

Who causes the most trouble and are the most difficult people to deal with in the workplace? Is it clients, colleagues, subordinates or 'the boss?'

When I first started offering my *'Dealing with Difficult People'* seminars, I assumed that 'off the wall' clients would be the most difficult group to deal with in the workplace. My second guess - was difficult colleagues. I was wrong in making those assumptions. My research has proven (confirmed by the more than 54,000 participants of my seminars) that the most difficult people faced by those in the workplace are not clients, colleagues or subordinates - but overwhelmingly, the employees' supervisors or managers!

Why is this the case? Because those who are responsible for completion of tasks by others, have not obtained proper supervisory training. Even though these people have titles such as: supervisor, foreman/woman, manager, superintendent, department head, vice president or even C.E.O. most have not received the basic training necessary to enable them to successfully supervise others. Some believe that if they have a BA or MBA degree, they have received adequate training. However, basic supervisory training is not part of most BA or MBA degree programs.

These difficult supervisors (I use the word supervisor - but this includes all the above titles) make mistakes such as:

- Discipline their staff in front of workmates or clients.
- Harass staff (either through bullying or sexual harassment).
- Have temper tantrums.
- Are moody - have unpredictable behaviour.
- Label their staff's behaviour (stupid, dumb) or make sarcastic remarks, instead of trying to correct the actual behaviour of the staff member.
- Don't value or respect others opinions (especially their subordinates).
- Don't provide the necessary training to fill the gap between the job requirements and the employee's skills.

Dealing with Difficult Situations

- Are not available when their staff need their help.
- Don't give recognition for a job well done. Instead of concentrating on the 98 per cent their staff do right, they concentrate on the two per cent they do incorrectly.
- Don't back up their staff when dealing with customer complaints. (The customer complains and instead of backing their staff, they commiserate with the client and don't give their employee the opportunity to defend his or her side of the story.)
- Don't provide an up-to-date job description with key performance indicators (KPIs) and standards of performance for the tasks performed to achieve those KPIs.
- Conduct performance appraisals on staff without a proper job description upon which to base their evaluation. (If staff members don't know what's expected of them and neither does the supervisor - how do supervisors have the audacity to attempt an evaluation on how well their employees performed their duties?)
- Use the same leadership style on all staff members, even though a different leadership style is required. (Some need step-by-step instructions - others just need an outline of what is required to complete the task - Theory X vs. Theory Y management styles).
- Have one set of company rules for staff - another for themselves (do as I say - not do as I do). They bend the rules when clients go over the head of front-line staff, causing embarrassment for staff member.
- Don't provide policy and procedure or employee manuals that outline the company rules and regulations for all staff.
- Have poor work ethic.
- Do nothing to improve the employee's interest in their jobs (lack of development).
- Won't listen to their staff's suggestions about better ways to complete tasks.
- Have a negative *'That will never work'* attitude toward changes suggested by their staff.
- Are perfectionists and expect everything to be done perfectly.
- Are workaholics and expect their staff to be the same.
- Use authoritarian management style, which just results in resistance from staff.
- Don't step in to resolve personality conflicts between staff.
- Abuse their position power.

Dealing with Difficult Situations

- Don't know how to handle the problems that occur when promoted into a position where they're supervising former peers.
- Upper management have not given these supervisors the full responsibility to perform their duties properly (i.e.: Delegate and check staff's work, complete performance appraisals on employees reporting to them, discipline employees as required and preferably hire their own staff).
- If staff member's behaviour requires correction, the supervisor either ignores the issue (hoping it will go away) or bungles the disciplinary interview that results in retaliation - rather than a needed change in the employee's behaviour.
- Show favouritism to 'pet employees' (socialise with only one or two of their staff) or show bias (either gender or race related) towards staff members.
- Poor role models.
- Don't know how to manage their time and become a bottleneck to productivity of their employees. Staff either don't have enough to do or are kept in a panic to complete last-minute assignments.
- Allow nepotism with all its unique problems.
- Don't keep promises.
- Too immature for a supervisory role - use poor judgement when making decisions.
- Are wishy washy - can't say *'No'* to requests, so overload staff with assignments.
- Bring personal problems into the workplace.
- Promoted too soon - did not receive proper training to fulfil the obligations of a supervisory/management position.

If this describes the actions of your supervisors or managers - seriously consider providing them with the necessary tools they need to do their jobs properly. Will this take a long time and cost too much? No - learning the basics of supervision won't involve as much time as you might expect - and look at the rewards - an effective, productive environment and highly motivated staff!

Here are some examples of these aforementioned problems:

Dealing with Difficult Situations

Disciplines in public

'My boss has a habit of disciplining his staff in front of clients and co-workers. This happened to me last week and I'm still seething. It's affecting my work and I can't change how I feel until I do something about this. But what do I do to make sure it won't happen again?'

This is an example of bullying so, before you do anything about this situation; prepare yourself for the eventuality that things might get worse before they get better. Check your company policies and procedures manuals to learn how bullying is handled in your company. Document what happened to you and when it happened. Talk privately with your supervisor using feedback to let him or her know how the behaviour has affected you.

Say, *'I have a problem and I need your help in solving it. I'd like to talk to you about something that's affecting my productivity. Last week you disciplined me in front of clients and colleagues. I found this very demoralising and embarrassing. I'd like to request that if you need to correct my behaviour in the future, that you do so in private, where your comments won't be overheard.'* Then show him/her the company policy relating to bullying.

The three steps in the process of feedback are as follows:

PROCESS OF FEEDBACK

a) Describe the problem or situation to the person causing the difficulty. Give examples.
b) Define what feelings or reactions their behaviour causes you (sadness, anger, anxiety, hurt or upset).
c) Suggest a solution or ask them to provide one.

The Problem: *'Last week you disciplined me in front of clients and my colleagues'*

Your feelings or reactions: *'I found this very demoralising and embarrassing.'*

The solution: *'If you need to correct my behaviour in the future, that you do so in private, where your comments won't be overheard.'*

Dealing with Difficult Situations

If the supervisor refuses to change and continues to discipline you in public, go higher up the chain of command. Here are the steps to take:

1. If this is the supervisor's normal behaviour with all his/her staff, have a meeting with the affected staff and ask whether they're willing to complain as well. If they agree that they too want the behaviour to stop, have them write down their complaints and sign the complaints (so they won't back out later). They would include details of what happened to them:

   What was said?
   When it happened;
   Who was involved?
   Damage to customer relations;
   Loss of productivity; and
   What has been done so far to try to stop the unacceptable behaviour?

2. Ask for a meeting with the supervisor. All complainants will attend and discuss your collective complaints.
3. If the supervisor doesn't listen or change his/her behaviour - as a group go to the supervisor's boss or to your Human Resources representative with your complaints. Identify your supervisor's actions as bullying and ask them to ensure that the bullying won't continue.
4. If your boss's boss and the Human Resources representatives don't (or won't) solve the problem, ask for a transfer to another department away from the bully.
5. You may decide bite the bullet and take the next step and take your boss to court for bullying.
6. As a last resort you may have to leave for greener pastures elsewhere. When you feel your boss has removed all the pride and pleasure you get from your work - it's time to leave.

The bullying boss - Tantrums

'My boss is a tyrant and a bully. He even has temper tantrums. You'd think we were on a football field the way he treats his employees. He disciplines in public, hollers at employees, belittles staff and is patronising and chauvinistic towards women. He's hated, rather than respected, by the entire staff. How should I deal with him?'

Dealing with Difficult Situations

Bullying is a learned behaviour and unless it's stopped when they're children, this behaviour can become a way of life. Bullying at any level is a play on power and is unacceptable everywhere in society. And when the victim complains about the bullying, they're often labelled a 'woos' or a 'sissy' by the bully. How dare these bullies try to make their victims feel guilty when they're the ones who are in the wrong! Bullies are cowards who don't play fair. They use their power (be it perceived or real) to lord it over others and desperately need anger management.

Unfortunately, in Australia the bullying laws are still in their infancy and there is little legal protection for workers. If workers do take the bully to court, they face hefty legal bills with no assurance that they will be reimbursed for those expenses. Many just throw up their hands, leave the company and learn from the experience - and the bully gets off again. This is the new millennium and yet some companies are still operating with cavemen/women mentalities. I've witnessed bullying in the workplace so often that I've come to believe that this draconian style of behaviour is not only tolerated, but seems to be the norm, rather than the exception in Australian companies. But is that any excuse for not stopping this unacceptable behaviour?

Some companies have policies on how to deal with bullying but don't follow-through and protect their workers against it. Hence the employee is forced to take it to court. Victorian laws are making a stab at dealing with this unacceptable behaviour but these changes fall short of the mark by insisting that bullying must be repetitive and ongoing. To the victim - one incident of bullying is enough and should have all the protection of the law to deal with it. There should be zero tolerance to bullying - by society, companies and the law.

If you've already talked to your boss about how repulsed you are by his/her bullying and nothing has changed - you have no choice but to go over his head. However, be prepared - because even his/her superiors might do nothing to stop the bullying. You may have to leave your employment and look for work elsewhere (with no guarantee that you won't run into it in the new company). The other alternative is to prepare for a lengthy and costly legal battle in the courts. It's your choice.

Now how to deal with the tantrums. Don't try to stop him in mid-stream of his tantrum. Simply listen and force yourself not to be affected by the anger and frustration he's trying to thrust upon you. When he finally finishes his tirade say, *'I can see you're angry about this. Why don't I give you a chance to calm down – then we can discuss this issue.'* Then walk away. If he continues to behave in this manner say, *'I'm very uncomfortable being around you when you're out of control. This is unacceptable behaviour and is a form of harassment and bullying. When you've calmed down, I'll be glad to discuss this rationally with you.'*

Make sure you document each incident where his behaviour is unacceptable (having a witness helps) and either go to his superior or to your Human Resources representative to initiate charges of harassment.

Sexual harassment

'Our company doesn't have a sexual harassment policy. My boss is constantly telling dirty jokes at work, but I don't have any guidelines to follow so I can deal with it.'

Organisations have a responsibility to ensure the workplace is free from harassment. Sexual harassment is a term covering unwelcome sexual behaviour and is unlawful, direct discrimination on the ground of sex. Co-workers, as well as superiors may be responsible and charged for acts of sexual harassment.

A complaint of sexual harassment does not necessarily mean that sexual harassment has actually taken place. Organisations have been charged with reverse discrimination. This happens when employees don't receive merited promotions and bonuses. Instead, a workmate receives them in return for sexual favours given to a supervisor.

No longer can others in positions of power 'look the other way' and ignore that sexual harassment is occurring. For instance, if I'm a supervisor and do nothing when I see another person sexually harassing an employee, it's believed that I've condoned the action. If the employee knows that I saw or know about the situation and do nothing, s/he can charge both the offender and the witnessing supervisor (me) with sexual harassment.

Each incident in itself may be relatively minor, but if continued over a prolonged period, can be very stressful to the victim. Harassment can produce a hostile work environment that can adversely affect the terms and conditions of employment and make it impossible for the

Dealing with Difficult Situations

person to continue employment. Sexual harassment amounts to unlawful sex discrimination if an employee is obliged to continue to work in an environment which is generally hostile demeaning or intimidating.

In Australia, it's been established that most sex discrimination is against women. An employer has a legal responsibility to ensure that there are no policies or practices operating within an organisation that directly or indirectly discriminate against women. An employer can be vicariously liable for the actions of an employee even if the employer was unaware of the actual actions of the employee. If your company doesn't have a sexual harassment policy - insist that they prepare one and make it available to all staff members. Many companies have sexual harassment advisors.

Research shows that seventy to eighty per cent of women have experienced one or more forms of sexual harassment while working. Fifty-two per cent of them lost a job because of it. This is criminal and needs swift action to eliminate such future harassment.

It's important to take steps to prevent sexual harassment in the workplace. Line management needs information about what harassment is and how to receive, investigate and resolve complaints. It's also essential that managers are aware of their responsibilities and the organisation's policy on sexual harassment.

If you believe you have been sexually harassed, it's up to you to check your State Harassment laws. Should you be the object of sexual harassment you should:

1. Tell the person that you object to whatever s/he's doing or saying. *Let him or her know you really mean it!* If necessary, explain that his/her behaviour is a form of sexual harassment and you expect it to stop immediately. Record everything that happens - date, time, events, witnesses, etc. Recognise that you're probably not the only one who's been sexually harassed by this person. Find out if there are others so you can lodge a group complaint.
2. If the person does the same thing (or something similar) again, repeat your earlier objections. Back this up with a written letter or e-mail. Relate to your earlier verbal complaints. State only the facts, not assumptions. Make at least four copies of this letter. Send one copy to the offending person; one to his or her supervisor, your supervisor (and the Chief Executive Officer of

Dealing with Difficult Situations

your company if you think it's appropriate). Keep one copy for your records

3. If the behaviour continues or the company or union has not dealt with it, lodge a formal complaint with your local Equal Employment Opportunities Commission. When in doubt, call your local E.E.O. office and talk to a trained counsellor. If the situation involves physical assault, involve the police by lodging a sexual assault charge.

Note: If the first incident is serious enough, object verbally, send a letter (with copies to applicable parties) and lodge a formal complaint with the Equal Employment Opportunities Commission. *See Chapter 6 for more on this topic.*

Are moody, have unpredictable behaviour

'I can never predict what kind of day I'll have because of my boss's moods and unpredictable behaviour. How can someone with that kind of temperament be in a position of power? Because she's my boss - I need to know how I should deal with the behaviour.'

Most moody people are very immature, have low self-esteem and many feel they have to take every affront personally. Follow above instructions on feedback and start documenting her behaviour in case you decide to take further action.

Boss labels me doesn't value or respect others' opinions

'My boss is hypercritical of my work and uses labels to describe my behaviour. He uses such words as 'stupid' and 'dumb' to describe my behaviour. On my performance appraisal he said he didn't like my 'attitude.' How can I get him to concentrate on the 98% of the work I do right - instead of labelling me and concentrating on the 2% I do wrong?'

The boss who labels employees (rather than deal with their behaviour) is bound to de-motivate his or her staff. Talk to your supervisor privately. Say, *'I have a problem and I need your help in solving it. On my performance appraisal, you put down that you didn't like my attitude, but when I asked for specifics you refused to give them to me. And the last few times you've corrected my work you've said that I was 'stupid' and 'dumb.' I'm upset that you've*

Dealing with Difficult Situations

given me those labels and I don't know how to improve my performance or what you really want from me.

I'd like to go back to the comment from my performance appraisal about my 'attitude. What did I do wrong that you objected to?'

Her supervisor replied, *'Well, you were rude to Mrs. Brown.'* (Rude is another label that does not discuss her behaviour.)

'What specifically did I say to Mrs. Brown that was rude?'

'You told her that you had better things to do with your time other than listen to her constant complaints.'

Now the employee knows what is wrong with her 'attitude' and can change her behaviour accordingly.

The employee did the same with the other two labels and was able to determine the exact behaviour that was not suitable. Only then did she have something she could deal with and change.

At a later meeting with her supervisor where he complimented her on a task well done, she replied, *'Thanks for the compliment. I have to admit that I'm so used to hearing about the things I do wrong that it's a pleasure to receive confirmation about the things I've done right.'*

Lack of proper job descriptions

'My company doesn't think it's important that we have proper job descriptions. Mine just generalise in a paragraph what I am supposed to do. I'd like to have a better one, but don't know how I should go about it.'

Many companies use position descriptions that are disgustingly inadequate and don't include the essential information needed in today's workplace. Some only have a paragraph describing what the person does and others go a bit further to include Key Performance Indicators (KPIs), so believe their job descriptions are adequate. This is not enough. In addition to other pertinent information, a proper job description includes the following.

- A general description of what the person does (in paragraph form),
- A list of Key Performance Indicators.

Dealing with Difficult Situations

- Under each KPI is a list of the tasks that are performed to ensure that the KPI is reached.
- Each task includes benchmarks or standards of performance that are measurable (rather than subjective). These measures include quality, quantity, time and can include cost if relevant.

Use the following to convince your company why the above type of position description is essential for the smooth running of the company:

- It's the primary tool to determine qualifications for recruiting new employees.
- It's an excellent training tool to compare an employee's capabilities against those required by the position allowing the company to determine the required training to fill that gap.
- Many government training grants to companies require a detailed job description so they can determine what is required of employees compared to their present level of knowledge and ability.
- Both the employee and employer know exactly what the employee is to do and the employee's performance can be measured against clear written objectives.
- Duties do not 'fall through the cracks' and eliminates the expression, *'I didn't know I was responsible for that!'*
- Morale of employees normally rises 100% when it's clear what their employers expect from them.
- Company performance appraisals will be based on objective, rather than subjective measures. There are no surprises at performance appraisal time, because it's clear to both the employee and their supervisor exactly what is expected of the employee.
- If it becomes necessary for a supervisor to correct an employee's behaviour, it can be done based on objective (rather than subjective) reasons. Should the employee be terminated, the employer can show exactly what standards of performance were not met by the employee and the documentation to prove that the employee had an opportunity to improve his or her behaviour or performance.
- It's a vital tool for manpower planning that helps determine the gaps between the employees' skills and abilities and those required to fill their next promotional position.

Employee development and training

'I've been trying to get ahead in my organisation but find that the men are given training and the women are not. I've made sure the training department and my boss know that I want to get ahead and am interested in relevant training - but I'm still overlooked. I've asked for training on my past three performance appraisals, but still no training. What do I do next?'

This could be a case of sexual discrimination. Many organisations offer a variety of on-the-job training for their employees, but frequently, women are denied access to these training courses. Their managers make incorrect or stereotypical assumptions about the working patterns of women and the number of years women intend to remain in the workforce. These assumptions are applied to all female employees - regardless of the actual job performance or career ambitions of individual women. Consequently, the organisation may not provide the information or facilities for these women to participate in training programs.

Your first step is to establish an Affirmative Action Program in your organisation. Contact the EEO (Equal Employment Opportunities) representatives in your area to assist in setting up such a program. This program will assess the skills, qualifications and ambitions of women employees so their training needs are realistically identified and will outline the employer's responsibility in providing equitable training opportunities for both male and female employees.

In assessing the training opportunities for women within the organisation, the following factors should be examined:

1. How is information on internal training courses made available throughout the organisation?
2. Is information on the content of the training courses and the potential benefit it may provide to the career path of individual employees easily available to all employees?
3. Are supervisors or others who are responsible for the selection of employees to attend training courses fully aware of the organisations' Affirmative Action program and the need to fully utilise all the talents and skills available to the organisation?
4. Are all employees actively encouraged by management to use all opportunities for training and development when they arise?

5. Are training courses conducted in convenient locations to ensure that employees with childcare or domestic responsibilities are not automatically precluded from nomination and selection?
6. Are employees encouraged to self-nominate for courses that they believe will be of benefit to their job opportunities, rather than waiting for supervisors to nominate them?

Won't back up staff

'My boss always takes the clients' side when they complain about something I've done. I don't condone the 'the customer's always right' philosophy. They're often wrong or see things only from their point of view. For once, I'd like the opportunity of giving my point of view!'

When your supervisor receives a client complaint, the first thing s/he should say to the client is, *'Let me investigate this and I'll get back to you.'* The supervisor mediates between what the client believes and what the staff member believes and come to a compromise or solution. Both the supervisor and the employee must understand that if the staff member caused the problem - the client deserves TLC (tender loving care) in the form of extra services or action. If the employee is right, the supervisor must defend his/her side of the issue and explain to the client what they can do about solving his/her complaint. This often involves suggesting two or three alternatives that will solve the client's problem.

Performance Appraisals

'My company doesn't have regular performance appraisals. My last one was two years ago. How can I convince my supervisor that I should have one?'

How often should performance appraisals be conducted? There's quite a bit of flexibility here, depending upon the needs of the position. The recommended times are: Shortly after the employee is hired, the first part of the probationary performance appraisal (which lists the expectations) is completed.

Two weeks *before* the employee's probationary performance appraisal period is over - the performance appraisal meeting is held. This is the time when the supervisor makes a decision about whether

Dealing with Difficult Situations

the employee will be accepted by the company as a permanent employee.

If the employee is accepted as a permanent employee, a new performance appraisal is started for the next evaluation period.

There are two methods of determining the employee's yearly performance appraisal thereafter: It can be held on the anniversary date of when the employee started with the company; or it could be held once a year at the same time for all employees.

Some companies have bi-yearly performance appraisals. Many companies do performance appraisals before and after every special project the staff member completes regardless of the time frame of the project. The company must decide which method is best to meet their staff's individual needs.

Performance appraisal systems that evaluate such subjective things as judgement, initiative, attitude or interpersonal skills are not fair appraisal systems and should be replaced.

There are many advantages of doing regular performance appraisals:

- Putting things down on paper makes people more specific about what they expect.
- It allows the staff member to take part in setting standards they feel they can meet.
- Makes people more productive and motivated to do a good job.
- New ideas and methods for completing tasks can be discussed and encouraged.
- Keeps people from being buried or lost in the system.
- The 'good guys' or high achievers don't get passed over.
- The 'bad guys' or low achievers and those using unacceptable behaviour, don't get to hide.
- They improve communication between supervisor and staff members. The more the employee is involved in setting his or her own standards, the more likely s/he will react positively. Employees are often their own worst critics, so should not be allowed to set unrealistic standards of performance.

If the employee doesn't measure up – s/he knows s/he's failed <u>before</u> review date. There are no surprises at performance appraisal time.

Dealing with Difficult Situations

'Even though I supervise a staff of four, my manager insists on doing my staff's performance appraisals. I think this should be one of my responsibilities as a supervisor.'

Supervisors have many responsibilities, including delegating and correcting work, conducting performance appraisals and disciplining staff that report to the position. Unfortunately many are given the title 'supervisor' but not given the authority to carry out their duties. I believe that the title 'Lead Hand' should be abolished because many just have two responsibilities - that of delegating and checking work.

Unless those who are responsible for supervising others have all four major responsibilities, their company is setting them up to fail. Supervisors should also discipline their staff (up to termination when experts step in) and do performance appraisals on all staff who report to them. A desired additional responsibility should be hiring their own staff (after the company Human Resource department or recruitment firm has chosen a short-list of suitable candidates). This way the supervisor is ensured that the candidate is in sync with both him/her and the existing staff.

Leadership style of supervisor/manager

'My boss must think I'm daft because he treats me as if I'm ten years old. I have been in the workplace for ten years and don't need to be told step-by-step how to do everything. I work in a very creative field and am creative myself. How do I let my boss know that all he has to do is explain what he wants to achieve and let me do it?'

There are many leadership styles in management - each suitable for different situations and personalities. It sounds as if you're the kind of person who needs lots of 'rope' and loose supervision. Your supervisor is leading you with a style that's more suitable to someone who has an absolute need to know exactly what steps s/he needs to take to accomplish a task. Let your boss know the kind of leadership you need from him.

You might start by saying, *'I'd like more freedom when accomplishing my tasks. I'm a creative person and usually can visualise what you want and will ask questions to clarify my picture of that. I'm uncomfortable with step-by-step instructions - and like to*

Dealing with Difficult Situations

use my own resources to do tasks. Would you feel comfortable giving me that leeway?'

Other employees may not feel comfortable unless they receive detailed instructions on how to complete tasks. They usually love routine and are knocked off-balance when changes occur. You on the other hand, love variety and will seldom do a task the same way twice. You're probably entrepreneurial and can see all kinds of ways things can be improved. If your employer doesn't allow you to use your creative juices, you'll likely go elsewhere.

Do as I say - Not do as I do

'The other day I spent half an hour explaining to a client why I couldn't do something for her because of a company regulation. She decided to go over my head to my boss. My boss gave into her. On her way out of the store the client made a point of letting me know what had occurred. There seem to be two sets of rules in our company - one for front-line staff and another for the supervisors!'

Rules and regulations of a company <u>must</u> be adhered to by <u>all</u> employees - including supervisors. Talk to your supervisor and go over his/her head if necessary to confirm company rules and regulations. Start by speaking to your supervisor,

'I have a problem and I need your help in solving it. I was upset yesterday after I'd spent half an hour explaining to Mrs Smith that I couldn't do what she wanted me to do because of a company regulation. As you know, she went over my head to you - and she made a point of letting me know that you let her away with it. Can you imagine how I felt when she made a point of telling me that? I need to know whether this is a rule or not so, I won't have the same thing happen in the future.'

Lacking company policies and procedures

'My boss called me into the office last week to let me know that I had broken a company rule. I didn't even know about the rule! She told me that it was 'standard practice' in her industry. Shouldn't there be some kind of list of company rules and regulations available to employees so this doesn't happen again?'

Progressive companies not only have detailed policy and procedure manuals, but they provide employee handbooks that explain the

Dealing with Difficult Situations

company rules and regulations to their staff. New employees receive a copy of this handbook on their first day of their employment and are encouraged to ask questions about the contents. Many companies have the employee sign a document stating that they have read and understand the information. Then, if they break a company rule or regulation, they can't say *'I didn't know about that rule/regulation!'*

You might suggest to your employer that you take on the task of preparing an employee manual for your company employees. You would start with the company policy and procedures manuals and only include the information necessary for employees to understand company rules. This will also encourage your company to update the company policies and procedures as well (this should be done at least annually).

Poor work ethic

'My boss is the laziest person I know - she delegates everything to others and does nothing herself. She seems to spend most of her time at management meetings and preparing reports rather than doing any work herself. I get so mad at her when she dumps another task on my desk that I find it difficult to do a good job.'

There are two kinds of supervisors; working supervisors and those who are solely responsible for delegating tasks to others. If she's a working supervisor, she will likely be doing the same type of tasks as her staff along with her supervisory responsibilities. It sounds as if she is the second type. It may seem as if your boss is not doing her share, but if you look behind the scenes, those meetings and reports she is preparing are as much work for her as your tasks are for you.

And if you do a poor job of completing your tasks, you are not only making yourself look bad, but you're making her look bad as well. If your performance slips far enough, you will leave her no other choice but to reprimand you. Remember, your main function as an employee is to make your boss look good. Her job is to give you the tools you'll need to allow you to do this.

No development - Low interest in job

'My job is so boring - I hate coming into work every day. I do the same thing all day every day! I have few skills, so am not trained to do other things, but there must be something better I can do.'

There are two solutions to this problem. Solution One is to prepare for another kind of position where you won't be so bored. Have you had career counselling to determine the kinds of occupations you may be good at? Once you've determined this, take relevant courses in the evenings or take time off and go back to school full-time to gain the ability to enter a new field.

Your employer can supply the second solution. Many use job rotation to keep their employees motivated and happy. All rotated tasks are at the same skill level, but involve different tasks. An extra plus for the companies who use job rotation is that this practice keeps employees from daydreaming on the job or possibly having accidents if they work in a dangerous environment (such as carpentry). They can also fill a position when others are away.

Supervisor unavailable

'My supervisor says she has an 'open-door policy,' but most of the time when I need her advice to solve a problem - she's not available.'

Plan ahead and arrange a set time every day when you can speak with your supervisor. Many use first thing in the morning or just after lunch for this. Another is to leave an e-mail message or place a note on her desk outlining your problem and a time when you *must* have a resolution.

You might ask yourself whether you should be making more decisions on your own. Talk to your supervisor and establish your decision-making limits. Prepare sample questions you want to ask including how you think you should handle the problem. You might find that you had the answers all along and just needed your supervisor's approval to use your own initiative to deal with such issues. Your supervisor might be pleased with this sign of initiative or will make herself more available if she doesn't want to delegate extra authority to you.

Won't listen to my ideas

'I have many years of experience in my field, but find that my employer won't listen to my ideas even though they really work. The company's existing ways seem to take so long and cost so much! If I hear, 'it's not in the budget,' 'that won't work,' or 'we tried that

Dealing with Difficult Situations

before,' one more time when I make suggestions - I'm going to scream! How can I get my company to implement my ideas?'

Start by writing down the existing way of doing things. Then add the advantages and disadvantages of doing it the existing way. Do the same with your new way of doing things. Try to concentrate on the cost savings of your plan - in time and money. Because most companies are money-driven - they'll likely listen if you can prove that your way will save the company money.

Boss is a perfectionist

'My boss is a perfectionist. Everything MUST be right - or it's sent back. I'm pushed to the limit meeting deadlines, so can't spend the time required to make sure that every 'i' is dotted and 't' is crossed!'

Talk to your boss. Ask him whether he would rather have things absolutely correct and have you get behind in your work or continue meeting your deadlines but have a few minor mistakes. You may be surprised at his answer - he may not have realised what kind of pressure you're under and the deadlines you're forced to meet.

He may be a perfectionist in everything he does. This could be a compulsion that he can't or doesn't want to change. If this is the case you'll have adapt, by improving your diligence by double checking your work before submitting it to him.

Workaholic boss

'My boss is a workaholic and expects her staff to be the same. I have a young family and many home responsibilities because my wife works too. On top of that, I'm taking evening courses twice a week. How can I convince her that I can't put in the extra hours she expects of me?'

At an employment interview, it's important that all prospective employees ask what hours they're expected to work and whether there is much overtime. Many companies state they want their employees to have a work/life balance, but in practice, their staff find it impossible to get their work done in the established business hours. Many are putting in sixty-hour weeks and find themselves taking work home each evening and on the weekends.

Dealing with Difficult Situations

Start by discussing your dilemma with your supervisor. Outline your obligations away from work and ask her what she expects of you at work. She may not know that you're juggling things so much and give you pointers on what is and is not crucial to be done at work. You may have to put off your evening courses, if the company can't be flexible.

Supervising former peers

'I was chosen to take over the position of supervisor when my boss had a transfer. Ten of my colleagues and I applied for the position. Since starting the job, I've run into lots of resistance from those who worked the closest with me in the past. They seem to have problems accepting me as their supervisor. How can I turn things around to improve their productivity?'

Those who find themselves supervising former peers are faced with many negative feelings from their former colleagues such as:

- Jealousy/envy/anger;
- They know your weaknesses;
- Lack respect;
- Sabotage your efforts;
- Gang up on you;
- Expect favouritism or bias; and are prone to back stabbing.

If you're younger than your staff they may not give you the respect you need to get tasks completed. Or if you're a woman supervising men, your subordinates may balk at accepting a female boss (even females staff members may do this). Your supervisor should have already talked to each unsuccessful candidate to explain why s/he wasn't chosen for the position. Then on your first day as supervisor, your manager would set up a meeting with your new staff to introduce you. S/he would explain to your new staff that they were expected to give you the same respect and productivity as they did to their former supervisor. S/he would then turn the meeting over to you and leave the room.

How would you start your first meeting where you were supervising former peers? Start on the right foot by acting like a supervisor. After your opening statement, add these comments, *'I'm really counting on all of you to help me make this adjustment.'* Then

Dealing with Difficult Situations

looking each staff member in the eye and ask, *'How about you Bill - can I count on your support?'*

Do this for each person in the room. Inevitably there will be one (or even two) who make it obvious by their body language that they're agreeing under duress. You will need to take further steps to deal with these staff members.

Also state, *'Although I've worked alongside all of you since .... I know little about your individual skills and abilities. In the next two weeks, I'll be looking over your personnel files and will have a discussion with each of you to learn your career plans and know more about your skills and abilities.'* During those meetings with the dissenters, spend time trying to smooth the waters for them. If their productivity drops, take steps to correct their behaviour.

I know you can't go back to your first day on the job as a supervisor, but you could implement these ideas so you can become the supervisor they need.

Won't Discipline Staff

'My supervisor really needs training in how to discipline staff. One of my colleagues is constantly coming in late, forcing the rest of us to cover for her. She has said nothing to correct this behaviour, but last week she called me into her office and took a strip off me for something I had done. I admit I made a mistake, but her behaviour really ticked me off. I don't mind being corrected about my behaviour, but I don't like being treated as if I'm a criminal. It was just one mistake!'

To be effective, discipline should be aimed at changing undesirable behaviour - not at initiating retaliation. This supervisor on one hand did nothing about the late issue and over-reacted about the mistake you made. She obviously had not received training on how to discipline staff. See solution under 'Disciplines in Public.'

Manager lets staff by-pass me

'I'm a new supervisor and am running into a problem I didn't foresee. My manager is allowing my staff to bypass me and go directly to him. I think he should send them back to me so I have a chance to deal with the issues. If I run into problems - I feel it should be me going to my manager for help to solve the problem if it's

Dealing with Difficult Situations

required. He's delegating tasks directly to my staff that is causing serious time management difficulties. It's close to Performance Appraisal time and he's said that he will be doing the Performance Appraisals for my staff. How can I deal with this kind of behaviour?'

I'm aware that you're a female supervisor in her first supervisory position. Unfortunately many male managers feel a need to protect their female supervisors by allowing this to happen. Deal with it right away. This can't continue.

The majority of companies work under the hierarchal system where each level is responsible downward for the next level. No one is expected to infringe on the 'turf' of the other, unless serious problems surface.

Talk to your manager stating, *'I have several problems and I need your help in solving them. Yesterday Staff member #1 was stretched to the limit to meet some deadlines. I learned that you had delegated another task to him and he didn't know how to fit it in. On the other hand Staff member #2 did have time to do your task. In the future could you give the task to me and I will delegate it downward to the appropriate staff member?'*

Then add, *'When my staff come to you with problems concerning me, would you please ask them whether they have discussed the problem with me? If they haven't, could you please send them to me for a resolution to their problems?'*

'Because it is one of my responsibilities as a supervisor, I'd like to confirm with you the dates I will be conducting the Performance Appraisals for my staff.'

Authoritarian Style of Management - Abuse of Power

'I foolishly accepted a position without meeting my immediate superior. My supervisor turned out to be a domineering tyrant whose authoritarian style of management puts everyone off (that's why the last person in my position left). How do I deal with his behaviour?'

This person is only happy when the 'pecking order' is established. Domineering tyrants must be king of the mountain and anything that gets in his way - he'll crush. He'll use others to get where he wants to go via intimidation. Everything relates to power and many of these people are allowed to climb the corporate ladder because of their ruthlessness. Are they liked? Not by many - but their companies love them because they force their employees to constantly be on their toes. The hair on the back of his staff's neck will automatically rise when he's nearby and their senses will instantly be on high alert preparing them for his next intimidating move.

Speaking to these tyrants about their behaviour will not change their attitude - they don't care what you think. So the only alternative is to do some sleuthing to find out how many people have left the company because of this tyrant and the approximate cost so far in productivity, unhappy employees, absenteeism because of stress of his staff etc. and approach upper management with the facts. And even when the facts are given, some companies may not act to remove the person (see section on bullying).

Personality Clashes

'Two of my colleagues are constantly at each other's throats which makes the work environment very tense. It's got so bad that I hate to come into work - and am thinking of looking for work elsewhere. Why doesn't my supervisor step in and stop this from happening?'

Use feedback to explain your frustration to your supervisor. This might stimulate her to take action. This is another sign of poor supervision and especially for the lack of discipline given to the two staff members who are making life difficult and affecting the morale of everyone nearby. The supervisor should call them both into her office and explain her displeasure at their actions.

She would outline the behaviour she objected to by stating, *'This hostility between the two of you can't go on. It's affecting your co-workers and your work. The atmosphere is intolerable and serious. I know you don't like each other and I don't expect you to do so, but unless things change and this problem is solved, I'll have to start disciplinary procedures. I'm going to leave you two alone and want you to spend the next ten minutes discussing what you're both going to do to solve this problem. When I return, I want you to tell me what you've decided to do to solve this problem.'*

She would then leave the room and return ten minutes later. *'What have you decided?'* By this time, they should have resolved their differences. They would discuss the employee's plans to alleviate

Dealing with Difficult Situations

the problem and the supervisor would then ask them, *'Can I count on you to do what you say you're going to do?'*

Once they give their assurances the supervisor would add, *'I want you to know that if you revert back to your old destructive behaviour I'll have no other choice but to put written warnings on your file. Do you both understand this?'* The supervisor will have to keep a close watch on the situation and call further interviews if warranted.

If they hadn't resolved the problem by the time the supervisor returned, she would take on the role of mediator so that the underlying problems were discussed. If they refused to discuss their differences, then she'd reiterate the earlier comment, *'Unless things change and your behaviour improves, I'll have no other choice but to start disciplinary action. I'm counting on you to not make this necessary.'*

If the behaviour doesn't improve - she must follow through with the appropriate action. *The employees must know that the supervisor will not tolerate the situation remaining as it is.*

Favouritism and Bias

'My boss doesn't seem to like me because I'm of a different ethnic origin than he. On the other hand he shows distinct favouritism towards his 'pet' and allows him to get away with things I'm disciplined for. What do I do to stop this from happening?'

Supervisors are human and have their favourites and biases - however in the workplace, this is absolutely unconscionable. All employees must be treated equally. Have others noticed this behaviour? Are they willing to speak up on your behalf? If so, you could use them to be a witness to the behaviour to back up your allegations. Once this is established, ask for a meeting with your supervisor. Take your witness with you.

State to your supervisor, *'I know that you're probably not aware of it, but you are showing discrimination and bias against me and favouritism towards Charlie. Here are some facts to back up my allegations.'* Hopefully you won't have to take this to your employee relations or Human Resources department, but be ready to do so. If your allegations are warranted, you are protected from discrimination by law.

Dealing with Difficult Situations

Poor Role Model

'My boss breaks most of the rules you've mentioned and is the worst role model I have run into. Why do companies keep these kinds of supervisors on staff?'

Read information on bullies and authoritarian style of management - because many of these bad role models are also bullies.

Can't Manage Time

'At work we're either sitting doing nothing or are rushed off our feet and it's mainly because of our supervisor. She lets things pile up and is often a bottleneck for us to get the work. This means that we often have unexpected overtime. This disrupts the plans I might have had for my evenings and weekends. How can we help our boss to be more organised?'

A boss who isn't organised is often one who has chaos in his or her department. Why not ask your boss if you could help her manage her time better. Suggest that she start a 'to do' list in the morning that identifies all the tasks he needs to finish by the end of the day. S/he would then prioritise each of these tasks into A, B, C and D tasks.

- 'A' tasks must be done right away, by either her or by her staff;
- 'B' tasks are tackled after 'A' tasks are completed;
- 'C' tasks are done whenever she can fit them in; and
- 'D' tasks usually should be ignored or thrown away.

When delegating tasks to her staff she could label each request with a coloured tag. Red means that it must be done right away (giving a deadline for completion). Orange means it must be done today and green - to be done when staff has time. This way, her staff don't have to go through their entire in-basket or e-mails to determine the priority of tasks.

Why not suggest an early morning meeting where you can discuss your day's assignments and anything you can do to get some tasks on their way (that she's hoarding on her desk to dump on you later when you're rushed)?

Nepotism

'I work in a company that encourages nepotism. It seems as if most of the people here are either related or have been able to have their

Dealing with Difficult Situations

personal friends hired by the company. I'm one of the few who has obtained my position because of my merit - not because of my genes or who I know. How's a person to survive this kind of environment when people run in packs and outsiders aren't included in their inner circle.'

You've identified one of problems that can bring on the downfall of a company. Employees should be hired because of their abilities - not who they know or who they're related to. It's hard fighting this kind of battle and it's too bad you didn't know what you were stepping into when you accepted your position. Unless you want to spend your time alone and fighting the majority - it's far more reasonable and practical to look for work elsewhere.

Won't Keep Promises

'I've been promised that the company will implement my new way of doing a task, but I've waited for four months waiting for this to happen. I was also told that I could have my annual leave in June, now find that the supervisor has cancelled all leaves for the month of June. It seems as if she breaks her promises for no reason at all.'

Supervisors should not make promises unless they intend to keep them. In the future, try to get these promises in writing (CYA - cover your ass) and follow-through later if promises aren't kept. Keep asking your supervisor when your new way will be implemented and describe the hardship cancelling your annual leave is having on your family. When the supervisor makes promises in the future say, *'Can I count on you to do this, because I'll be very disappointed if you renege on your promise?'*

Immature Supervisor

'Even though my supervisor is in her thirties and is ten years older than me, I find that she's very immature in how she approaches her job. She gives instructions, then ten minutes later changes the way she wants to have the task completed. She gossips with her staff, tells jokes and visits with her staff to discuss family issues. Before accepting assignments for her staff she doesn't stop to think whether we can handle the extra load or not. She's very wishy-washy and seems incapable of saying 'no' to others. I don't think she has what it takes to be a supervisor.'

Dealing with Difficult Situations

Some who are in their early twenties make wonderful supervisors, while others in their forties or fifties still don't have enough maturity to supervise staff. It sounds as if she hasn't had supervisory training and seems to be unsure about how she should be doing her job. You won't likely have to do anything about the situation - she will tighten the noose on herself without any help from you. Upper management will soon see that she's not the person for the position.

Why don't you prepare yourself for her downfall by getting the supervisory training yourself, so you're ready to step in when she leaves? Or why not suggest to her that you both take the training (therefore you won't set yourself up to feel guilty later if she fails).

CHAPTER 2

DIFFICULT SITUATIONS - SUBORDINATES

I hate being a supervisor!

'I didn't realise the responsibilities I accepted when I agreed to take a promotion to the position of Office Supervisor. This position wants more from me than I expected.'

Most supervisors (at some time or other) ask themselves, *'What was I doing when I accepted this position? It demands from me twice as much as I thought it would! Everyone's pulling at me - my boss from above, my staff from below and my new co-workers (other supervisors) from the side - and then there's the union! How's a person to cope?'*

If feel you're in 'over your head,' make sure you immediately take a supervisory training course. Companies that appoint an employee to a supervisory or management position without providing them with adequate training are setting the employee up to fail.

The secret to this transition is knowledge. Knowing what you're expected to do and how you should handle different situations are the keys to successful supervision. No longer are you only responsible for your own actions, but you're responsible for your staff's as well. This is the big difference between being a worker and being a supervisor. Supervisors must also be good leaders, good time managers and problem solvers, have high interpersonal skills and be able to chair meetings.

What is a Supervisor?

A supervisor is anyone who is responsible for getting work done through other people by planning organising, staffing, directing and controlling. This includes clerical supervisors, foremen, managers, executives and C.E.Os.

Supervision isn't easy - it's difficult for some to make the transition from being told what to do, to making decisions for others. It's also difficult to rely on others to complete assignments for which you (the supervisor) are held accountable.

Here are some terms that relate to supervision:

Dealing with Difficult Situations

Responsibility:

These are the actual tasks that require completion by either yourself or a member of your staff.

Authority:

This means the person given the responsibility to complete the task and the authority to complete the assignment. The supervisor delegates this authority to the staff member. For example: You have given one of your staff the responsibility of ordering office supplies for your unit. The employee makes a list of what other staff members require and takes that list to the Supply Depot. The Supply Clerk refuses to fill the order and says, *'You don't have signing authority.'* You made a serious mistake, caused embarrassment to your employee and wasted valuable time because you didn't give the person the authority to complete the task.

Another supervisor asked one of his staff to go to the Human Resources Department to pick up a staff member's personnel file. Because the file was confidential, the department required written permission to release it. The employee returned without the file. So, make sure your staff has not only the responsibility (the task itself) but also the authority to fulfil the obligation.

Accountability:

Many supervisors believe that if they delegate a task to an employee, they can divorce themselves from the responsibility for that task. This is not so. There are two levels of accountability:

1. Delegated Accountability:

The supervisor gives the responsibility (task) to the employee and makes the employee accountable for the task.

2. Final Accountability:

The employee is accountable to the supervisor for the task, but the final accountability remains with the supervisor who delegated the task. Because supervisors have this final accountability, staff have the ability to make their supervisor look good or bad. That's why it's essential that supervisors have the ability to discipline staff and conduct performance appraisals when tasks have not been performed properly.

Dealing with Difficult Situations

Supervisor has tantrums

'One of my supervisors has tantrums. He swears, slams down the phone, throws things at the wall and has a shouting match with anyone within earshot. He berates his staff and disciplines them in public. My staff become very upset when they're exposed to his actions (and so do I!)

I know I have to step in to stop this from happening in the future, but I lack the management know-how to deal with a problem of this magnitude. What should I do to stop this kind of disruptive behaviour?'

How did you ever hire such a tyrant? Someone slipped up when making reference checks on the employee. This employee is using aggressive behaviour and is misusing his position of power. He has likely been doing this in his past positions as well. If you allow his behaviour to continue - you are setting your company up for a bullying or harassment charge so you must stop his behaviour - now.

Adults who still resort to temper tantrums to get their way, haven't grown up. They use tantrums, because they've learned that they get what they want if they yell and carry on. They often lack the communication skills that enable them to use tact and diplomacy to get work done through their employees. They love the control they have over others and enjoy watching everyone jump to do their bidding. Most of them desperately need anger management counselling.

Don't wait for the next explosive episode to erupt. Call him into your office and confront him with your knowledge about his behaviour. Use facts. Relate exactly what you witnessed and heard. Then relate the repercussions his behaviour caused not only to his co-workers and staff, but to your clients who may have been within earshot. Ask him to explain why he acted the way he did.

Explain that you feel he's abusing his position of power and that his behaviour is a form of bullying and harassment. His actions are so serious that you'll be putting a written warning on his file. Recommend that he obtain counselling on how to handle his anger. Be clear about the consequences if he repeats his destructive behaviour.

Dealing with Difficult Situations

There can be a positive element to this kind of dialogue. Your confrontation about his actions could start a dialogue that will make him see how destructive his behaviour is, not only to his career aspirations, but to his relationship with others as well.

If he uses this type of behaviour again, follow through with your consequences. This type of behaviour usually warrants one or two written warnings and then the person is usually terminated. Along the way it's essential that you keep detailed, factual documentation of what transpired in case he decides to take you to court and charge your company with wrongful dismissal.

Helping your employees accept change

Bill Evans had decided to upgrade his computer system to take advantage of a new computer program that would save time, effort and money. His concern was that his assistant was the kind of person who balked at every change. He wasn't looking forward to telling her about the upgraded equipment and systems he was planning to install.

When supervisors want to make changes in the methods their subordinates use to complete assignments they're often surprised by the resistance they meet. This is especially true because of the rapid changes in technology that can take considerable effort and time to put in place.

One of the main things people do when they want or have to implement a change is to dive right in and simply do it. Unfortunately, most end up running into resistance from those who are personally affected by the change. Supervisors need to be aware of the stages people go through when adjusting to change so they can help their staff make the transition as smoothly as possible. There are four major stages people go through when change is implemented:

1. *Unfreezing.* During this initial stage the employees need to give up their regular way of doing things and identify new methods. This involves breaking old habits. Detail-oriented personalities will likely resist.

2. *Changing*. The supervisor explains the new pattern of behaviour or new way of doing something. Before doing this, the supervisor should identify the advantages of the change and

Dealing with Difficult Situations

be prepared for resistance by determining ways to overcome those expected objections.

3. ***Refreezing.*** Employees' use of the new method is monitored until it becomes automatic. Supervisors must watch for die-hards who may be determined to continue doing it the old way. This can take up to three months of constant surveillance.
4. ***Commitment.*** People are ready to use the new way and it becomes automatic.

Planning before implementing your change will eliminate many obstacles. Here are the steps to take when it's necessary to implement change:

1. Write down the existing way the task is performed. Be specific including the what, where, when, who and how's.
2. Identify the pros and cons (advantages and disadvantages) of doing the task the old way.
3. Write down the new way - be specific.
4. Identify the pros and cons (advantages and disadvantages) of doing the task the new way.
5. Brainstorm (alone or with others' help) to find solutions to the disadvantages of doing things the new way.
6. Anticipate and prepare for as many objections as possible. Pinpoint the objections and try to develop a plan for handling each objection or minimise its adverse affect.
7. Consider bringing up significant objections yourself, instead of waiting for others to do so. Then explain how these can be overcome.
8. Ask your employees to explain their objections in very specific terms with examples.
9. Don't be content with superficial reasons for resistance to a change. Dig until you discover the real reasons.
10. If you possibly can, work out a practical way of overcoming each objection.
11. If you're unable to overcome an objection, try to find a way to compensate for it.
12. Rally enough benefits to win the person's support and co-operation despite his/her objection.
13. Find a way to ease the person's mind, to make it less risky to go along with you, despite his/her objection.

Dealing with Difficult Situations

14. With habitual or chronic objectors, introduce your idea gradually. Don't try to get immediate acceptance or compliance. If necessary, spoon-feed the idea to them, giving them a chance to gradually get used to the new idea. Their objection may be nothing more than a delaying tactic - the person's natural resistance to change.
15. Introduce the change.
16. Follow-through to make sure that your staff don't slip back to the old way of doing things.

Bill Evans's employee will need to be assured that she will receive adequate training and will have assistance at her finger-tips should she run into problems. Most computer companies who provide new hard- and software have twenty-four hour help lines for just this kind of situation. Make sure there's plenty of time for her to make the transition from the old system to the new. She'll likely need regular reassurance from you that you're confident she'll succeed in making the transition.

Young female supervisor

'Because I have several years' experience in an office and have completed supervisory training, I've been appointed to a position as supervisor of our marketing division. I'm only twenty-seven years old and am running into resistance from women I supervise - many of whom are old enough to be my mothers. Several of them have ten or fifteen years' experience, but I was appointed because none of them had supervisory training. Some of my staff are openly hostile to me and won't co-operate. I'd hate to start disciplining them, but I might have to because they're making me look bad. How can I deal with this kind of problem?'

In the past, most women were not considered for supervisory positions until they had many years of experience. Because women these days are becoming more educated - instead of starting their working lives in support positions, they are appointed to a first-line supervisory position. This can cause some unique problems. One is the dilemma of supervising women old enough to be their mothers.

Traditionally, society taught us that the older woman - the mother or the aunt - knows more, so therefore is to be treated with deference and respect. Switching roles is upsetting to both the young female supervisor (who's suddenly in the position of the parent) and the

Dealing with Difficult Situations

older female employee (who's now in the position of the child seeking approval).

Lydia, the young supervisor, soon realised that she had to clear the air with her subordinates. She called a meeting with her staff and asked them how she could ease the transition for them. At first there was dead silence, but eventually Betty (one of the less hostile women) explained that they had all been upset when she had been hired. Most of them felt that one of them should have been promoted to the position when it became vacant.

'Do you know why that didn't occur?' asked Lydia.

No one seemed able to answer so Lydia added, *'I was appointed specifically because I've received supervisory training. Have any of you had training in that area?'*

'I was put into an acting supervisory position when my boss was away sick,' one employee replied.

'That's excellent developmentally, but unless you've had proper supervisory training, handling a supervisory job can be overwhelming. How many of you applied for a supervisory position?'

Three women replied that they had done so.

'Would you like to make certain that you're not overlooked in the future?'

There was a resounding, *'Yes!'* from all three.

'Well, let's see if we can put you into the supervisory training program. That way, you won't be overlooked in the future. I'll do everything I can to help you obtain such a position, but you'll have to do your share by performing well and obtaining the necessary training.' She added, *'I'm counting on all of you to co-operate and do your work properly.'* She then asked each staff member, *'Can I count on you to do this?'*

One employee, Julie, appeared reluctant to make a commitment to her, so Janet knew she would have to watch her performance. Soon the woman's low productivity and poor work habits made it necessary for Janet to counsel her on her behaviour. She again explained what she expected from Julie and what the consequences would be if she continued to produce sloppy reports. Unfortunately,

Dealing with Difficult Situations

Julie never did accept Lydia as her supervisor. She continued to produce sloppy work and eventually had to be fired.

Lydia fared better with the others. When she noticed a change in their attitude and productivity, she thanked them for their understanding and co-operation. Two of the women asked for and were given supervisory training.

Another problem that female supervisors can run into is the difference in the service provided by support staff (mainly women). In the past, most went out of their way to keep their bosses (usually male) organised, on time and comfortable. They nurtured their bosses (brought them coffee, reminded them of appointments, opened and sorted their mail). But when a woman's promoted to that same position, the nurturing may stop unless she's on top of the situation. She'll have to let her staff know that she expects the same kind of treatment given to the former male supervisor.

Women Supervising Men

'I have no trouble supervising women - but sure do when it comes to supervising men!'

Angela is a designer who supervises four male technologists. Even though she clearly explains how she wants tasks completed, the men kept doing things 'their' way. Fortunately, before accepting her position she had obtained supervisory training that prepared her to act confidently.

When one of her male subordinates refused to do a task her way (which was an act of insubordination - a serious enough infraction to have him terminated) Angela conducted a disciplinary interview. She carefully documented the interview and placed a written warning on his file that identified that his employment with the company would be terminated if a similar incident happened in the future.

If you're a woman, would you have felt confident doing this on your own if you were supervising men? If you're planning to climb the corporate ladder, it's a distinct possibility that you <u>will</u> be supervising men in the future. Make sure you're prepared to handle it.

Dealing with Difficult Situations

Hired the wrong person

'Two months ago I hired an employee, but he's turned out to be completely unacceptable. How can I be sure that next time I will choose the right person?'

If recruiters, supervisors and managers don't take enough time when hiring employees, they'll find they've set themselves up for a period of misery. Problems can occur if:

- The right questions aren't asked on the interview;
- The interviewers aren't knowledgeable enough to hire competent personnel; or
- References aren't checked properly.

Companies may end up with a real loser, who instead of helping their company with production, cause more work in the long run. Have you hired someone and found that:

a) They lied on the interview about how long they'd worked for a company?
b) They told you they had more experience than they actually had?
c) They didn't fit in with the existing staff?
d) Their work ethic left much to be desired?
e) They weren't able to handle the duties of the position after considerable in-house or professional training?
f) You were on a different wave-length than they and found it difficult to get them to do things your way?
g) You required a self-starter and the employee required very detailed instructions to get anything done?
h) The person who was hired to work on the front lines dealing directly with clients, doesn't have the people-skills you require?
i) The person has a negative attitude, who gripes and complains about everything which eventually affects his/her co-workers resulting in low morale for all your staff?
j) Your company has installed a new computer system, but the new employee is unwilling or unable to pick up the new technology.
k) The person looked very presentable on the interview, but their day to day appearance leaves much to be desired even after several talks you've had with him/her.
l) The person puts things off so long (procrastinates) that project deadlines aren't met?

Dealing with Difficult Situations

m) The employee is a perfectionist in everything they do, which holds up progress?

n) Employee is a know-it-all, doesn't follow directions, does things his/her own way and bucks the system?

I'm sure you've run into the above kinds of employees in your daily work situation. It's hard to evaluate people's ability to fit the needs of a particular position. Unless you've had years of experience, it can be a very intimidating experience. Proper interviewing, screening and especially reference checking of the above employees would have eliminated most of these problems. So doing things correctly *before* they're hired is crucial. If this requires recruitment interviewing skills training - make sure you obtain it so you don't hire another 'dud.'

Reference Checking

Employment application forms

The following information should be included on company employment application forms that will protect companies from being charged under the privacy act:

****

I certify that the statements made by me in this application are true and complete. I understand and agree that a false statement may disqualify me from employment or result in dismissal.

Permission is granted for {your company name} to contact my past employers for references.

Date: _____

Signature: _____

****

When conducting reference checks start with the last supervisor/manager and work backwards chronologically. Contact at least two, preferably three former managers. It's best to speak with the applicant's former managers rather than someone in the former company's Human Resources Department.

Those who have worked closely with a former employee know far more about his/her work habits than the Human Resources

Dealing with Difficult Situations

Department personnel might know. However, if the former supervisor is not available, contact the Human Resources Department. References that are ten years or older do not normally warrant reference checks.

Problems may occur if candidates don't want to jeopardise their present position and may have been with their present employer for several years. The candidate can be asked if there is a member or former member of his/her company who would comment on his/her performance and yet not jeopardise his/her position with the company. There is considerable risk in hiring someone who will not agree to the above.

Treat all reference checks as highly confidential. They're to be kept locked away in private files - not the employee's subsequent personnel file. Former employers may hesitate to say anything that might spoil the applicant's chance of earning a livelihood, even though his/her record with them may have been poor. If former employers appear to be hedging with their answers, explain to them that the information is strictly confidential and **keep it that way**. Explain that you require their assistance in assessing the former employee honestly and without prejudice.

Make sure you identify yourself and the company when making reference checks. Start your conversation by stating *'Mr/Ms ……………..has applied to us for a position and has given me permission to contact you to verify some information s/he has given us. Do you remember him/her?* Examples of the questions that can be asked when conducting a reference-checking interview are:

- Did they report to the referee?
- Dates of employment;
- Position held;
- Duties of position;
- Did applicant supervise staff?
- Salary: (be sure to distinguish between base salary and any fringe earnings);
- How did the applicant relate to peers? Subordinates? Clients? Supervisors?
- How was employee's attendance? Punctuality? General health? If unsatisfactory, why?
- How would you rate applicant's technical knowledge?
- Any problems or deficiencies?

- Quality of work?
- Quantity of work completed?
- Personal grooming;
- Dependability;
- Cooperativeness;
- Creativity (if applicable);
- What company did s/he work for before joining your company?
- What company did s/he go to after employment with your company?
- Why did applicant leave your company?
- Is there anything else you could tell me about the candidate?
- Would you re-hire?

Other questions would relate to concerns that were identified at the time of the interview and can be added to the Reference Checking Form before commencing the interview. Be sure to note the date, name, position, company name, address and phone number of the person giving the reference. End the interview by thanking the person for answering your questions.

Aggressive Worker

'One of my employees seems to have a chip on his shoulder and takes offence at every word I speak to him. He argues with every comment others make and is generally a pain in the neck. I've inherited him - I certainly wouldn't have hired him, but I'm stuck with him and have to deal with his aggressive behaviour.'

The feelings that cause an aggressive attitude in employees are deep rooted. The supervisor faces the problem of either changing them (which admittedly is difficult) or re-directing them to the advantage, not only for the company, but for the employee as well. Some job-related causes of aggressive behaviour on the part of employees could include:

1. Insecurity on the job.
2. Employee's lack of qualifications or credentials.
3. Little recognition for employee's achievements.
4. Under-utilisation of their abilities.
5. Lack of acceptance with work groups (including racial and cultural differences).
6. Failure to feel settled into their occupations.

Dealing with Difficult Situations

Those who don't believe they fit into their positions could become aggressive towards their immediate bosses, the company, top management, the job and fellow workers. Some effort can be made toward directing the negative attitudes of aggression toward a work-related goal if the attitude can't be changed. Techniques a supervisor might use are:

1. Show employees how their fellow workers count on their efforts and how important their jobs are to the company.
2. Make problem employees feel secure in their jobs.
3. Indicate that with their training and other qualifications, they have the capability to do more than a satisfactory job.
4. Give recognition more frequently to aggressive-tendency employees.
5. Bring them into group conversations: ask for their advice.
6. Identify their responsibilities and set performance standards.

If the supervisor's attitude indicates that s/he feels the problem employee has much to contribute to the entire group's productivity, the employee is likely to assume such a role. Most aggressive employees are very success-oriented. Their drive for recognition could cause the employee to set high goals for him/herself in order to achieve further recognition. Channelling this energy in the right direction can be a major step in the right direction for this type of employee.

Low Productivity

Dr. Daly asked how he could motivate one of his employees, a receptionist-nurse who had worked for him for three years. Her performance was quickly going downhill. She was lethargic, lacked initiative and her sense of urgency was completely missing. Because of the economic situation, he had not been able to give her a raise for over a year and the situation wasn't likely to change in the near future. What other things could he have done to motivate her to be a better performer?

Much more is involved in supervising employees than simply assigning and checking work, assessing performance and disciplining employees. Supervising people is an art that depends to a great extent on how well staff can be motivated.

Dealing with Difficult Situations

Supervisors must watch for the 'Pygmalion effect' when trying to motivate staff. If a supervisor believes employees are smart, s/he will treat them that way. If a supervisor believes employees are capable of independent thought, s/he will treat them that way. Unfortunately, if the supervisor believes they are lazy, dumb or slow to pick up new ideas (or have any other undesirable attribute) s/he often treats them that way too. People respond to what they perceive is wanted from them. If supervisors expect high achievement, that's likely what they'll get. If supervisors expect low productivity, that's likely what they'll get as well.

Do you need to change your attitude towards the abilities of your staff? Are you letting the Pygmalion effect influence how you supervise your staff?

Has Dr. Daly checked to see that his employee has an accurate up-to-date job description with standards of performance for each task? She may not know what you expect from her, so this is the place to start. Talk to her to find out what she has to say about her lethargic performance. Some people are motivated by their interest in the work itself. She may be bored with her job and need stimulus to do better work. If this is the case, see if there are any of your duties you could delegate to her so she'll continue on a learning curve. If this isn't possible, job rotation is another motivator because it keeps employees from being bored with their assignments. This also has a spin-off benefit that if one employee is away sick, another is qualified to take over for the absent employees. This ensures that work does not pile up for the absent staff member.

Could your employee be having problems being accepted by her peers or could she be in the throes of a personality clash with another employee? Try to help your employees to work together as a team by giving them team projects. If the latter problem is the case, step in to stop the conflict.

Could she have concerns about the security of her position? Has it been necessary for you to cut staff or put some of your staff on part-time employment? Don't overlook the possibility that this is the reason for her lack of motivation.

Those who believe their positions are in jeopardy will often stop taking any kind of risk when performing their tasks. Many will resort to helplessness and appear to need far more direction from their

Dealing with Difficult Situations

supervisors. Rather than make a wrong decision, they revert to 'playing it safe' and get every new task approved by their supervisors.

Staff Motivators

Other motivators are the desire or need for:

Money: Many supervisors feel this is the only incentive that would really motivate employees. For some, this is true - but for the majority - it's not true. In others, just the opportunity of making more money can be a motivator (such as a possible promotion).

Recognition: This is probably the best motivator of all. It's very high on employees' lists for more favourable behaviour that in turn allows them to receive more recognition. A well-timed pat on the back can turn around even the most lethargic, aggressive or demanding employee. If you want even more impact, put your praise down on paper, so the recipient can save it and read it whenever s/he wishes.

Seniority: Employees receive special company benefits because of long-term employment. This could be a bigger office, more company benefits, a company car, etc. However, this can de-motivate other more conscientious or high-achieving employees who see seniority as a negative reason for recognition and more perks.

Merit System: This would make sure that employees would receive a salary in ratio to their productivity, rather than to their seniority with their company. This cuts out much of the 'deadwood' in corporations. Those who've always expected their company to protect their employment simply because they've worked for the company for a long time - fear this method.

Status: This would be the title of the position or the employee's perceived importance to the company. For instance, do you think a staff member would prefer the title Junior Clerk or Administrative Assistant? I'm sure you'll agree that Administrative Assistant sounds more important.

Challenge: The opportunity to grow, to stretch, to use their full potential is *the* motivator for many employees. The idea of winning is a definite turn-on to many who enjoy the gamble.

Competition. To those with a competitive nature (most sales types) competition is a definite turn-on to higher productivity. They thrive on the excitement of the challenge.

Security: For employees who believe their jobs are in jeopardy (or those waiting for a pending lay-off) letting them know that their job is secure (and the company is solvent) may be the only motivator they

Dealing with Difficult Situations

need to do a good job. Security applies to other safety issues such as air pollution and smoking issues.

Lack of security: If their job is on the line because of poor productivity or behaviour, they'll likely clean up their act and produce more. This is a negative motivator, but may be the only motivator for your lazier employees or those who lack direction and goals.

Responsibility: Doing only part of the job can be a turn-off to some employees. When they have the full responsibility for the completion of a task, they feel a much higher sense of achievement. They say, *'I was in charge of that project. My boss said I did a good job.'*

Promotional Opportunities: This is a turn-on to the high achiever or someone who really wants to get ahead in a hurry. For those who are at the minimum wage level, it can be an incentive to work harder, so they can earn more money.

Training: When companies supply training to their employees, the employees feel that the company cares about them and are interested in their well-being. Companies that implement manpower planning use training to make sure their existing staff are ready for promotional opportunities. This also encourages longevity with the company. They provide for development of employees' talents and abilities and allow them to use the training on the job.

Achievement: Many companies make public announcements when their employees accomplish something unexpected. *'I'd like to congratulate Patti Smith who was able to resuscitate Mrs. Jones when she had a heart attack in our company parking lot. Congratulations Patti!'*

Awards: Companies give perfect attendance awards, sales awards, charity awards and give recognition for work above and beyond the call of duty.

Extra privileges: Employers might decide to let their employees go home when they've complete their allotted work. There are no specific hours of work - just allotted amount of work.

Additional Benefits: This could include a company car, an expense account, a corner office, their own personal assistant, company credit card, season's tickets to concerts or sporting events or the use of a condominium on the Gold Coast, etc.

Leadership style of supervisor: A good leader can motivate employees to give their best effort, simply because they respect their leader and want to do their best for him/her. In return, they want their supervisor to be proud of them.

Dealing with Difficult Situations

Hours of work: Companies have implemented flex-time and find it to be a great motivator. Their early risers start at 7:00 am and leave at 3:00 pm. Late starters start work at 10:00 am and leave at 6:00 pm.

Job Sharing: This occurs when two employees share the responsibilities of one (normally full-time) position. Some split the duties with one person working in the morning, another in the afternoon. In other cases, the employees may work two days one week and three the next. It's an ideal set-up for many working mothers with young children. Salaries and benefits are also split in half.

Company Social Events: The opportunity for workers to associate with each other socially is a good motivator for some employees. This could be having a company sports team, company picnic, barbecue or other social event.

The work itself: Job rotation often reduces the boredom of repetitive tasks. There's another spin-off benefit - that of having more than one person qualified to take over the duties of a position for an employee who's on vacation or away because of illness.

Be aware that it's not possible to motivate everyone - you just *can't* motivate some people. With this type of unsatisfactory worker, start by explaining exactly what you expect of them (document your requests properly) and make sure they have a good job description. Then give them ample opportunity to improve their performance. If they refuse to conform, replace them with good workers. There are too many excellent people who are unemployed, for companies to keep foot-draggers on the payroll. They just de-motivate everyone around them.

I lead - but they won't follow!

'There's something wrong with the way I'm dealing with my staff. They seem to resist my efforts to keep things streamlined in our office. What am I doing wrong?'

Your problems could stem from the manner in which you lead your staff. Every member of your staff might have to be treated differently. For instance, one employee may need constant help from you, need step-by-step instructions and balk at any sign of changes. Another might just want you to explain the task and let them do things their own way. They'll want you to be available if they require assistance, but they don't want you to 'hover' over them while they perform their tasks.

Dealing with Difficult Situations

Here are seven methods of leadership behaviour. You will likely use all seven, but most supervisors these days find that they prefer styles five, six and seven the most. The leadership styles go from boss-centred leadership to employee-centred leadership. It's up to you to decide which style suits each situation:

1. ***Supervisor makes the decision and announces it***
   In this case, the boss identifies a problem, considers alternative solutions, chooses one of them and then reports this decision to the subordinates for implementation. They may or may not give consideration to what they believe their subordinates will think or feel about the decision. In any case, they provide no opportunity for them to participate directly in the decision-making process. Coercion may or may not be used or implied. An example of this would be when a new company rule or regulation is being set into place.

2. ***Supervisor sells the decision***
   Here the supervisor, as before, takes responsibility for identifying the problem and arriving at a decision. However, rather than simply announcing it, they take the additional step of persuading their subordinates to accept it. In doing so, they recognise the possibility of some resistance among those who will be faced with the decision and seek to reduce this resistance by indicating, for example, what the employees have to gain from their decision. In the example given above, the supervisor would give reasons why the new rule or regulation is being implemented.

3. ***Supervisor presents ideas, invites questions***
   Here the boss has arrived at a decision and seeks acceptance of his/her subordinates and gives fuller explanation of the thinking and intentions of the supervisor. After presenting the ideas, questions are invited so that associates can better understand what they're trying to accomplish. This 'give and take' also enables the supervisor and the subordinates to explore more fully, the implications of the decision. The staff is invited to ask questions about the why's and wherefore's about the new rule or regulation being implemented.

4. ***Supervisor presents a tentative decision subject to change***
   This kind of behaviour permits the subordinates to exert some influence on the decision. The initiative for identifying and diagnosing the problem remains with the boss. Before meeting

Dealing with Difficult Situations

with the staff the manager has thought the problem through and arrived at a decision - but only a tentative one. Before finalising it, the supervisor presents the proposed solution for the reaction of those who will be affected by it.

The supervisor says in effect, *'I'd like to hear what you have to say about the plan that I have developed. I'd appreciate your frank reactions, but will reserve the final decision for myself.'*

5. ***Supervisor presents the problem, gets suggestions and then makes the decision***

Up to this point, the boss has come before the group with a solution. Not so in this case. The subordinates now get the first chance to suggest solutions. The supervisor's initial role involves identifying the problem. The supervisor might, for example, say something of this sort: *'We're faced with a number of complaints from newspapers and the general public about our service policy. What's wrong here? What ideas do you have for coming to grips with this problem?'*

The function of the group becomes one of increasing the supervisor's range of possible solutions to the problem. The purpose is to capitalise on the knowledge and experience of those who are on the 'firing line.' From the expanded list of alternatives developed by the supervisor and the subordinates, they then select the solution that's regarded as the most promising.

6. ***Supervisor defines the limits and requests the group to make a decision***

At this point, the supervisor passes to the group (possibly including themselves as a member) the right to make decisions. Before doing so, however, they define the problem to be solved and the boundaries within which the decision must be made.

An example might relate to how the staff deals with unruly children. The boss decides that this is something that should be worked on by the people involved so they can come up with a plan that would be workable for all the staff. Right now, each staff member deals with the problem independently, with little guidance or consistency with other staff members' methods. Because this is such a touchy issue, the boss decided that a policy must be written and implemented. This way his staff would feel more comfortable dealing with unruly children on company premises. At a meeting of his staff, he explains the problem and everyone is invited to brainstorm to come up with suggestions (some might be fairly hilarious). Each serious suggestion would be discussed, the pros and cons of each suggestion would be outlined and then a decision would be made by the group about which method they would use.

The same tactic could be used to implement flex-time - who wanted to work from seven to three; eight to four; or nine to five. Because the entire group is involved in making the decision, there were few grumbles after the system is put in place.

7. ***Supervisor permits the group to make decisions within prescribed limits***
This represents an extreme degree of group freedom, only occasionally encountered in formal organisations, as for instance, in research groups. Here the team of managers undertakes the identification and diagnosis of a problem, develops alternative procedures to solve it and decides on one or more of these alternative solutions. The only limits directly imposed on the group by the organisation are those specified by the team's boss. However, if the team's boss participates in the decision-making process, s/he'll do so with no more authority than any other member of the group and will commit him/herself in advance to assist in implementing whatever decision the group makes.

You could use this system when one staff member wishes the rest of the staff to know important information that may affect their jobs. For instance a staff member becomes aware of changes in the company's reporting system and calls a meeting to describe it to the rest of the staff. Another staff member may call a meeting to discuss the changes that are going to be made to their filing system. Another person may be in charge of keeping track of holiday time, so calls a meeting to ask the staff when they plan on taking their annual vacation.

When I was Human Resources Manager, I used this method when I was in charge of setting up an orientation program for my company. The senior staff was invited to a meeting where they discussed what should be included in the orientation package for new employees.

Dealing with Difficult Situations

Coffee and Smoke Break Abuses

'One of my technicians abuses his coffee breaks. He's away longer and longer every day and is setting a bad example for the rest of the staff. Another employee takes five minute smoke breaks every hour.'

Studies indicate that some sort of break in the work schedule increases production. Some firms permit their employees to have their coffee and snacks at their work stations or desks. No particular time is set for the break and it tends to fit into the normal flow of work. Any congregating is discouraged. Many employees will not interrupt the flow of work, either because they use the more slack moments for the snack or because frequently they don't care to have something to eat.

The second type is a work stopping time where everyone congregates in one area - a lunch room or cafeteria. Supervisors must discourage employees from slowing down in anticipation of the coffee break. At the conclusion of the break, the resumption of work must be commenced; otherwise, the fifteen minute coffee break can extend by five minutes beforehand and then at least five minutes afterward (bathroom break). The supervisory personnel should be visible immediately before and after the coffee break. They can make direct observation of abuses and encourage more productive use of time. Handing out assignments, checking on progress and other supervisory functions can be accomplished prior to and right after the break.

Despite efforts, some employees will look upon the coffee break as an opportunity to socialise and waste time. Only a conscientious effort on the part of the supervisory personnel to observe abuses and restrict excessive break activity will cause the segregation of those who occasionally abuse, from those who will consistently abuse the time allotted.

Those who smoke should know that they are given the same total time during the day as are allowed for coffee breaks. Therefore, if the coffee breaks are normally fifteen minutes in the morning and the afternoon - the person would be entitled to the same breaks during the day - but no additional time off for coffee. You'd have to make sure that the employees did not take additional time for breaks.

Dealing with Difficult Situations

The Overlong Lunch Hour

'Marty, my accountant constantly takes extra time during his lunch hour. What should I say to him?'

Abuses such as washing up and preparing for the break and getting organised after the actual break, adds up to a lot of lost production time. In addition, the actual time off the premises or at the cafeteria seems to grow when no effort is applied to monitor this abuse. While a manager may close his/her eyes to the lost time as being of small consequence, the few employees who get away with the extended lunches will generally cause adverse affects on employee morale. It's always better not to hedge. Get to the issue - no games. The supervisor should confront the person openly and tell him/her that they are abusing the lunch hour privileges.

After lunch, the supervisor should be available to assess late employees. Several discipline possibilities exist, including docking or lateness, minimising overtime and changing the hour for lunch for some of the employees who are problems.

Start by stating, *'Marty, I see you're still having difficulty getting back on the job at one o'clock. Starting tomorrow, let's try having your lunch hour start at twelve-thirty and see if that's better.'*

Personal phone calls

'One of my staff - Shelly - spends far too much time making or receiving personal phone calls.'

To supervisors, nothing can be as annoying as watching an employee receiving or initiating an excessive number of personal telephone calls. It's not just that the company's phone lines are being tied up, but their workflow is being interrupted. An employee's personal calls should be held to a minimum. After all, s/he is at a place of business and personal requirements should wait until breaks or after work.

You might say to the phone abuser, *'Sally, when you use company time to conduct personal business, whether it is a telephone call, gossiping or just discussing what you did on the weekend, you're using part of my office budget without anything productive coming back.'*

You might also:

Dealing with Difficult Situations

1. Ask her to advise her friends and relatives about the company policy. Reserving the phones for important or emergency calls may not eliminate the frivolous calls entirely, but it will make fair minded employees follow the rules.
2. If you don't have voice mail, have the receptionist ask an incoming caller for his or her name and say, *'Can you tell me the reason for your call or is this a personal call?'* Nothing further needs to be ventured by the receptionist. The question may be enough to embarrass the caller without being too nosy. Such a question tends to reduce the calls and their duration. Or the receptionist might keep track of such calls for one or two days and submit the report to you. Have follow up interviews with employees who continue to make excessive personal telephone calls and start placing written warnings on their files.

Ethnic problems

'One of my employees is constantly making ethnic slurs towards a co-worker. I know I have to step in, but what should I say to her?'

Most work forces (if they're in compliance with the law) are a mixture of individuals of different ethnic backgrounds. Turning the other cheek or tolerating an ethnic slur, whether against a co-worker, a supervisor, a client or someone in the general public, is poor management. An ethnic slur is destructive of the public-good portion of the company image and can undo the efforts put into the human relations among employees.

Jokes at the expense of someone else are not jokes at all. Sometimes the joke-telling gets out of hand and someone's feelings are hurt. Comments of this sort should be discouraged as soon as someone starts *'Did you hear the one about the ...'*

Management should never knowingly joke about someone's background or personal appearance, nor should they condone such behaviour on the part of their employees. One can't judge on the surface how a joke in poor taste might affect an individual. Ethnic comments stem from prejudice - not facts. Prejudice presumes that there's a stereotype of an ethnic group and disregards its members as individuals with different characteristics. Use such reminders as: *'I didn't think that was funny, Paul ...'*

This shows your disapproval and makes the employees more aware that you're monitoring such kinds of jokes. A supervisor's put-down of a slurring joke is indicative of top management's attitude towards any kind of prejudice. Sometimes a private session with the offender is necessary. The supervisor should deal swiftly if the employee insists that the remarks are 'harmless.'

'Tammy, if they're harmless - then they're pointless, so keep your thoughts to yourself.'

If the problem continues, the supervisor should say: *'Tammy, a note is made on each performance appraisal on how employees get along with the other employees (or clients, etc.). I wouldn't like to place a comment on your personnel record that you don't get along, but that's what I'll have to do if you keep making those remarks that I warned you about. Do you understand?'* Or, conduct a formal disciplinary interview explaining the consequences to Tammy if she continues to act as she has in the past.

Buck-Passing Employees

'Maria has a habit of passing-the-buck to other staff members when she's responsible for an error. How can I get her to own up to making mistakes?'

Buck-passing employees can become experts at determining why certain tasks are someone else's responsibility. They say, *'I didn't know I was responsible for that!'* when you'd spent hours explaining the task to them. Others refuse to admit they've made a mistake. They say, *'Who Me? I didn't do that!'* when you both know they were at fault.

Most people take the full blame for their own errors. However, in our more complex managerial environment, it's becoming increasingly important to avoid even minor errors. Buck-passing is often caused by a supervisor's failure to properly delegate responsibility and/or a lack of up-to-date job descriptions. All employees must have a definition of duties set down in the form of a job description manual. Each task should have a performance standard established so that both the employee and the supervisor can monitor how well the employee is doing. This description should be updated regularly (preferably at performance appraisal time).

If not handled correctly, buck-passing can lead to lying, cheating and deep-sixing of mistakes so that no one will find them. The

Dealing with Difficult Situations

concealment of operating mistakes causes irreparable harm to the company. Service failures can be costly in the short- and long-term dollars. Firstly, there's the cost of the immediate replacement of the service. Secondly, the quality image of the company is impaired so the ultimate sales or services are reduced.

The responsibility definition for each employee is not limited to job training, but should be reinforced from time to time. A typical example might be: *'Maria, you're responsible for correctly matching the freight bills to the duplicate of the receiving report.'*

'What if there are differences?'

'It's part of your duty to note the differences on the voucher to Accounts Payable. Any mistakes in matching will be your fault. Any questions?'

Even if Maria is very suited to the job, she will make mistakes. However, she will make fewer and fewer mistakes and will not attempt to pass the buck on occasion if she's reminded of her responsibility and if she's not over-disciplined for any errors. Over-disciplining may cause such excuses as:

'The dispatcher said it's okay to approve trucking bills - so I thought this was okay too.'

'Don't blame me for that one! John said that it was okay to approve it.'

Setting an example is important. Supervisory personnel will discourage buck-passing by employees if, from time to time (in the presence of their subordinates) they admit to making mistakes themselves. Not every mistake need be admitted to in front of subordinates - however, the admission of an occasional goof on the part of the supervisor will demonstrate to others that passing-the-buck is not desirable.

Work Avoidance

'I have a lazy employee who thinks up many ingenious ways to get out of work. How should I deal with employees who don't do their share of the work or deny making mistakes?'

The first step would to be to check to see that the employee's job description was adequate. Then have a meeting and discuss what your expectations are.

Dealing with Difficult Situations

Disciplining employees can be a problem, whether you manage a business office or supervise a loading dock. Employees use a variety of tactics to avoid work. Being habitually late and being away from their desks are two of the commonest ploys. Deal with these employees by obtaining as much factual information as possible so you can make concrete accusations. Express your concerns over their need to cover-up or deny their mistakes. Explain that you feel it's acceptable for them to make mistakes, but unpardonable for them to try to cover up for those mistakes.

Interrupters

'Sally is constantly interrupting her colleagues with small talk and interferes with the work flow of others.'

This can be a particularly annoying staff member. A certain number of interruptions are part of any job and no one expects workers to refrain from some social exchanges. It's when interruptions get out of hand that action is required. Start by keeping a log to determine how often the person interrupts others, when it happens and for how long. Then explain to Sally what will happen if it continues.

Supervisors may also find that a large portion of their day is spent dealing with their staff's interruptions which are often because they don't rely on their own abilities to make decisions. When an interrupter comes to them with questions, instead of automatically giving the answers to their questions, they should ask the staff member, *'What do you think you should do?'* Their employees usually know what they should be doing, but seek their supervisor's approval anyway. Giving them the chance to learn that they knew the solution before they asked it; is the solution to this annoying habit. Soon, they'll realise that they have the ability to make many more decisions without bothering their supervisor about them.

On the other hand, if supervisors feel that their employees are keeping them from doing your 'real' work - they may need to change their attitude. Perhaps dealing with those so-called interruptions is really an important part of their job - as important as dealing with clients or completing reports. In that case, supervisors need to remind themselves, *'That's my job calling.'* Possibly they're not providing the proper training to help their staff become independent enough to not need their constant approval.

If the above applies to you, try the following:

Dealing with Difficult Situations

- Plan short meetings to discuss problems and find solutions to employee concerns.
- Set time limits for meetings and stick to them.
- If your staff is unsure of what to do or their authority level, they may need to have their job descriptions updated.
- Ensure that your staff is adequately trained to do their jobs and give them the authority to handle tasks that really don't need your input or approval.

'The Silent Treatment'

'Jane uses the silent treatment to get her way. If she's upset about something, she clams up and refuses to talk (which can go on for days). What should I do to change her behaviour?'

In modern society, studies show that men and women use the 'silent treatment' equally and both need to be discouraged from using this form of indirect aggression. Ignoring others by refusing to discuss issues is manipulative and unfair and results in a no-win situation for both parties. This isn't to say that people can't walk away from an argument until they calm down, but they must return within a reasonable length of time and resolve the situation with the other person.

Let staff members who use such techniques know that their behaviour is an act of indirect aggression. Explain that they should discuss and resolve annoying situations immediately so they don't accumulate and end up causing a major blow-up later.

When women are asked why they use the silent treatment on men, many reply, *'He never listens to me, so why should I bother to express my opinion?'* This assumption by women comes from differences in male/female communication styles.

Research shows that women face each other directly with eyes anchored on each others' faces when conversing. Men sit at angles to each other and look elsewhere in the room, periodically glancing at each other and often mirror each other's body movements. Men's tendency to face away from women in a conversation, gives women the impression that the men aren't listening. Women also nod their heads much more often than men to show that they're listening and make far more 'listening noises' such as *'um hmmm.'* It's worth taking the effort to explain these differences to both your male and female employees.

Dealing with Difficult Situations

Difficult Counselling Interviews

'One of my staff members, Joe, is going through a rough time at home which is drastically affecting his performance at work. It looks as if his marriage is breaking up. How should I approach him to let him know that even though he's going through a rough time, I still need him to do his work?'

'One of my employees, Sandra, is obviously going through a tough time in her personal life. Her elderly mother lives with her and she has to decide whether to put her in a nursing home or not. Her productivity is slipping and she's very withdrawn and doesn't have the same enthusiasm she used to have when dealing with clients. I'd hate to add to her problems, but must see some improvement.'

Personal problems of various kinds can interfere with an employee's performance at work, including:

1. High absentee record;
2. Requests to leave work early;
3. Lateness at the start of work and around coffee and lunch breaks;
4. High number of personal telephone calls;
5. High error rate and breaking of company or safety rules;
6. Little response to group effort;
7. Reduced production;
8. Increased fatigue;
9. Reduced availability for overtime;
10. High 'Sickness' days off;
11. Loss of initiative;
12. Expressions of irritability to co-workers;
13. Requests for irregular vacation time;
14. Antagonism toward supervisor or management;
15. Lower training/learning capability;
16. Low company loyalty; and
17. High grievance rate.

These personal problems may surface that warrant a counselling interview such as:

- family break-up
- alcoholism
- drug abuse

Dealing with Difficult Situations

- illness in the home
- problems with children
- problems with spouse
- elderly parents living with them

How should supervisors deal with these problems? Are they qualified to handle them? In most cases - *no* they're not! This is why supervisors should keep abreast of where their staff can go to obtain counselling to solve these kinds of problems. Help them obtain this help - then back off. Make allowances on the job if necessary, but eventually stick to performance issues. Remain objective. Keep emotions in check. It's difficult to think and respond to an employee's need, if you react with emotion yourself.

When dealing with issues of this kind, <u>confidentiality is a must!</u> The employee should be advised that if possible, the matter will go no further than the supervisor. Don't discuss these issues with others unless they're critical to solving the problem. The supervisor can point out the extent to which the employee's performance is below average. Comparisons to previous records can be made. The supervisor can offer assistance in solving the personal problem, but, must stress that suitable performance from the employee must be the end result. For instance:

'I know you're having a bad time right now Joe, but I still need you to keep up our production quotas. Can I count on you to do your share?' Or:

'Sandra, I know that you're capable of better work. Is there some way I can help you to get back on the right track?'

Keep in mind that the problem is the other person's - don't take responsibility for it. Do however try to help him/her get through the problem.

Occasionally counselling interviews can turn out to be difficult ones because of other reasons. A supervisor notices that an employee is snarling at other employees or observes that an employee seems lethargic and their job performance is below normal. The supervisor calls the employee in for a counselling interview. When asked, *'What's the matter?'* the curt reply may be, *'It's none of your business!'*

Dealing with Difficult Situations

What would you reply if you were this employee's supervisor? You should say, *'Yes it is. Whenever your behaviour affects your productivity or those around you, it **is** my business.'* Then encourage him/her to discuss the problem.

If s/he still refuses, add, *'You have two choices. Give me a chance to help you with your problem or get along better with your workmates and improve your job performance (or whatever was the problem). Which have you decided to do?'* Wait for an answer. Then, let him/her know that you expect his/her behaviour to improve and give the consequences should s/he not be willing to change.

What do you say if an employee brings others into the discussion? For instance, *'Joe does that all the time - why are you picking on me?'* Your answer should be, *'We're here to discuss **your** performance - not Joe's.'*

You should then:

- State your perception of the problem and allow the person to think about it.
- State your expectations and keep the door open for further discussions when the employee has cooled down.

This will allow the employee to settle his/her temper and be less emotional or angry when s/he decides to deal with the issue. When you call an employee in to discuss a behaviour or production problem, keep in mind what you wish to accomplish - a change in the employee's behaviour and/or productivity – not retaliation.

Upon becoming aware that the supervisor has noticed a change in attitude or lower performance, the employee may push to solve his/her own problem or at least learn to live with it so it doesn't affect his/her work. The supervisor's duty is to assist a subordinate who has a personal problem, if such assistance is wanted and is possible.

Second, there is the obligation to the company, which requires the best performance possible from each employee. The time to butt into an employee's personal problems is when the supervisor feels s/he can accomplish both these objectives by rendering assistance while maintaining production. A little caution is advisable; *the supervisor should not become directly involved other than as a possible source of advice.*

Dealing with Difficult Situations

Sick Leave Abuses

When Bruce entered his office at the beginning of the day he learned that two of his staff had phoned in to say they'd be away from work that day. This seemed to be a regular occurrence and happened far too often. He checked the employee's attendance records and one employee in particular, had been absent more than 21 days that year. This had not been for any lengthy illness, but was scattered with absences of two or three days at a time.

A large contributor to the breakdown of employee morale is the fact that some employees get away with calling in sick, get paid for the day, when they weren't the least bit ill. While it's difficult to determine completely who is truly ill and who isn't, steps can be taken that will likely ensure that the privilege of sick leave with pay is not abused.

Most employees will go to work even with a runny nose and fever and refuse to take advantage of sick pay policies. Many feel that they don't wish to take sick leave for minor ailments because they may need the leave when they're 'really' sick. Others feel that, *'No one can handle my job as well as I can'* and feel some responsibility for their performance. To them, it's part of the ethic of being a good worker. The supervisor should recognise the sacrifices made. When this type of employee calls in sick, s/he is generally too sick to perform any kind of work at all.

Other employees will be out for any and every minor ailment. They view sick leave as a right and want to take full advantage of any accrued leave. They demonstrate little responsibility for their required productivity. The fact that other workers have to carry a larger workload or that their company will suffer economically is of little concern to them.

How many times a year does an employee pull that line before s/he may be considered a chronic absentee? One company says that eight or more absences during a twelve month period indicate a problem employee.

When this type of employee calls and says, *'Sorry boss, but I can't make it in today.'* A seemingly good reply may be: *'Sorry you're ill - stay out until you're feeling better.'* However, don't say that. Don't worry: chronic absentees will stay out until they feel a lot better.

Dealing with Difficult Situations

Why should they have to knock themselves out? And besides - they view sick leave as their right.

For those suspected of abusing this benefit, the supervisor should call the employee at the end of each work day to ask: *'Orson, how are you coming along? I'm calling to see if you expect to be at work tomorrow.'*

Two beautiful spin-offs benefits can result. First, it has been determined that the absent employee is really at home. (Of course s/he could have been at the doctor's - but *every* time s/he was called?) Second, the employee who becomes aware of the procedure may be discouraged from taking sick leave for seemingly minor ailments or to accomplish some personal chore.

It's generally agreed that innocent absenteeism, even if it is excessive, can't be grounds for disciplinary measures. On the other hand, it's generally agreed that an employee's inability to report for work on a regular basis (for whatever reasons) can be grounds for discharge.

Where the company is faced with the problem of an employee who has been absent from work for excessive periods of time, (i.e. the chronic absentee) s/he may be discharged if the company is able to demonstrate that it's unreasonable for the employment relationship to continue. In such cases:

a. The employer must be able to document the employee's absences, demonstrating not only that they can readily be seen to be well beyond what any reasonable person would consider acceptable, but also that the employee has deviated substantially and unduly from the average level of attendance of other employees;

b. The employer must be able to demonstrate that the excessive absenteeism problem has been persistent and has continued despite documented attempts by the employer to have it corrected. The supervisor must document his/her efforts to counsel the employee and determine underlying reasons for absences. S/he must also be able to show that s/he has had every degree of compassion and has taken into account any 'extenuating circumstances' for excessive absenteeism and has been patient with the employee in attempts to have the problem corrected.

Dealing with Difficult Situations

c. The employer must be able to present convincing reasons explaining why s/he feels that there is little or no likelihood of a reduction in the excessive absenteeism in the future. In this regard, the employer is often best advised to provide medical evidence in support of this conclusion.

One employee had been enrolled in a drug rehabilitation program because of abuse of prescription drugs, but still had many days absent from work. The employee always gave a doctor's certificate, but his supervisor wondered how authentic they were. How could he make sure that his staff's absences were because they were legitimately sick and not taking the day off because of other reasons or had slipped in their rehabilitation program?

Many employees abuse a company's sick leave by using sick leave for one of the following reasons:

- their children are sick;
- their spouse is sick;
- they just wanted a day off;
- for 'personal reasons' (too varied to list); or
- had abused drugs or alcohol.

Should a supervisor pay his or her staff when they're away for these kinds of absences? It depends on the supervisor and their office policy and award agreement. Unless covered by an award, sick leave is given to employees for their own illness, not for the sickness of someone else or for other reasons. Other companies provide additional paid leave such as compassionate leave (for critical illness or death in the family) or jury duty leave. Still others allow a set number of days for family emergencies or sickness. This is often put into a broad category entitled 'general or personal leave.' This can be used for family or personal emergencies, but again employees are cautioned not to abuse the privilege. They must require the day off because of a legitimate emergency.

So what can a supervisor do if s/he feels employees are abusing their paid time off privileges? Usually a simple reminder about the abuse of the sick leave policy will stop the abuse. If the absences become chronic, it's generally agreed that an employee's inability to report for work on a regular basis (for whatever reasons) can be grounds for termination.

Dealing with Difficult Situations

In industries where there is a heavier reliance on individual performance and any absence is a disruption in the flow of service to customers, management has to rely more on stiffer illness verification procedures including the following:

1. Required doctor's certificate for three or more consecutive sick days.
2. Doctor's certificate for any absence due to illness before or after a holiday weekend.
3. Complete physical examination by the company doctor if the employee is out more than ten days in any one year.

What should the supervisor do, when forced to question a doctor's certificate verifying the employee's illness? S/he should investigate. When an employee is found guilty of falsifying a doctor's certificate, s/he can and should be disciplined. The degree of discipline depends on the circumstances of the particular case.

The Alcoholic Employee

'One of my staff - Charlie - has come back from lunch under the influence of alcohol. I have sent him home when this occurs, but it's become a regular thing with him. He's been away several days around the weekend, which I suspect have been because he was drinking and had to sober up. How am I to deal with an employee who appears to have become an alcoholic?'

Experienced supervisors will advise that any promise by an employee that s/he can control his/her alcoholic habit must be viewed with suspicion. S/he would not admit to him/herself (much less to the boss) that s/he has a drinking problem. This makes for a strong distinction between the alcoholic and the other types of problem employees who frequently admit to their shortcomings.

Most people drink and even though some may be considered heavy drinkers, not all become alcoholics. The few that do can be helped more successfully if help is offered in the early stages. Generally the drinker who has become an alcoholic will begin to incur a heavy absentee record - not necessarily typified by the Monday and Friday syndrome. (Frequently s/he has dried out by Monday and if Friday is payday s/he needs the cash). Partial attendance can be expected.

Dealing with Difficult Situations

Either related illness forces him/her to be late or s/he leaves after lunch break. Sometimes food has made the employee ill or s/he may wish to indulge the weakness.

When questioned about the absences or the partial absences, the alcoholic can't be expected to admit to the real cause, but will offer any excuse. Supervisors must realise that this kind of problem is beyond his/her realm of responsibility. Employees with this problem must be encouraged to obtain help from their family doctor, Alcoholics Anonymous or any other source available to him/her. The supervisor must, however, be very firm in stating to the employee that failures in performance must be corrected and it's up to the employee to find a way to accomplish this.

When an employee's problem of excessive absenteeism is due to drug or alcohol abuse, the employer may discharge the employee if s/he is able to demonstrate that the 'employment relationship' cannot reasonably be reconstructed. In such cases, the employer must be able to define that decision in relation to the type of criteria noted above. As well however, the employer must show that s/he has recognised the alcoholic problem as an illness and has made every effort to assist the employee in efforts to correct the illness. Any rehabilitation efforts will be carefully reviewed and the company must be convinced that further efforts at rehabilitation are not likely to be successful.

A frequent attribute of the problem of the alcoholic employee is that many co-workers and supervisors wish to conceal the problem. They have a desire to 'help' the employee by not permitting the higher levels of management to be aware that one of their employees is an alcoholic. For some reason, this type of cover-up is not tried with other types of problems, but genuinely peculiar to employee alcoholism (and drug abuse). Some of the reasons used for covering up for the alcoholic include:

1. Charlie's a good worker.
2. He needs the job and getting caught would sink his ship.
3. He has a lot of problems at home.
4. He would help anybody he could.
5. It's an illness that can't be cured by letting management know.
6. It will only take a short while to sober him up.
7. The job caused him to drink.

Dealing with Difficult Situations

In circumstances such as these, the employee may run circles around his/her supervisors and co-workers who mistakenly believe they can help the employee by covering up his/her actions. One way of overcoming the willingness to conceal the alcoholic employee is to set the record straight with regard to all alcoholics:

1. If the alcoholic employee drives to and from work or uses a company vehicle, s/he may be a deadly menace to him/herself as well as to others on the road.
2. The alcoholic is a threat to his/her own safety and that of others while on the job. *If an alcoholic injures him/herself at work while intoxicated, s/he generally cannot obtain worker's compensation for any job-related injury.* Also: *Other injured employees may not recover worker's compensation and may have to lodge a personal law suit against the alcoholic to pay for any time off because of an injury.*
3. An alcoholic doesn't get cured by someone's covering up for him/her. S/he continues to be a problem both at work and at home.
4. The company's community relations suffer if other organised groups in the community see in the company image, a tolerance for alcoholism.
5. If an employee has customer contact while intoxicated, s/he will cause a loss of sales and company image.
6. Many employees, clients and parents of some of the younger employees, are offended by the presence of an alcoholic employee on the premises.
7. An alcoholic can only be cured with the assistance of experienced persons who are skilled in such matters.
8. An alcoholic employee, besides problems with tardiness and absenteeism, may:

    o Disregard safety rules;
    o Be indifferent to productivity requirements;
    o Have a higher error rate;
    o Drink on the premises;
    o Steal company and/or other employee's property; and
    o Encourage others to violate company rules.

Managerial and other personnel will do well to advise the alcoholic employee that drinking is a problem that s/he hasn't been able to handle on his/her own; that they understand that s/he has a problem

Dealing with Difficult Situations

and will do what they can to help. While only s/he can stop the drinking, the associates should applaud the alcoholic's effort to overcome the problem.

Supervisors and other management personnel should be made aware that cover-up of the existence of alcoholic employees will not be tolerated and that the company has rules regarding the handling of employees who drink on the job. If an employee is interested in helping the alcoholic, there are ways - not by trying to cover up for him/her, but by encouraging him/her to seek assistance.

Messy work area

'Darren is a very messy person and his work area is a disaster waiting to happen. How can I get him to tidy up his work area?'

This is a necessity under work cover regulations. Many think that having a messy work station is not a requirement of the job. They consider it window dressing, for they believe that an operation can be just as productive no matter what the housekeeping conditions are. However, some of the characteristics that do affect efficiency and are evidence of poor housekeeping include:

1. Missing records or files.
2. Lost or misplaced tools or equipment.
3. High supply costs.
4. Improper mix of parts and inventory.
5. High contamination of product.
6. High scrap and rework costs.
7. Poor balance of finished products inventory.
8. High machine down-time.
9. Poor safety record.
10. Low employee morale;
11. Disinterest in working overtime.
12. Discipline problems and labour turnover.

One way to motivate the employees to maintain a tidy work area is to set an example. If the supervisor's office is neat and clean, then good housekeeping habits are more easily encouraged among the rank and file. Encourage daily clean up at the end of the day. If the supervisor spots someone whose workstation looks messy heading for the door, s/he should stop the employee and ask him/her to organise his/her workstation before leaving. For more difficult

Dealing with Difficult Situations

problems, a written checklist of housekeeping activities could be given to messy employees.

Sloppy or Careless

'One of my staff completes her work so poorly, that someone else has to re-do her effort. This often takes more time than the original task. I'd hate to have to fire her, but unless her productivity improves I'm afraid that's what I'll have to do.'

Have you been clear to her what you expect from her? Is her job description adequate? Does it outline the tasks she must do and have standards of performance or benchmarks that she's expected to reach when performing those tasks? If not - the fault could be yours.

Or it's possible that she has been in a 'rut' for so long that it will take considerable effort for her to 'dig herself out.' Unfortunately, she possibly doesn't perceive that she's in a rut and plods along, day after day, year after year, often performing tasks she can barely tolerate doing. Her entire life may be routine and mundane and she may not have considered there are other options open to her.

Short of putting a bomb under her, there's not much you can do to get her motivated. Motivation has to come from within herself, but start by letting her know what is expected of her. Then be ready to initiate the disciplinary process outlining the consequences she will face if she does not improve her performance.

The Bottleneck Employee

'The work isn't getting out because George isn't doing his part!'

Bottlenecks are a frequent management complaint. The causes could be attributable to either the management's design of the work flow or to an employee's poor work habits. Management's poor design of the work flow can be detected by a simple test. Have another employee assume the duties of the employee in the problem area. If there's still a bottleneck (after the training period) then changes may have to be made to the work flow arrangements.

Here are the typical characteristics of a bottleneck employee:

1. They have poor time management skills.
2. Too many items are held up because of relatively minor problems.

Dealing with Difficult Situations

3. Have not had enough training.
4. Have low decision-making capability.
5. Are unaware of supervisor's expectations.
6. Square peg in round hole - qualifications don't fit requirements of the job or they lack teamwork skills.
7. Feel threatened by job insecurity.
8. Have an unusual fear of making mistakes. Or,
9. Involved in personality clashes with supervisors or colleagues resulting in a lack of cooperation between staff.

Where there's no indication that the employee is being a deliberate bottleneck, some additional on-the-job training may be in order to ensure employee understands what the job entails. During this re-training, the supervisor can see if the employee understands his/her job responsibilities. S/he can demonstrate to the employee how to perform the various tasks and then guide him/her under direct observation. Little techniques that speed the job along should be emphasised.

If employees are more aware of what functions are performed before or after theirs, they can use their judgement and understand the consequences of their own performance. Employees will learn how their jobs fit into the total picture and what contribution they're expected to make.

Most 'sticks-in-the-mid' don't really want to be 'sticks-in-the mud.' Nearly everyone wants to feel that s/he is co-operating to achieve common goals. The ploy is to make everyone in the work force have a common goal. Other employees can be encouraged to assist:

'Tom, can you show Rick how he can move that project faster?'

'Rick, let Tom show you a couple of techniques for pushing the stuff through that we need now.'

Encourage the problem employee to want to put the work out faster. The paying of a few compliments here and there improves confidence among slower employees. It permits them to have a greater feeling of job security and certainly reduces tensions. The bottleneck employee can become less fearful of incidental mistakes, thus reducing his/her own built-in need for more control of his/her work.

Dealing with Difficult Situations

Error-Prone Employees

'Phil is our departmental disaster who makes so many mistakes I often wonder if he isn't doing so on purpose to evade doing his job. He's an intelligent man, but still makes the most unusual mistakes. How can I turn him around and improve his accuracy rate?'

Just as auto insurance companies recognise that some drivers are more prone to having accidents than the general population of drivers, some recognition must be given to the fact that some employees are more likely to make mistakes than others. Of course, deliberate mistakes are a cause for the use of disciplinary measures up to and including firing the errant employee. However, most mistakes are not intentional. They are caused by a variety of reasons, including errors of judgement on the part of management.

There are two basic kinds of mistakes; system mistakes and human mistakes. The first results from the design of a system. Constant improvement of the system will reduce the error rate.

No matter how well the system is designed, there is a certain amount of reliance on the human factor. That factor is the one to which line management personnel have to apply a great deal of attention. The system's designer may also be at fault of the 'human' mistakes. Some of the following conditions may also exist:

1. Inadequate job training.
2. Limited written instructions.
3. Large number of subordinates reporting to one supervisor (12 should be the maximum number of subordinates reporting to one supervisor).
4. Too few intermediate levels of supervision.
5. Dull working environment.
6. Job boredom.
7. Poor analysis of error cause.
8. High employee turnover.

Most employees like to feel that they're earning their pay. Part of that feeling of pride stems from their opinion that their work has few if any errors. Therefore, they appreciate help - when offered gracefully - to improve their own pride in their work. One method of attack is to provide an employee-coach for the error-prone employee. A senior employee, who is proficient in his/her job, will be able to isolate the causes of the problem employee's errors and provide instruction in special techniques to either avoid such errors or catch the mistakes and take corrective action. To minimise carelessness, the problem employee has to be shown at which points in the process, some additional attention should be applied:

'Arnold, could you spend a little more time rechecking your work?'

'Donna, can you pay a little more attention to these types of items?'

Employee Daydreaming

'Mary has just announced that she's engaged to be married. This is great – but she spends too much of her time thinking and daydreaming about her wedding and is so distracted that her work is suffering. How can I get her back on track?'

We all daydream, but some people do it to excess - to a point where it interferes with work or productivity or becomes a dangerous safety problem. In this case Mary is distracted because of her wedding. Speak to her and let her know that her productivity is down and that you're counting on her to give the same work as she did before the announcement of her wedding. She must know you're serious and will have no choice but to start formal disciplinary matters if her productivity doesn't improve.

Some jobs lend themselves more to employee daydreaming than others and have to be monitored more carefully. It's not always fair to pin the blame for daydreaming on the employee. His/her job may be so boring the employee can't keep his/her mind on it. Machine-like functions tend to create opportunities for daydreaming. Where greater worker attention is required, daydreaming can result in loss of productivity, errors and even accidents. The problem may be that the job was not designed to hold the employee's attention.

The design of the work area can reduce the tendency to daydream. Operations that must be performed while standing, tend to discourage day-dreaming. The work area decor is of some importance. Desks or work areas need not be all the same colour. Attempts should be made to eliminate monotony in the work environment. This is why job rotation is so popular.

Those work situations that require a higher degree of creativity on the part of the employee should have an environment that's conducive to creativity. If there's any flexibility in the method of

Dealing with Difficult Situations

performing the task, add that flexibility to the task description. This will allow the employee to decide how to handle particular steps by using his/her initiative in selecting his/her production process. Such flexibility permits the employee to think about how s/he wants to handle a particular job and therefore increases his/her alertness and reduces monotony.

No matter what efforts are made to dispel daydreaming potential, some employees seem to be lost in the clouds. Only constant supervisory attention can dispel the problem and keep the employee on his/her toes. Sometimes, a discussion between the supervisor and the employee is in order.

Show-offs

'I have an employee who is a real show-off and at our training sessions, he's the class clown. His actions interfere with the smooth-running of our department and training sessions are almost a waste of time because of his antics.'

Show-offs must be the centre of attention. They play games on others - interrupt them with childish antics. They can have the 'class clown' mentality where they seek others' attention by fooling around. Getting them to accomplish tasks can be a heavy chore. They accomplish this by escalating the value of what they do, where they've been and whom they know. They exaggerate their own importance to win admiration or attention and have the habit of snubbing people they don't think of as important. They're snooty and snobbishly superior. Being high achievers, they put themselves high on their own list of priorities.

Make sure he doesn't take an unfair share of credit for assignments done in a team environment. He needs praise, so give praise where praise is deserved and correct him when he tries to exaggerate his contributions. If he acts up at meetings - take him aside. Use feedback to explain what his behaviour does to others and the hardships it causes to his other team members. A clearly defined job description about how he is to complete tasks is a must. If his behaviour continues - begin disciplinary steps with written warnings.

Won't answer phone calls and emails

'Two of my staff are terrible communicators. One doesn't return phone calls - the other doesn't answer e-mails.'

Dealing with Difficult Situations

The possibility is that you might be communicating to them using an incorrect 'sensory language.'

When we say two people have 'rapport,' we usually mean that their relationship is harmonious - we get into someone else's world. We can enhance this rapport by determining another's primary sensory language. Most of us are a mixture of all three, but one usually stands out as being our primary sensory language.

People process information in different ways. They are primarily visual, auditory or kinaesthetic (muscular movement) in the way they process information. Each type uses distinctive words that reflect their preference. To create rapport with people, listen to find their primary mode of communication then mirror their language. Here are examples of these:

The visual person might say:

'I get the picture.'
'I see what you mean.'
'Let me see what the job looks like.' or,
'My perception is....'
The auditory person uses such phrases as:
'That sounds good to me.'
'I hear what you're saying.'
'That rings a bell.'
'I hear you loud and clear.' or,
'Let me explain how this works.'

Typical phrases for kinaesthetic would be:
'Show me how to do this.'
'That doesn't feel right.'
'Hold on.'
'I'm comfortable with that.'

'That's a rough problem.' or,
'You have a heavy task.'

Is it possible that the one who doesn't answer his/her phone calls is a visual person and the one who doesn't answer his/her emails is an auditory one? Just changing your method of communication might be the answer to these problems.

Dealing with Difficult Situations

CHAPTER 3

DIFFICULT SITUATIONS

- COLLEAGUES & OTHERS

Answering Phone Messages

'I'm a receptionist and find that some people don't return their phone messages. Mr. Bailey had tried five times to reach Mr. Smith and I placed the messages on his desk throughout the day. I know Mr. Smith wasn't very busy that day and had ample time to answer the messages. The fifth time Mr. Bailey called; he accused me of not passing on his messages. I've had enough of this person's poor business practices, but don't know how to approach him about the problem.'

Most companies these days have voice mail. Why has your company not installed this device? However, this doesn't answer your request. Use the following technique whenever anyone is making your life miserable - whether it is someone who isn't returning phone calls or doesn't have his or her information ready for your department's monthly reports.

Say, *'I have a problem and I need your help in solving it.'* Then discuss the problem. *'Mr. Bailey called and left messages for you five times today. I placed those messages on your desk. The last time he phoned, he accused me of not passing your messages on to you. What should I tell him the next time he calls?'* This way, you dump the problem on the lap of the person who caused it and most feel obliged to help you solve the problem. It's far better to use this tactic than saying, *'You turkey – why don't you answer your phone calls?'*

Dysfunctional childhood

'My co-worker, Bill, grew up in a dysfunctional environment. He was beaten and yelled at most of his life and suffered from a barrage of constant put-downs. Repeatedly, he was told he was 'stupid, dumb and wouldn't amount to anything.' He firmly believes that his future won't be any different from his past so resists making decision that

will alter his life. How can I make him see that his future is what he makes of it and his past is not a blueprint for his life hereafter?'

Many people spend their lives reliving the past. They get into a mental rut that concentrates on what was, rather than what will be. Many of their comments start with the prefaces, *'I should have ...'* Or, *'If only I had ...'*

When people drift through life, rather than controlling it, I think of them as 'stuck.' They'll remain stuck where they are, unless *they* do something to change their lives. They waste their lives by getting in a rut and staying there or making feeble stabs at changing their lives. The least kind of opposition sends them scuttling back towards their safety net of sameness. These people hate getting up in the morning, because there's not much that's exciting or stimulating in their lives. One day is just like another and the future's likely to be the same. These people need a jolt to get them living again. Just as heart-attack victims need a jolt of electricity to get their hearts restarted; these people need a jolt of reality to put them back into the land of the living.

Let's put ourselves into Bill's shoes for a while and feel what he might be feeling:

He accepts criticism as always being true. Not only does he accept criticism from others willingly, he's the one who criticises everything he does himself as well. The little voice in his head is always ridiculing him about his perceived failures. He punishes himself with statements such as *'I'm too old ... I'm not smart enough ... I'm not good at that.'* What he's stating is, *'I'm a finished product in this area and I'm never going to be different.'*

His fear of failure is very often the fear of someone else's disapproval or ridicule. Failure is someone else's opinion of how certain acts should be completed, so he doesn't attempt anything new or challenging. He'll shun experiences that might bring failure and avoids anything that doesn't guarantee success. He may turn down excellent opportunities, but can't explain why he's doing so.

He hasn't learned how to be assertive - to stand up for himself. Inexperienced in the art of getting his own needs met, he allows others to manipulate him. He's unable to make decisions that support his own wishes, values and feelings. The result is that he feels bad about himself without knowing why.

Dealing with Difficult Situations

He constantly compares himself to others. Others are always happier, more famous, more successful or worth more. Others' successes only make him more depressed at his own status in life. He may feel that if he fails at something, that he's a failure as a person. Instead of trying another avenue or another way of doing something, he quits trying.

Using 20/20 hindsight, he can probably see exactly where he went wrong - on a job interview or in a love relationship. These thoughts can cause immobility and make him remain in the negative rut he's in.

So how do you help this kind of individual? Encourage him to stop thinking of life in black or white terms. There are many grey areas in between. Deal with him by having a heart-to-heart talk with him. Identify his negative behaviour and ask his permission to bring this behaviour to his attention if you hear him running himself down or reliving his past. Once a person is an adult, there's no excuse to blame a terrible childhood or a failure at school for what's going to happen in their future. He must change his attitude about this to become 'unstuck.'

If life doesn't come up to his expectations, console him with the idea that it's never too late for conditions to change. Instead of dwelling in the past, he needs to concentrate his energy on building a better, happier life and make the most of the present moment.

He can't acquire the trait of extending himself to the utmost overnight. Confidence is a cumulative feeling. There will likely be setbacks and disappointments, but:

Someone who tries to do something and fails is a lot better off than the person who tries to do nothing and succeeds.

Encourage Bill to get professional counselling to counteract his dysfunctional childhood and introduce him to good role models. Your moral support will make this transition considerably easier for him.

Serviceman gets uncivil treatment

'I'm a serviceman for business machines and find myself becoming angrier and angrier by the attitude of the people I've come to help. I'm blamed because the machine has broken down, but they often

Dealing with Difficult Situations

don't stay around to explain the exact problem they're facing. This means I have to check out the entire machine that costs the companies much more. My second beef is that I'm treated as if I'm a non-person or as if I'm part of the machine. It's no wonder that service people don't last long in my business!'

We all need to look at how we treat people who work in the service industry. Ask yourself whether you commit the following actions that are degrading and can have devastating effects on others:

1. Do you release your frustrations about the broken business machine on the service representative? *'It's about time you got here. This machine hasn't been working properly all day!'*
2. Do you fail to recognise service people by treating them as if they weren't there?
3. Do you fail to keep them informed about problems you're facing or have faced in the past?
4. Do you forget to thank them for fixing your problem?

If you're guilty of the above actions, try a little empathy and realise that the service representatives are doing their best to keep your machines in working order. If you're the service representative, say, *'I'm doing my best to help you, but you're not making it very easy for me to do so. I need to ask you some questions, so I can hone in on the problems you're facing. Then I can fix your machine and allow you to get on with your work.'* This should at least get some of the help you need to get the job done.

'My problem is that clients come on to me and make passes when I make service calls. How can I deal with this without offending the client?'

This is a problem faced by both men and women when they enter the domain or 'home turf' of clients. Be as businesslike as possible when visiting clients. If the client shows signs of being amorous, (such as suggesting that you get together for lunch) explain that you'd rather not mix your business with your personal life - and stick to it.

If they persist and become aggressive in their advances, more drastic actions are required. Say, *'Your actions are upsetting me. I've told you twice that I'm not interested in pursuing a personal relationship with you. If you continue to talk and act in this manner, I'll have no other recourse but to charge you with sexual harassment.'*

Dealing with Difficult Situations

In the latter case, you would document the incident. Tell your supervisor that you were forced to threaten the client with sexual harassment charges and give him or her, a copy of your documentation. If your supervisor is enlightened, s/he will follow-up with a verbal or written confirmation to the client about your treatment and reinforce your actions. If I were your supervisor, I'd also talk to the client's superiors and make them aware of the problems the employee is causing to the staff member. It's likely that this client treats other people in a similar fashion and their employer will likely want to take steps to stop his/her behaviour before the situation ends up in a court battle.

Customer Service

'One of my colleagues embarrasses me by the way he treats customers. He's rude, gives poor service and generally makes our department look bad.'

Customers are no different from anyone else in that they appreciate courtesy. One thing a salesperson must never forget is that the customer is number one. Sadly, some salespeople give the impression that looking after the customer is an interruption to their 'real work.' Such behaviour implies that the salesperson is doing clients a favour by helping them. In reality, the customer's needs should take precedence over any other work they do.

Customer service of course, is not just important for those who work in stores and restaurants. Every kind of organisation that exists in society needs proper customer service. Rudeness, impatience and insensitivity are not compatible with good, professional sales. Even so, salespeople sometimes display these negative traits. Discourtesy, disrespect, indifference, slow service, ignorance of the services offered by the company, errors and negative behaviour repel customers and leave bad feelings. Customers often respond to the bad feelings by simply staying away.

Customers gravitate to places where they get the most positive feelings. The way salespeople act with customers is far more important than all the company money spent on advertising and image building. The most successful members of service organisations share common traits. They learn everything they possibly can about their organisation and how it can serve its clients better.

Knowledgeable salespeople know:

- What their organisation does.
- Who their key personnel are.
- Why the organisation works the way it does.
- What services or products it offers.
- What common questions or problems are likely to arise
- How they can help clients more effectively.

Show your colleague where you think he's falling down in his service to the customers using feedback to explain how you feel when he does this. It just takes one inefficient salesperson to destroy what has taken your company years to build and you don't want to be part of the problem by ignoring his poor service. If he refuses to change, document the bad service he has given and explain your concerns to your supervisor.

Colleague has tantrums

'Sue, one of my colleagues has tantrums. You've told us how to deal with bosses who have tantrums - but how do you deal with colleagues?'

Keep in mind that someone who is having a tantrum is not acting reasonably. Anyone who is not acting reasonably is temporarily insane. If you yell back at them - all you have is two people having an insane conversation. Your goal when coping with a person having a tantrum is to help them re-gain control. So:

1. Keep your cool and be firm. Make it clear that you intend to cool down the situation before continuing your discussion.
2. If Sue won't calm down, ask her what she would call such behaviour if one of her children acted the same way. Threaten to walk away from her if she won't calm down. Follow-through if she continues.
3. If she does calm down, ask for facts about the situation.
4. Listen carefully and then do what you can to resolve the dispute.
5. She may regret her outburst. Be ready to deal with her guilt feelings.

Obviously, she doesn't know how to handle anger; otherwise she wouldn't allow herself to get to this stage. Most tantrum givers have feelings of fear, helplessness and frustration. They have low self-esteem and many take every affront personally. As a child they likely found that tantrums allowed them to get their way - so why stop doing something that's so effective? This disruptive behaviour often continues into adulthood, but at that stage of their lives, their tantrums produce a greater backlash of anger and resistance than any of the other difficult behaviours.

If the situation is repetitive and on-going, it's likely that this person has tantrums in front of others as well. So ask for others' help in stopping this unacceptable behaviour.

What a chauvinist!

'He did it again! He made another chauvinistic remark! He insists on calling me 'his girl.' Well I haven't been a 'girl' since I was twelve! Where has he been for the past twenty years? I'm so tired of chauvinistic men!'

Bill, a senior officer in her organisation had embarrassed her again at the last manager's meeting. She had made a minor mistake on a report. He patted her on the head and said, *'It's okay. You're very smart for a woman.'* She was so shocked that she couldn't reply.

Chauvinism is behaviour displayed by both men and women who believe that the world should be male dominated and that men are superior to women. This can still be a serious problem for women in the work place.

There are two forms of male chauvinism. The first kind is blatant. The woman *knows* this man is out to make women feel bad, to put them down and to keep them in their 'place.' They may refer to a woman in a management position as their 'token woman.' Women should stick to the facts when dealing with this kind of individual. If a man says, *'You're earning a good salary for a woman.'*

The woman should reply, *'You believe that women should earn less than men?'*

He says, *'Yes, I do.'*

She says, *'I hear what you're saying. I believe women deserve an equal chance to earn the same kind of salary as men. Women pay rent like men, pay the same for food as men and definitely pay taxes like men. What are the reasons for your belief that women should earn less than men?'* This starts a dialogue instead of ending up in a confrontation.

Why do some men feel the need to use this intentional type of chauvinism? They use it to put women down, which in turn makes *them* feel more important. So how should a woman respond to intentional chauvinism? A calm, *'That was a very chauvinistic remark you just made. What did you really mean by that comment?'* Or, *'That was a very sarcastic and hurting remark you just made. Can you explain why you felt the need to make such a comment?'*

Another tactic is, instead of reacting to the chauvinistic remark, tune it out and ignore it. By remaining calm the victim maintains control. The true chauvinist can't handle this behaviour, because the woman isn't drawn into playing the game. It's no fun any more - so they take their chauvinistic remarks elsewhere.

The other form of chauvinism is more subtle and is used by men who often aren't aware that their actions could be classified as chauvinistic. These are usually older men, who are sixty years of age or older or men whose upbringing or home situation conditioned them to believe that they are to protect and care for women. Many of these men call women 'dear' because women *are* dear to them.

Because these men don't use this type of chauvinism to hurt women, a gentle response from women is advisable. They often don't know that what they do or say may be offensive to women. Unless the women let them know there's a problem, they're not going to change, so it's up to women to speak up. *'I don't know if you're aware of this or not, but many women would find your last comment to be chauvinistic or patronising. I'm not offended by your calling me 'Dear,' but other women might be.'*

If a woman is promoted into a senior position and finds she is the only female at that level, she may suffer from isolation. The male managers have coffee and lunch together and may not think to include her in their plans. This leaves her with the choice of having breaks with her female support staff or finding other senior women in her company (or others) for socialising.

Sarcasm

'Will I never learn? Why did I let him goad me into getting mad again?'

Dealing with Difficult Situations

Paul, a co-worker was the most sarcastic person she knew. He threw his barbs at Sandra relentlessly. Their last exchange went as follows:

Paul: *'Give women an inch and they'll take a mile. Pretty soon we won't have any say in what's happening in the world.'*

Sandra retaliated with: *'Well, with 52 per cent of the population being women and only 48 per cent men, what do you expect - the same paternalistic society we've suffered through for centuries?'*

Who was in control of this sarcastic exchange? Sandra, the recipient of the sarcasm is - until she replies. Did Sandra respond correctly by using sarcasm herself? No - she relinquished the control, which will likely not stop Paul's barrage. Sandra could have stopped the sarcasm by sticking to facts and determining what Paul was trying to tell her. If she'd done this, the following conversation would occur:

Paul: *'Give women an inch and they'll take a mile. Pretty soon we won't have any say in what's happening in the world.'*

Sandra: *'What's happening that you object to?'*

Paul: *'Women want too many extras in the work place.'*

Sandra: *'What extras?'*

Paul: *'Day care, for instance. Why is it necessary? Too many women work. They should be at home with their families.'*

Sandra: *'How many women do you think work because they have to?'*

Paul: *'Not many.'*

Sandra: *'Over three-quarters have to work because their families can't survive without both incomes. Over half of working women are the sole breadwinners for themselves and their children. These children need adequate day-care. It's not a frill, but a necessity for most women. Do you feel women should be shouldering the full responsibility or should the men be taking part in this?'*

You can see that Sandra is combating the sarcasm with facts, not emotions and keeps Paul on topic. As the conversation progresses, he uses less and less sarcasm and they end up in a discussion rather than a debate.

There are two basic kinds of sarcasm. Some sarcasm is nothing more than harmless kidding that's humorous for all concerned. Many

Dealing with Difficult Situations

comedians use it, as do good friends. It's non-threatening because the speakers make fun of themselves or situations. They do not use it to put others down. Strong laughter at a joke can relieve headaches and lower a person's blood pressure and create bonds between people. The urge to share a joke of this kind is almost irresistible.

The second kind is hurtful and designed to make others feel small - the kind Paul used on Sandra. This type of sarcasm occurs because it's no longer acceptable to hit others with fists, so cutting words (sarcasm) is used instead. It's a form of indirect aggression; one of the most manipulative methods of getting one's way. Those using it feel a sense of power at seeing other people squirm, pointing out and laughing at others' shortcomings.

Because their jest is often subtle and open to more than one interpretation, it can be used to communicate taboo interests and values, to probe for what the other person is thinking or to make a suggestion the joker is not sure will be accepted. Through their joking comments, they can mention forbidden subjects, engage in offensive or childish behaviour and even step out of the bounds of good taste.

It's important that we look behind the reasons people use the hurting, cutting kind of sarcasm. It's because it makes **them** feel more important. Emotionally, they don't feel very good about themselves, so they put others down to make themselves feel more important. The game continues when others respond defensively or act hurt. They're happiest when others get angry and defend themselves.

These people resort to the hurting kind of sarcasm to express negative emotions. They're usually reluctant to confront the cause of their sarcastic remarks directly. They accomplish this through pranks, ridicule or jokes at someone else's expense. Examples of conversations using hurting sarcasm are:

'You finally decided to honour us with your presence.'

'That outfit looks like it came off the ark.'

'Ray did such a good job on his last project that the company demoted him.'

'If you're so smart, why aren't you my supervisor?'

'You're not exactly Mr. Efficiency yourself!'

Dealing with Difficult Situations

'Mark's so smart - he got forty per cent on his last marketing exam.'

You've just tipped over a cup of coffee. Comment, *'You didn't miss any of us with your coffee this time did you?'*

You ask a person to repeat a comment. They reply, *'Is English your second language?'*

Instead of reacting to his sarcasm - she should turn it off. If she can't stay quiet, has tried logic and feels his actions warrant an answer, she could try, *'Your last comment was very sarcastic and a put-down. Put-downs hurt. Can you explain why you said what you did?'* Or, *'Why did you feel you had to give me a put down like that?'*

Another approach to sarcasm is to say, *'That was pretty sarcastic. What did you really mean to say that you're covering up with sarcasm?'* This should at least cause him to analyse why he made the remark and what he really meant to accomplish with his remarks. This makes him account for his actions. He might not be aware of how destructive his behaviour is to others.

Use the following comments *only* if you don't want the person to speak to you again say, *'Your last comment was very sarcastic and a put down. What is it about me that makes you feel so intimidated, that you use such cutting sarcastic remarks?'*

Sarcasm can also be a defensive move and Paul may have felt the need to defend himself. Could Sandra have put Paul on the defensive with her actions or could he perceive that she was responsible for a putdown he received? Was she better looking, did the vice-president of the company like her better or did she get the promotion he wanted? When she understands the hidden motives behind his sarcasm she should be able to handle it better.

She also needs to be aware that men and women use sarcasm differently. For instance, men are often very sensitive about baldness, so, when a man's buddies notice a small bald patch on his head, he'll likely receive a new nick-name, 'Baldy.' Could you imagine what would happen if women did this to each other? For instance, can you really picture one woman saying to another, *'How are you doing today, flabby thighs?'* It's likely that the other woman would never speak to her again!

Unless women grow up with brothers who use this form of sarcasm, they react as if the man has hit them. In a way he has - verbally, so many act hurt and become defensive. The man's reaction to her behaviour is often, *'Can't you take a joke?'* Women should ask the giver of the sarcasm to explain the 'joke' to them.

Power Trips

'One woman at work is power-hungry. Even though Jennifer has a junior role, she tries to lord it over her co-workers and makes us know that she expects to be our supervisor soon. Why does she do this and how can we deal with her awful attitude problem?'

Power is influence over other people or can just be not being dependent on others. Those who are overcome with their own power stay preoccupied with their own needs and are often oblivious to the wishes and desires of less powerful people. They must be in charge of every transaction whether they have the authority to do so or not.

Should Julie be placed into a supervisory position, she would have trouble adjusting to how she should act and misunderstand her role. She's obviously observed other manipulative managers who misused their power by their domineering, intimidating and even bullying behaviour. She needs to understand that her present display of strength and power is probably due to and used to cover up for how inadequate she feels.

Co-operation is the name of the game and gives a person true power and influence over others. Only when trust is established will people want to follow the person's lead. You cannot buy respect, but she seems to think she can do so by her constant need to be in charge.

Leadership can be demonstrated with a simple piece of string. Pull it and it will follow wherever you wish. Push it and it will go nowhere at all. If people don't follow a supervisor's lead voluntarily - if they always have to be forced - that person's not a good leader.

When socialising, this kind of person is the one who treats service people like dirt. She does everything she can, to make their jobs difficult, yet complains if the person retaliates with less than his/her best service.

At present, she may not even be aware that she is antagonising others. Don't let this tyrant continue to use this behaviour in your presence. It's up to you to bring this offending habit to her attention.

Dealing with Difficult Situations

If she tries to lord it over you at work - let her know that you don't appreciate her behaviour. If she belittles service staff - do the same.

PROCESS OF FEEDBACK

1. Describe the problem or situation to the person causing the difficulty. Give examples.
2. Define what feelings or reactions his/her behaviour causes you (sadness, anger, anxiety, hurt or upset).
3. Suggest a solution or ask them to provide one.

The problem: *'Last week you belittled both me and other service staff in public. You don't have the right to do this.'*

Your feelings or reactions: *'I found this very patronising and embarrassing for everyone.'*

The solution: *'In the future I won't put up with such behaviour and will challenge your right to use such manipulative tactics.'*

What she does about it is her business, but at least she will know that you won't tolerate that behaviour any more. If all her co-workers use this tactic, she will soon stop the behaviour because she'll realise that all she's doing is making enemies. The supervisor should have stepped in and dealt with the problem.

Problem Meeting Participants

'I hate our weekly meetings! We never accomplish anything and we waste so much time and people walk in late. And those who come to the meetings aren't much help either with the bickering, procrastinating and promising they'll do something when everyone else knows they'll renege as usual.'

Meetings are notorious for wasting time. Many shouldn't be held and others could use conference phone calls to settle issues instead of people having to fly from far off branches to attend meetings. Do suggest alternatives to those who hold these unnecessary meetings. Be sure to outline the advantages and disadvantages of having the meetings at such set times and those for having meetings only when they're necessary. Here are some guidelines on how to deal with the

Dealing with Difficult Situations

bickering, procrastinating and people who promise but don't follow-through:

Dealing with problem participants at meetings

Participant is: Overly talkative - to the extent that other participants do not have an opportunity to contribute.
Participant may be: An 'eager beaver,' exceptionally well informed; naturally wordy or nervous.
What to do: Interrupt with *'That's an interesting point ... Let's see what everyone else thinks.'* Directly call on others. Suggest *'Let's put others to work.'* When the person stops for a breath, thank him or her, restate the pertinent points and move on.

Participant is: Engaging in side conversations with others in the group.
Participant may be: Talking about something related to the discussion; discussing a personal matter or uninterested in the topic under discussion.
What to do: Direct a question to the person. Restate the last idea or suggestion expressed by the group and ask for the person's opinion.

Participant is: Argumentative – to the extent that others' ideas or opinions are rejected or others are treated unfairly.
Participant may be: Seriously upset about the issue under discussion; upset by personal or job problems; intolerant of others; lacking in empathy or is a negative thinker.
What to do: Keep your temper in check. Try to find some merit in what's said; get the group to see it too and then move on to something else. Talk to the person privately and point out what his or her actions are doing to the rest of the group. Try to gain the person's cooperation. Encourage the person to concentrate on positives, not negatives.

Participant is: Unable to express self so that everyone understands.
Participant may be: Nervous, shy, excited or not used to participating in discussions
What to do: Rephrase, restating what the person said, asking for confirmation of accuracy. Allow the person ample time to express his or herself. Help the person along without being condescending.

Dealing with Difficult Situations

Participant is: Always seeking approval.
Participant may be: Looking for advice; trying to get leader to support his or her point of view or trying to put leader on the spot.
What to do: Avoid taking sides, especially if the group will be unduly influenced by your point of view.

Participant is: Bickering with other participant.
Participant may be: Carrying on an old grudge or feeling very strongly about the issue.
What to do: Emphasise points of agreement, minimise points of disagreement. Direct participants' attention to the objectives of the meeting. Mention time limits of the meeting. Ask participants to shelve the issue for the moment.

Participant is: Too quiet, unwilling to contribute.
Participant may be: Bored, indifferent, timid, insecure; more knowledgeable or experienced than the rest of the group.
What to do: Direct questions to the person that you're fairly sure s/he can respond to. Capitalise on the person's knowledge or experience by using them as a resource person.

Participant is: Seeking attention.
Participant may be: Feeling inferior or hiding a lack of knowledge by clowning around.
What to do: Keep reminding the person about the topic being discussed. Talk to the person privately. Point out what his or her actions are doing to the rest of the group.

Participant is: Uninvolved and unwilling to commit to new tasks.
Participant may be: Lazy; too busy already or feeling s/he should not have been asked to the meeting in the first place.
What to do: Ask for facts concerning the person's schedule. Ask the person to volunteer for tasks (others in group must as well). Make sure you ask the right people to future meetings.

Participant is: Already too over-committed to other things to take on new tasks.
Participant may be: Unaware of own skills and abilities or lacking in organisational skills.
What to do: Ask for facts concerning the person's schedule. Ask the person whether s/he is already over-committed. Tell the person

Dealing with Difficult Situations

you're counting on him or her. Send the person to a time-management seminar.

Participant is: A buck-passer who blames others for anything negative that happens and doesn't accept new tasks readily.
Participant may be: Unable to admit to making mistakes or afraid to take risks.
What to do: Make the person account for his or her actions. Ask for facts to back up allegations. Privately ask why the person won't accept new tasks.

Late start to meetings

'I waste a lot of time going to meetings. I'm always on time, but others just drift in. I have to chair a meeting myself but don't know how to make sure everyone come on time.'

You can make sure meetings start on time by:

1. Schedule meetings at odd times. A meeting scheduled to run from 10:15 - 11:00 am will get people's attention, especially if previous meetings were scheduled for a full hour.
2. Start on time - no matter who's missing. If you don't - you set a too-casual tone.
3. Close the door at the appointed hour. This will stress the importance of starting on time and signal to latecomers that lateness is disruptive.
4. Cover the most important items first. If the significant business is discussed last, then timeliness is not as well rewarded as it should be. Plus, people are freshest at the meeting's start.
5. Items of interest to habitual latecomers should be raised early. Not to be nasty, but to motivate people to be there on time because there are things they want to hear about.
6. Speak privately to offenders. An occasional lapse doesn't merit a tongue-lashing. But a chronic lateness habit may be broken if you take the time to explain that it's not just a matter of enforcing the rules, it's that you value the person's input.
7. Make staff presentations part of meetings. Participation breeds greater enthusiasm. People tend to listen closely to their peers, especially when they know that they too, will be speaking.

Dealing with Difficult Situations

Why are some men intimidated by assertive women?

'I'm a new female manager and am running into resistance from the other male supervisors.'

How might a man feel if he's confronted by a woman in what he thinks of as male territory at work? Let's put this in another environment (away from the workplace):

Let's say a man's working in his backyard (workplace) and he spots a strange animal (a female manager) in his yard. This animal isn't like those he normally finds in these surroundings. He knows he's seen this type of animal in another environment (support position) but doesn't quite know how it will behave in the present situation. He's rightfully careful. He doesn't make any moves towards it (ignore the new female manager) and merely stands back, watching and studying it. If it shows anger or defensiveness toward him, he gets ready to defend himself. If it shows intimidation, he takes advantage of it.

This is the effect a woman has on a man when she enters a male-dominated work environment. The man doesn't know whether the woman is dangerous or not. She seems to be doing things - that to him - don't make sense. He has a hard time figuring her out. Naturally he reacts defensively!

Women entering supervisory or management positions need to understand these men's inner turmoil. Help them adapt to your presence (often unwanted) by earning their trust and respect. Don't expect immediate acceptance. It's been said that a woman not only has to be as good her as male counterparts, but she has to be better for her to be accepted as an equal or gain respect from male associates.

To continue with our hypothetical situation, the man is still standing back, studying the animal. He has his defences up, so that he's ready to protect himself if necessary. When the animal (the woman) makes funny sideways moves toward him (using feminine behaviour) he's even more wary.

Now the animal helps itself to some piece of food (part of his job) off his patio table. He's naturally annoyed. (This is what some women do - they do part of someone else's job thinking they're 'helping.')

Dealing with Difficult Situations

In a home environment, women are conditioned to the idea that if she sees a task that requires action, she simply does it. In the workplace, this can step on the toes of other (mainly male) employees.

I could go on with this comparison, but I think you get my drift. Women *do* act differently when they're in supervisory or management positions.

A variety of things may cause men to be intimidated by an assertive woman. Heaven forbid, she may turn out to be better at supervision than he is! Some men who feel intimidated by women try every ploy to get rid of them. This type of man refers to all women in derogatory ways, by attempting to put them in their 'place.' For instance, they describe mentally strong women as, 'Pushy,' or 'Castrating.' On the other hand, most women are referred to as 'girls' and the majority of them haven't been 'girls' since they were thirteen years of age or so.

Male subordinates have another perceived problem. It's almost impossible for most of them to visualise themselves reporting to a woman. They think of women supervisors and managers as mother figures - and they're big boys now! They also might be intimidated by the fact that they don't know where women are coming from - they seem to play by a different set of rules. So how is a woman to deal with difficult male subordinates?

Here is how one new female supervisor dealt with this problem. Colleen was given a senior position, with several men reporting to her. One man objected because he had applied for her position. His behaviour bordered on insubordination and Colleen had to deal with it.

She said to him privately, *'I know you wanted my position, John and I can relate to how you must feel. I too know what it feels like to be overlooked for a promotion. I want and need your co-operation and I'll try to make it possible for us to work together harmoniously, but I won't tolerate any more negative behaviour from you. Can I count on you to change this?'*

John's behaviour improved and he became a productive employee. Later Colleen helped John identify why he had not been given her supervisory position. She was able to make sure he obtained the necessary training to equip him for the next promotional opportunity.

Staff object to my style of management

'I have difficulty supervising my male staff. They seem to ignore my instructions.'

Men are comfortable telling people what to do. If female supervisors request them to do a task, men believe they have the right to accept or refuse the woman's request. An example of this: A female supervisor wanted Mark to help Joe get a job done, so said, *'Joe looks as if he could use your help.'*

Mark replies, *'You're right he does seem to need help.'*

Later, the supervisor became upset when she found Joe still struggling along and learned that Mark had not offered to help. Mark thought that she was just making conversation, not asking him to help Joe. Because he had other, more pressing tasks to do, he'd thought her comment was not important.

The supervisor should have been clearer in her communication with Mark. She had supervised women in the past and that was the style of management that worked best with them. She didn't understand that men required a different kind of direction from her.

She should have stated, *'Mark, Joe needs help so I want you to leave the Miller report and help him until he completes his assignment.'* Mark would then know that she had prioritised Joe's project over the one he was working on and would have immediately helped Joe.

'It's difficult supervising my female staff. They accuse me of being too autocratic and demanding. How can I get them to do what I need them to do without offending them?'

Women supervise differently than men and don't like to pull rank, so they request, rather than demand. If a female supervisor uses a male type of supervisory method with women (ordering them to do tasks) the women feel as if the person is pulling rank and being bossy.

Dating colleagues and clients

'I'm trying to get over an office romance with my boss. Can you discuss office romances and explain whether you'd recommend

Dealing with Difficult Situations

them? What should I keep in mind for future possible office romances?'

It's amazing how fast colleagues catch on to the 'office romance.' You may think you've pulled the wool over everyone's eyes, but your body language will probably give you away and there will be subtle differences in how you interact with each other.

Most people believe that this kind of arrangement is fine - that it won't affect their chances of doing well with their company - but it does. Others may assume that any promotion you receive was because of your personal relationship with a person from upper management (should this be the case). It can be uncomfortable for co-workers throughout the romance because they may perceive that you are a pipeline to the upper level - and may tell about any difficulties they run into. They're also uncomfortable if and when the romance breaks up - and many don't know how to handle the situation. To be safe, stay clear of dating anyone you work with or have as a client. This is especially deadly if you work in the middle or upper management levels.

What causes or initiates most office romances? It's caused simply by proximity and availability to those of another gender. If they're doing basically the same kind of work - there can be a team spirit that can't always be matched by a spouse. How much time do you think most employees spend (awake) with their spouses? Married employees spend just about the same length of time (often more) with other sex colleagues as they spend with their spouses!

Occasionally office romances might work out - but the odds are that they won't. Beware of letting your hormones take over; think of the consequences should the romance break up. Inevitably, it will be difficult for both of you. When the romance sours and one of you decides to leave the company, more often than not, it's the woman, because she's likely in a more junior position. If neither employee goes, it will likely cause a serious strain on their office relationship with each other and with colleagues.

Dating Mentors

'A man I worked with became my mentor and lover. He helped me learn the ropes in our department, so I welcomed the advice he gave me. Our relationship went on for over two years, but I'm serious about my career and unfortunately our relationship went sour when

Dealing with Difficult Situations

I received a much-wanted and hard worked-for promotion. He seemed to be jealous of the progress I was making in our company. What are some of the things I should be looking for in my next mentor?'

If the person you're having the romance with was your mentor, the break-up of the romance is bound to be even more traumatic. If you talk with successful employees, many will tell you that somewhere along the line they had a mentor (at least a part-time one).

A mentor is often an influential senior officer of the company s/he works for - who is possibly approaching retirement, but definitely committed to building the company by developing talented younger employees. They encourage what appear to be ordinary people to achieve success, because they see the hidden talent in these individuals. A mentor provides information and moral support to help younger employees through good and bad times. This person stops younger employees from making mistakes that they've seen others make. This allows their protégé to skip rungs in their promotional climb up the corporate ladder, but the mentor can 'pull them in' if the protégé is heading for trouble.

Unfortunately, male mentors for women are still a rare breed. Perhaps this is because such a relationship is still likely to attract gossip and speculation that sexual 'favours' may be part of the deal. However, if a man is willing to take this chance with his reputation, then the woman is encouraged to do so as well. For women, the pluses of having a mentor can far outweigh the minuses - unless there are sexual overtones mixed in with the help that's offered. Women should never accept the latter kind of 'help' up the ladder. The help they accept must have no strings attached!

There are many pluses to having a mentor, but occasionally there are negative sides as well. Because the mentor is often much older, they may not really be in touch with new technology or may retire while the protégé still needs assistance. Or, the mentor may have taken on a protégé for the wrong reasons - out of paternal or maternal feelings or to reinforce his or her own sense of power. Or the protégé may have been looking for a surrogate parent. Often a mentor may dump too many responsibilities and tasks on the protégé, who burns out and rebels, with negative consequences.

Watch that this person doesn't take over your life and make all the decisions for you. Listen to his or her advice, but remember that you should be the judge of whether to take that advice or not.

Should you date your mentor - decidedly *'No!'* The last thing you want to do is jeopardise your relationship by bringing romance into it. The break-up of this kind of romance can be very traumatic, especially for the protégé.

Occasionally, as a protégé progresses up the ladder, the mentor may become very critical of everything the protégé does. S/he can't seem to please the mentor - no matter what s/he does. The protégé could be getting too competent, therefore has become a threat to the mentor. The mentor reacts by making almost impossible demands. If this happens, the protégé must wean him or herself from the mentor. Very likely, they no longer need this kind of help anyway.

Fortunately, many mentors remain loyal and good friends - even when the protégé reaches the mentor's level. The protégé can now give the mentor peer support, which can be very valuable indeed.

Saboteur - or I'll go through the motions, but will fight you every step of the way!

'My secretary hates making coffee, but rather than admit this to anyone, she makes lousy coffee. One time she uses half a package of coffee, then one and a half packages, hoping that someone else will do the job.'

Obtain proof that she has done this. Ask her why she did what she did and explain your expectations. Tell her what the consequences will be if something similar happens in the future. Make sure this task is listed on her job description with standards of performance relating to how the coffee should be made.

Personality clashes

'One of my co-workers and I really don't get along, but when we're with others she pretends as if we do. How should I handle this kind of behaviour?'

Be gracious - she is trying her hardest to make the best of a bad situation. Say, *'I know you're not my greatest fan, so I appreciate your efforts to be friendly.'* This should at least let her know that you see she is trying to get along. You need to do the same.

Dealing with Difficult Situations

Communication is always a matter of give and take - make sure you're willing to give a little yourself to make the relationship more harmonious.

Always Slow

'We work in a team setting. A co-worker of mine is so slow completing her work that I wonder why she hasn't been fired. Sure she completes her reports, but it takes her so long to prepare it, I feel like taking over for her. She seems to have a low energy and often looks as if she's 'putting in time.' She's so disorganised that she's driving me to distraction because many of our projects are late.'

Her actions are affecting the entire team. Gain the other team members' assistance in confronting her. When parts of projects are allotted to team members, make sure she gives her word that she will have hers ready in time. Explain how disappointed you have been in the past when she has let the team down and explain that you're counting on her to do her share of the work. If she fails again say,

'We were counting on you to do your part. Can you explain why you have let us down again?'

If her actions continue, your team will have to discuss the matter with your supervisor (who obviously isn't on top of the issue).

Procrastinator

'I always get all the unpleasant tasks out of the way at the beginning of my day and feel good at the end of my workday. My co-worker puts these tasks off as long as possible and I see him getting testier as the day goes on because he still has to complete the disagreeable tasks. Why do people do this? They must know that this habit is adding to their stress level?'

There are two approaches to tackling distasteful tasks – doing them first or last. You've seen how effective the first way works, but obviously your colleague hasn't clued into this way of completing tasks. There may be several reasons why he puts things off.

One type of procrastinator says *'I'll do it tomorrow.'* They use passive resistance to get their way through game playing - the, *'If I put things off long enough, maybe they'll forget they asked me to do it.'* method. This is often the answer he'll give when he's snowed

Dealing with Difficult Situations

under with work. Or he may not have time to complete the task, but grudgingly accepts it anyway. He needs to stand up for himself if he finds himself with too many tasks to complete and how to say *'No'* when necessary.

Occasionally, the procrastinator is a perfectionist who believes he must be competent at everything he tries. If he isn't, he doesn't consider himself a worthwhile person. This is impossible to accomplish because of a constant fear of failure. This results in feelings of inferiority and the inability to live his life to the fullest.

He needs to learn how to enjoy the activity, rather than engaging in it solely for the results.

Employees, who consistently procrastinate when completing tasks, often find themselves the first ones fired. Companies simply can't afford to keep them on board. These employees look unprofessional, often become bottlenecks to others who are trying to get their work done and are a 'pain in the neck' to the more conscientious employees. Friends, family members and co-workers normally don't tolerate their excessive procrastination either.

How can you tell when procrastination becomes a problem? When people have something important to do, not much time to do it in, but find themselves looking for other activities to do instead. Or when *they* set deadlines and don't meet them! Procrastinators constantly delay making important decisions or work furiously at the last minute to complete crucial assignments.

There are five basic kinds of people who procrastinate more than average. Which type is your colleague?

The Hurry-up Type: He waits until the last minute and then works around the clock to meet deadlines. He needs to set concrete deadlines of when he must have tasks completed, giving a little leeway in case he runs into problems.

I'll Decide Tomorrow: He postpones decisions until events resolve the situation or others force a decision on him. He is normally a passive person who is a 'fence-sitter.'

Perfectionists: All tasks, no matter how small or insignificant he must complete faultlessly. He needs to select the tasks that are important and work hard at them. For the other assignments, he needs to know that it's okay ***not*** to do his best. When dealing with a perfectionist, identify for him when he can complete something in draft form. Let him know that you're not expecting perfection from him.

I'll Show Them! He delays tasks others give to him, as a way of retaining a sense of personal power and control. An employee does this when a supervisor delegates a task he doesn't think he should be doing.

Muddler: He puts off work because of bad habits, poor organisation or lack or direction. He goes around in ever widening circles, accomplishing little and always has an excuse about why he hasn't completed a task.

Which of the above describes your co-worker? Talk to him about what you've observed; help him see how his actions may be holding him back from a promotion and how procrastination can increase his stress level.

Lateness

'One of my colleagues is late for events she doesn't want to attend or is easily distracted and loses track of time. She disrupts meetings and lacks consideration for other people's valuable time. How can I tell her how annoying this is to others?

There are three basic kinds of time users. For instance, if there was a 2 pm appointment:

a. Person - arrives at exactly 2:00 pm.
b. Person - arrives at 1:50 pm (and gives the impression that she *just* made it!)
c. Person - arrives at 2:10 pm (and acts as if she's on time - gives no explanation for her lateness).

The type (a) person often cuts a fine line between being on time and being late. Occasionally, she slips into the (c) group. The (b) person's on time, but may arrive too early, so wastes valuable time while she waits. If she feels the need to be at least fifteen minutes early for an appointment, she should bring work with her to do while she's waiting.

The (c) person doesn't comprehend why others are hostile towards her and doesn't understand why those who're waiting are upset. By her actions, (coming in late) she's telling those who are waiting, that *their* time isn't important. She gives the impression that her time is more important, therefore it's all right for others to wait for her. Your colleague fits this category.

Explain how you feel when she's late (using feedback) and let her know why her behaviour is unacceptable to others and could result in disciplinary action from her supervisor.

Know it alls

'I have trouble dealing with the `know it all' type of person who asks me for information, then insists on giving me his/her version of what s/he believes is the answer.'

First, listen to their ideas. Then ask them for facts relating to their information (statistics, figures, etc.). Then, using information available to you, tell them the facts. Refer to rules, regulations, policies and procedure manuals or other written data if necessary. Most 'know-it-alls' can't back up their comments with hard facts and data.

Class Clown

'I don't need a company car often enough to have one of my own so use a car from the company car pool to visit my clients. Our company has a ruling that nobody is allowed to smoke in the cars and because I am a non-smoker that ruling is fine with me. However I seem to get one that reeks of smoke. I would like to refuse the car, but it is often the last one available. I know who smoked in the car. How should I deal with this?'

The person breaking the rules has all the attributes of a 'Class Clown.' He knows he was breaking the rules when he lit up, but refuses to stop smoking in the company cars. Whoever is in charge of allotting cars in the car pool should be informed of the problem. They are the ones who have the responsibility for dealing with the rule breaking. If that person refuses, talk to your supervisor.

Gossip

'A colleague of mine is forever interrupting my work with a juicy bit of gossip. I don't want to hear about her gossip and I've told her this several times. My resistance falls on deaf ears and before I know it, she's doing it again.'

Dealing with Difficult Situations

Gossip is another form of indirect aggression. When people pass on gossip from one person to another it's inevitable that the meaning of the words changes somewhat from person to person. The person talking behind the back of the other person doesn't allow the person to defend him- or herself. For instance, a co-worker states, *'Did you hear about Carmen's husband? The police picked him up for drunk driving last night.'*

How should she deal with the gossiper? She should either ignore the comments or suggest to the person that they both talk to Carmen about the information. To stop the gossip, she'd say to Carmen, *'I thought you should know there's a rumour going around that the police charged your husband with drunk driving last night. Were you aware of the rumour?'*

This lets Carmen know there *is* a rumour. You wouldn't ask Carmen whether it's true - you'd just let her know what's happening. The giver of the gossip soon learns that they won't get away with talking behind others' backs. It also stops gossipers from passing on unwanted gossip to this person.

There's also another serious issue here. While you are gossiping, you are wasting company time and money. If observed by upper management, it could keep you from receiving a promotion and you wouldn't even know why!

Sticky-Iffies (Backhanded compliments)

'The man I work with is forever giving me backhanded compliments such as, 'You earn a lot for a woman.' This isn't a one-time thing and he does it with everyone. Am I being too sensitive? How should I respond?'

He's giving you a compliment and then ends up giving you a put down. This discounts the positive statement, because he adds something negative to his comment as well. He's probably using these disguised or obvious put downs to hurt others. When dealing with him, use the following tactics:

1. After receiving the sticky-iffy or put down, reflect your understanding of the situation. Say, *'You feel ... think ... believe ...'* which confirms that you heard what they said to you (a form of paraphrasing).

Dealing with Difficult Situations

2. Then state, *'I understand ... perceive ... appreciate ... empathise with ... realise ...'* then express *their* point of view as you perceive it.
3. State, *'I think ... feel ... believe ... have ...'* and state *your* beliefs about the topic. Don't start your statement with such words as but, however, although or nevertheless.
4. Ask an open question (one that can't be answered by a 'yes' or a 'no.').

For example you would treat a discriminatory statement regarding gender:

He says, *'You're earning a good salary for a woman.'*

She says, *'You believe that women should earn less than men?'*

He says, *'Yes, I do.'*

You say, *'I appreciate what you're saying. I believe women deserve an equal chance to earn the same kind of salary as men. Women pay rent like men, pay the same for food as men and pay taxes like men. What are the reasons for your belief that women should earn less than men?'*

An example relating to age: They say,

'You're pretty young to be a supervisor aren't you?'

You say, *'You feel that I'm too young to be a supervisor?'*

They say, *'Well you are young!'*

You say, *'I realise that I'm young. I have six years' experience in this department, have a B.A. degree and have completed all the supervisory training provided by my company. What other prerequisites do you feel I need to handle my position?'*

An example relating to racial slurs:

They say, *'Every time I take a taxi, it's always people from Asia who are driving. Can't you people find anything else to do, except drive a taxi?'*

You say, *'You feel that people from Asia should have jobs other than driving a taxi. I realise why you must believe that. Many people from my country have to get extra education to work at their usual occupations in your country, so become taxi drivers in the interim. I'm taking university courses and will soon be working in my normal*

Dealing with Difficult Situations

type of occupation. What kind of special courses did you take to work in your occupation?'

An example relating to a person's size:

They say, *'You're in pretty good shape for a man your size.'*

You say, *'You think that because I'm a smaller man, that I'm not strong?'*

They say, *'Well, you are small to be able to lift that big barbell.'*

You say, *'I can see how you could come up with that perception. I'm sixty years old now and have been lifting weights since I was fifteen. I've won several weight-lifting contests and still work out every day. Can you see why I'm in good shape for a man my size?'*

Your tone of voice is very important in these exchanges. Your voice should not show defensiveness, but should state facts. This starts a dialogue where you can discuss facts rather than emotions. Use this technique for any sticky-iffy comments, disguised or obvious put downs.

Held back from promotion

'I've tried everything I know to get ahead in my company, but it seems as if they are reluctant to put women into management or senior positions in my company. How can I get the kind of job I know I can handle?'

Many women (often sole breadwinners) struggle to escape the pink-collar ghetto by obtaining supervisory or management positions. Here are some suggestions that may help you progress up the corporate ladder:

Step 1: Decide *where* you want to go by obtaining career counselling. Then investigate *how* you can get where you want to go. Will this be through on-the-job training or do you require formal education and/or training? Once you determine this, obtain that training, possibly while working at a junior-level position in the field of your choice.

Step 2: Document every task you do in your present position. Determine whether you're doing an important part of your boss's work. Look for those tasks that require independent action and/or decision-making on your part. You'll find that if you can identify the decisions you now make, you may be able to convince your

Dealing with Difficult Situations

employer that you're capable of making more major ones. You'll just be using different kinds of data. Look for duties where your judgement was crucial to the outcome of a task. Look for clear-cut areas of responsibility, authority and accountability. In other words, look for things you do on a regular basis in which *you* decide the outcome. These are the skills that those in management positions require and you'll be well paid for using them.

Step 3: Ask your boss if your talents could be utilised in other areas of his or her department. Explain that you're willing to take a cut in salary if necessary. Even a junior position (as long as it has a toehold on the bottom rung of the promotional ladder) is better than a support or clerical one.

If your boss doesn't think this is a good idea, talk to someone in your Human Resources Department. Identify the decision-making qualities you've developed and what specialty you would like to get into. Ask them to let you know about any positions that arise that would utilise your qualifications.

As backup, watch for job postings on your company's bulletin board and be sure to apply for positions you believe you can handle. Have the Human Resources Department explain why you're not suitable for the vacancies you're rejected for. This may be hard at first, but they'll explain where you need to improve your qualifications.

Step 4: Talk with someone in a high position in your company who's eager to see women progress in business and ask his or her advice about what kinds of experience or education you're lacking.

Step 5: When responding to ads, stay clear of those that describe the position or the candidate with words such as 'skills, right arm, high-class, bright, achiever, hard working, support services, assistant to or pleasant working conditions,' etc. These denote lower-level positions. Watch instead for words such as 'self-starter, career-oriented, challenging position,' etc.

Most senior positions identify their salary ranges as annual salaries - intermediate in monthly salaries and junior positions by hourly or weekly wages.

Step 6: Ask senior women in the company to help you reach your goal. Most of them will be glad to help you. Ask them how they got where they are and the route they took to get there. The saying, *'It's not what you know, but **who** you know,'* still plays an important part in being promoted.

Dealing with Difficult Situations

- Once you reach a higher position, here are some ideas that will help you succeed. Know your position duties and do them well. Always have areas you have to learn when accepting a new position. If you already feel you know all the duties of the job - you're probably overqualified already. If you resign from a position, never burn your bridges and badmouth your former company, boss or co-workers. You never know, ten years down the road when there's been a full turnover of staff, you may learn about a 'plumb' job, but won't be considered if they check your personal record and find 'sour grapes.'

- Make sure you receive equal training and educational opportunities as your peer group. At management meetings, when everyone's eyes rivet on you at coffee break, simply state *'I take cream and sugar.'*

- If asked to take minutes at a management meeting, get your personal assistant, explaining that you can't participate properly when taking notes. Learn to control your emotions such as anger, anxiety and fear (never use tears to get your way!). Be willing to express your ideas to your boss in private, but never criticise or challenge him or her in public.

- Never date a colleague or client you deal with on a regular basis.

- Know how your company deals with expense accounts (and don't always go bargain-express).

- Don't put yourself down. Learn from your mistakes and try to do better the next time. Learn the proper way to accept compliments for a job well done.

- If your boss is weak and indecisive - ask for written guidelines that identify where you have the authority to make decisions on your own. Explain that this is so that your boss isn't 'bothered' with trivial details. Not only will you be making more decisions, but your boss may be glad to toss them to you.

- Don't verbalise high personal ambitions to colleagues (especially men). Discuss this only with your supervisor or Human Resources representative. The time you should explain your full career plans, is during your interview and you're asked the question *'What are your career plans?'*

Dealing with Difficult Situations

Freezes under pressure

'One of my colleagues freezes whenever an emergency situation happens at work. He becomes immobilised – frozen to the spot. He also stays away from work if he's expected to make important decisions, so others are forced to make those decisions. In group situations he becomes mute and seems unable to speak. What's happening here?'

When his fight or flight response kicks in, instead of either fighting or running away from the danger, he simply freezes. He doesn't make decisions because he's afraid he'll make the wrong one. This again immobilises him. He becomes speechless because he seems to be highly prone to stage fright.

His behaviour is very passive, so suggest that he take an assertiveness training course. Help him learn how to make decisions. When he's forced to make a decision talk to him privately and ask him, *'What do you think you should do? Why did you make that decision? What other alternatives are open to you?'* If you're the one needing him to make the decision - give him deadlines and check with him along the way to see if he needs more information before making his decision.

These sound like well entrenched behaviours that may require professional help to overcome. He's likely had some pretty horrific situations in his past that have caused his immobilisation.

Bashful

'Sam is so shy that it's painful to watch him interact with others. The least little thing causes him to blush beet red, to perspire heavily and stammer his words. His colleagues and friends react by being super-careful while they're around him. Others evade him because of the guilt they feel when they inadvertently make him respond with this kind of behaviour.'

Bashful people readily show that they're greatly embarrassed by their non-verbal signals. They have nightmares about situations they might face the next day and by the time the situation occurs, they've worked themselves up until they're almost immobilised. These people are prone to a lot of teasing from stronger individuals and suffer terribly. To overcome: follow the steps for 'Freezes under pressure.'

Dealing with Difficult Situations

Self beraters

'One of my colleagues relentlessly puts herself down. She acts as if everything that's gone wrong must be her fault and is highly critical of her work and actions. She seeks daily reassurance from others that she's doing a good job and needs others to give praise for her actions (whether it's earned or not.)'

Most self beraters are average performers but they almost beg others to find fault with everything they do. They try to avoid receiving hurt from others by identifying their own faults, before anyone else can do it for them. If you decide to help her, she'll need a confidant who won't criticise, but will provide empathy. Help her realise what she's doing to herself with her constant self put-downs. Explain how others lose faith in her ability when she keeps running herself down. Your colleague desperately needs praise and recognition when her assignments go well. Make sure you provide this for her.

Uninvolved

'When it's time to go to lunch and I ask a colleague where she wants to go for lunch, her standard answer is, 'I don't care - wherever you want to go is fine with me.' I've tried to encourage her to state her preference, but still get the same response. Then, no matter where we go, she grumbles about the food or the service! How should I handle this?'

Start by using feedback to describe what her actions are doing to you and others when she plays games like she does. She probably isn't even aware that she's doing so, but there's a method to this madness. The deliberately uninvolved person is never wrong, but is never right either. She may say she doesn't care which decision is made, but her body language shows otherwise.

In the future, insist that she clearly states what she wants to do for lunch - that silence or *'I don't care - wherever you want to go is fine with me ...,'* is unacceptable. If she still won't state her opinion, say, *'So you don't care which restaurant we go to?'* Then point out that you don't want any grumbling about the food or service.

Sham assertive

'One would never know it by his behaviour, but Bill detests me. In private conversations he lets me know how he feels, but if anyone

Dealing with Difficult Situations

else is around, he's as nice as pie to me. I've recently learned that he's spreading lies about me.'

People in this category have problems in any but the most superficial relationship. They may seem open, assertive, warm and even extroverted, but this covers for a lack of honesty. Start by saying, *'I know you're not my greatest fan, so I appreciate your efforts to be friendly when others are around. What I don't like are the stories you're telling about me behind my back. If you have a beef with me - tell it to my face, so I'll have a chance to deal with it.'* Be polite and courteous with him at all times, but don't let your guard down. He could still be badmouthing you behind your back.

Bootlickers

'I'm rather amused at the games people play to get on the right side of their bosses. They fawn over them, giving passes to sporting events and doing special favours for their bosses. These things have nothing to do with work - so why do they do it except to curry favour with their bosses? I refuse to do this and am wondering if it is holding me back at work.'

These individuals are observed preening before entering their boss's office - doing up their suit jackets, slicking their hair, correcting their posture. Some resort to becoming the office tattle-tale - telling their boss all the gossip. They're manipulators who want to be noticed but use the wrong means.

Concentrate on your own behaviour instead of confronting bootlickers. You don't have to resort to the underhanded and ingratiating actions of a bootlicker. Instead, concentrate on doing the best job you can - so your boss looks good. Help your boss by keeping him/her informed about company issues s/he might have missed.

If you must speak to the bootlicker, take him/her aside and ask why s/he indulges in playing this game and what s/he expects to gain from it. Then explain your own aversion to that kind of behaviour.

Over-committers - Renegers

'Bob always has a smile and a friendly word to share and people instantly like him. However he promises that whatever you want

Dealing with Difficult Situations

from him - you'll get - then lets you down and doesn't deliver on his promises. I'd hate to hurt his feelings, but this kind of shirking of duty has to stop. I need to count on him when he says he's going to do his share of the work.'

Let him know that you're counting on him to do what he's promised to do. Say, *'You've let me down in the past by promising to do tasks you didn't have time to do. I'm counting on you to do this. If there's any chance that you can't deliver - I need to know now - not later when it's too late.'*

He may also need to know when you're happy with his performance. After all, he's trying to please others, but gets himself in over his head in the process, so may need reassurance that you're pleased with his work.

Other overcommitted people are prone to giving extravagant praise so they can use you. They believe if they constantly say things designed to please you (greatly exaggerating reality) you'll do as they ask. They're afraid their plan, procedure, policy or assignment can't stand on its own merit, so they use unwarranted praise to gain acceptance of them.

These are nice people who can't say *'No'* to others' requests. However they often find they haven't time to do what they promised. They make promises they expect to fulfil or they mislead you by breaking promises they hadn't planned to keep in the first place. They love harmony and hate to argue, so they'll agree to do what others ask them to do. They avoid confrontation hoping they won't hurt others' feelings. They promise too much or say they'll do something they don't really want to do. Unable to handle it all, they put off action or making decisions and break their promises. They don't hurt others intentionally, but often cause difficulty for others who are depending on them to follow-through.

Have him give either a verbal (in public if possible) or written commitment to you that he will complete the task. When necessary - you make the decision whether he does the task or not. If he does commit herself, explain that you're counting on him to follow-through. Let him know the consequences should he let you down in the future.

Dealing with Difficult Situations

Stalking Co-worker

'One of my co-workers began pursuing me two months ago. I'm not attracted to her and let her know that I'm not interested in a relationship. She hasn't been obvious, but I often see her watching me at work. What is of concern to me, is that I have seen her parked outside my apartment several times and have run into her at the supermarket too many times for it to be an accident. How can I get her to stop doing this?'

This is a case of stalking. Start by documenting every time you notice her stalking you. If others have observed her behaviour, have them document their observations as well. Then talk to her - giving her a copy of your documentation. Explain that her behaviour must stop. If it doesn't, speak to your Human Resources manager and/or union representative to have them speak to her about her unacceptable behaviour. If she still persists - speak to the police and obtain their advice on how you should be dealing with this situation.

Email abuses

'One of my colleagues is forever sending me smutty jokes over the internet. We have a company policy relating to this, but I'm reluctant to make a fuss.'

Make a copy of the company email policy and email it to this person. Explain that by accepting the unacceptable email, you are just as guilty. If the jokes continue to arrive, show your manager a copy of some of the offending emails and your request to have them stopped.

Chapter 4

UNHAPPY AT WORK

I hate my job!

'I'm so unhappy at work that I have to force myself to go to work every morning. It's because of management problems - they don't seem to care anything about their employees!'

Companies do many things to make life miserable for their staff and must be diligent to remove as many employee frustrations as they can. Some employees are de-motivated by companies who:

Use restrictive supervision

You'll likely obtain less job satisfaction if your supervisor gives you little chance to take an active part in how you complete your assignments. The more employees participate in *how* they do things, the more co-operative they will be.

The supervisor, who uses an authoritarian leadership style, is setting him/herself up to fail. If you have one of these supervisors, try feedback to alleviate the problem. If your supervisor won't listen, you may have to suffer for a while until a promotion's available. Other alternatives are; take a lateral move to another department or as a last resort, leave the company.

Lack of recognition

Supervisors de-motivate staff if they identify only what their subordinates do *incorrectly*. They should concentrate instead on what they do *correctly*, which will encourage better performance. When correcting behaviour, instead of saying *'You made a mistake'* they should say, *'The next time you do this, I'd like you to do it this way.'*

In the 'Old School of Management,' supervisors believed it was their *right* to take credit for any new ideas suggested by their subordinates. As expected, this just de-motivates employees and discourages any new ideas. Progressive supervisors are learning that if they give employees credit where credit's due, their staff is motivated to perform better. This also alleviates mediocrity and marginal production. Possibly, your supervisor isn't aware of how

Dealing with Difficult Situations

de-motivating his/her actions are. Use feedback to explain how his/her lack of giving recognition is affecting you.

Monotonous work

When companies implement 'job rotation' for their employees, they are attempting to make employees' jobs more interesting. Job rotation involves several employees who work at substantially the same class or level of work and pay range. Employers who use job rotation reap extra benefits because people can fill more than one job. Don't knock your company if they're doing this. They *are* trying to keep your work interesting. If they aren't; suggest they try it!

Little opportunity to try new ideas

Another prime de-motivater occurs when supervisors refuse to listen to their staff when they try to explain better, faster or more efficient ways of completing their work. They'll likely listen if you use comparisons, identify the advantages/disadvantages of both the new and the old ways and identify the cost savings of your proposed new method.

No new skill growth

At one time, companies spent training dollars on their people and still couldn't keep up with the demand for competent qualified people. Recently companies have had to tighten their training budgets. Companies may refuse to give training that they believe employees can't use right away. Employees whose promotions are six months to one year away may find it difficult to obtain preparatory training.

Employees, who find themselves in this position, would be wise to obtain and pay for this training themselves. This will ensure they *are* ready for the next step up (without their company having to put out the training money). This gives the employee an edge over competitors for the position who have not obtained this training on their own. These training dollars are well spent and a good investment by the employee. Often employers will reimburse such expenditures for related training if the training occurred while the employee was in another position in the company.

Dealing with Difficult Situations

Poor fit between abilities and job requirements

Before the economic downturn, many employees projected that they would climb the ladder in their companies very quickly. Many find they're over qualified for their present positions with little chance to move up in the company. If the expected promotion is still far in the future, they may be forced to move on to another company.

Anger expressed at work

'I have an employee whose productivity has plummeted. I know the problem doesn't stem from a personal or family problem, but the quality of her work has got to improve. How can I find out what's going on?'

Your first step is to have an interview with her and ask the reasons for her poor performance. Be prepared with facts to back up your belief about her work. You may find the following reasons behind her behaviour:

Direct 'Take that:'

Usually a person's first response to a negative working condition is to directly attack it. Often this leads to very productive and creative effort. New procedures can develop this way. 'Necessity is the mother of invention,' so some frustration can be desirable. However, if the blocking condition doesn't yield, she may openly show expressions of hostility, destructive in intent or she may use less direct methods.

Example: A manager fails to recognise an employee's ability to come up with new ideas. The employee quits giving new ideas. The employee knows how she can do a faster, better job but becomes frustrated because she can't complete a task her own way. She could become a 'middle of the road' employee with tunnel vision.

Sabotage - 'Let's get back at Them:'

Sabotage in the work-setting usually takes a much milder form than we typically associate with this word. Yet subtle forms of sabotage are very common. The work slowdown, the omitted procedure and the small 'error,' are all evidence of the frustration/anger model at work.

Dealing with Difficult Situations

Example: A personal assistant intentionally makes lousy coffee, because she doesn't drink coffee and feels coffee-making should not be her responsibility.

Over-Compliance 'If that's what you want ..:'

One excellent way of expressing anger at the blocking boss, is to do exactly what s/he asks regardless of the circumstances. The boss can't fault this practice, because after all, it's what s/he said, but s/he didn't mean to be taken so literally. Often when a union wants to make life difficult for management, the union starts going by the letter, rather than the spirit of the contract.

Example: You've given an employee a set of instructions on how to complete a project, you assume she will use her common sense and add pertinent information as necessary to complete the assignment. She doesn't, so the report is useless.

Emotional withdrawal - 'You aren't that important:'

One way to deal with continuing frustration is to deny the importance of the blocking conditions. This is the familiar 'sour grapes' attitude. We often see employees become apathetic and just 'go through the motions' on the job, by their actions saying, this job isn't that important; the really important things for me are outside the job. Productivity gains would be considerable if the interest and energy many workers spend on becoming star bowlers could be rekindled on the job.

Example: An employee follows her job description to a 'T.' As her manager, you know she's capable of much more.

Turning inward - 'It must be me!'

One of the most pathetic results of prolonged frustration is the tendency on the part of some to turn their anger inward upon themselves. Instead of venting their anger against the blocking conditions through direct or indirect means, such as already listed, the individual begins to attack him or herself and winds up with a feeling of 'I'm no good'. Turning such a person around is a management challenge of major magnitude.

Example: Employees who've taken risks and have been 'burned' may retreat into themselves and refuse to make decisions - use tunnel vision when completing assignments, won't take risks and

Dealing with Difficult Situations

must feel safe in any decision they make. Those who have written warnings on their file or who have been reprimanded in public will also react this way.

How to improve job satisfaction and productivity

So, how can you keep your employee wanting to contribute and be more productive?

1. ***Provide an atmosphere of approval:***

    a) An atmosphere of approval can be created by taking the following steps:
       - Recognise the importance of employee suggestions.
       - Listen to them – if not now, arrange to do so later.
       - Avoid Progress Killers such as: *'We've always done it this way!'*
       - Tell why their new ideas won't work. If employee gives a good idea, implement it as soon as possible and make sure you give the employee credit for the idea.

2. ***Allow them meaningful participation:***

    The evidence is pretty convincing that whenever people can influence their own work in a way that provides them with an opportunity to have a decisive voice, they will be more interested and involved. Employees will feel their participation is meaningful if you practice the following:

    a) Analyse *your* job and decide which tasks can be moved downward. If the task is easy for you to do - it can likely be delegated.
    b) Be willing to take the risk of more job involvement by your subordinates.
    c) Encourage your employees to volunteer for assignments they feel they can handle.
    d) Don't con your employees with the feeling that they're giving meaningful participation when a decision has already been made.
    e) When your decision has been influenced by the employee's ideas tell him or her.

Dealing with Difficult Situations

3. *Performance Feedback:*

   Some managers (and thank goodness they're getting fewer and fewer) believe that the yearly performance appraisal is all that's necessary for the employee to perform properly. Of course, along the way they believe that the employee must be corrected if s/he does something wrong, but otherwise they're 'on their own'. Employees that work for this kind of manager find:

   a) They don't have an up-to-date, accurate job description of the tasks they're expected to perform - and how they are to be performed.
   b) They aren't sure what's expected of them - therefore have no set objectives to meet.
   c) They seldom hear about what they did right (except silence), but appear to hear lots about what they did wrong.

4. *Consistent discipline:*

   If managers show favouritism or have a personality clash with employees, consistent discipline is usually a mirage. To ensure consistent discipline a manager must:

   a) Review rules and standards periodically to evaluate their relevancy to current situations.
   b) Ensure that employees know company rules and regulations.
   c) Reward or punish consistently.
   d) Be aware of extenuating circumstances.
   e) Document your action and the reasoning you used to make decision.
   f) Follow-up to see if the situation has improved.

5. *Right of appeal:*

   This is used only after serious attempts have been made by both the supervisor and the employee to settle a dispute. The third person (the mediator) is often a Human Resources specialist, a union representative or any other trained negotiator who can remain objective about the conflict. Companies that don't offer the 'Right of Appeal' (which are usually non-union firms) are missing a very effective management tool. Managers are advised as follows:

Dealing with Difficult Situations

a) You're not always right. Appeal procedures protect your people from your occasional lapses into biased opinion.
b) Be sure to listen effectively to your employee's reasoning behind their actions.
c) If you and your employee can't agree, involve another impartial third party.
d) Be willing to change your mind.
e) Welcome this appeal method as an aid, not a threat. Remember, you too will have access to this management tool!

Consider these ideas and see if they don't change your employee's productivity.

Mid-Life Crisis

Have you found yourself thinking, *'Is this all there is?'* If so, it's possible that you're trapped on a mid-life plateau in either your marital/family situation or due to the type of work you're doing. It's easy to get into a rut and stay there. So, if your marital or family situation is the problem - what could you do to put some spark back into your life? Or is the situation serious enough to consider family or marital counselling? If so, make that a priority for you to investigate and soon. Life is too short to waste life being happy.

Did work used to be exciting, but you now find it and your life to be boring you to tears? Every morning you get up and go to work, then come home? When you get home it's the same old routine - you read the paper, eat dinner, do some work, watch TV and go to bed. Then you get up and do it all again.

What are you going to do with the rest of your life? You hate the thought that your work is going to be like this forever, but you don't know how to break out of the rut or are afraid of failing in new ventures. If you're saying any of the above - you've plateaued (not going anywhere) and likely feel trapped. If you can accept that you're at the end of a phase, you can begin planning a new one.

For many of us, work is the basis of our identity and self-esteem - which is fine, as long as we're successful. But promotions do eventually cease, sometimes provoking a terrible sense of failure. Mastery of the work also may bring feelings of tedium. Dentists tire

Dealing with Difficult Situations

of filling molars, teachers become bored with their students and lawyers get weary of divorce courtrooms.

When this happens there's a good chance lethargy will set in; the person's productivity lessens and the joy of going to work ceases. Life becomes a tedious task - not a rewarding experience. Although different strategies work for different people, there are courses of action that can take them off that plateau. Here are some ways to leave it behind you and help you get on with your life.

Using skills in a different way

Plateaued people, who are unable to change their jobs, can benefit by using their knowledge and skills in different ways. One way is to be a mentor to younger people in your organisation. Being a mentor involves the challenge of being the wise teacher. Middle age is more likely to be a period of personal renaissance, especially if you encourage the creativity and growth of younger people. You'll create a new way to earn self-respect and will continue to challenge your abilities.

Another challenge is to become involved in your community and/or government. The volunteer sector can be as gratifying as your professional work, if you approach it with the same kind of commitment. Those who participate in the community, gain the opportunity of wrestling with different issues, having hands-on experience, being creative, exerting leadership and making a visible difference in society. It's another place where you can use your leadership and wisdom to help others.

Why do so many people find themselves in the wrong type of occupation? The following shows percentages of why people get off the track with their careers.

Reasons people choose the wrong career

1. They follow the advice of others instead of using their own instincts - 30%
2. Blind themselves to what the job will *really* be like - 25%
3. Assume they can live with a lower salary than they're used to - 20%
4. Don't check out potential problems and issues during their employment interview - 15%
5. Don't obtain career counselling.

Therefore, it's very important that you investigate the following:

1. Understand yourself - your wants, needs and desires.
2. Know what career options are open and available to you.
3. Know how to choose a suitable career path by evaluating your transferrable skills
4. Know where you can obtain the education and/or training you need to enter a new career.

Plateaued people often say, *'I do my job and just hope that something else will turn up.'* Those who work in large organisations are especially prone to being 'good' - waiting for the good fairy to notice them and reach out with a magic wand. However, if you wait for superiors (or fate) to create opportunities, you give others far too much power over your life. It's your responsibility to say what you want. You know your competencies better than anyone else. You're in a unique position to make a case for yourself, to change the design of your work, so that it's more challenging.

Think about the aspects of your work that give you intrinsic satisfaction and then enlarge on them. Speak to your supervisor or Human Resources Department about the steps you've taken to prepare yourself for your chosen career path. Make sure they know you're serious and want an opportunity to change careers. While you're unlikely to get everything you want, you're more likely to get something, than you are if you didn't speak up.

When I was working as a Human Resources Manager, a young woman came to me and explained that she was at the top of her clerical level and wanted to know what kinds of promotional opportunities were available to her within our company. I asked her where *she* wanted to go - what occupation she had chosen. She replied, *'I don't really care what occupation I get into, as long as it's a promotion and brings me more money.'*

I explained that she had gone as far as she could go as a generalist - that now she'd have to specialise. She still didn't appear to understand what I meant, so I suggested alternate careers. *'Are you interested in marketing, computers, human resources, accounting, sales, operations, production or any other specialty area?'* The woman just shrugged her shoulders and repeated her original statement about salary.

Dealing with Difficult Situations

She failed to understand that companies don't just offer jobs to people; she needed to do something to show her interest, aptitude and ability in the career she'd chosen. This woman should have prepared herself for promotional opportunities, rather than expecting her company to 'find' the opportunities for her. For instance: If she decided that she wanted to work her way up to a purchasing manager's position, she should have taken the initiative and enrolled in related courses. She could have taken these in the evening so she would be ready for the next junior buyer position that became available.

I sent her away to think about the area she wished to pursue, but never heard from her again - it was too much trouble for her to do this 'work' herself. She was unaware that I could have placed her into junior positions in most of the areas I'd identified.

When I was climbing the corporate ladder in Human Resources, I ran into a 'Catch-22' situation. I had asked my company if they would pay for the costs of supervisory training so I'd be ready for a pending supervisory position. Their reply was, *'We can't pay for that kind of training for you, because you're not a supervisor.'*

I debated whether I could afford to pay for the training. Because I was serious about being considered for this type of position, I took the initiative and registered for a six-week supervisory course that I could take in the evenings. When my company posted the expected supervisory position, I spoke to the manager in the area about applying for the position. His reply is still etched in my memory when he stated, *'We can't consider you for that kind of a position, because you don't have supervisory training!'*

I'd been prepared for this eventuality and produced a copy of my certificate of training. Because of this and my relevant experience with the company, they reluctantly hired me for the supervisory position: and became the first woman appointed to such a position in their company. If I hadn't taken the initiative, I'd likely still be in a clerical or low-paying position.

The amount I invested in this training has been repaid one hundred times over. So if lack of training is your problem, pay for it yourself. If your answer is that you can't afford the costs - you're making excuses. Have a garage sale or do without other non-essentials. The bizarre thing is, that my company reimbursed me for the cost of my

Dealing with Difficult Situations

training because it was training they would have paid for anyway after I obtained the position!

Career Decisions

There are five different types of career decisions a person could make in their lifetime:

1. Choosing an occupation.
2. Choosing a job.
3. Choosing an educational program (of study or training).
4. Choosing a career path (a series of jobs, occupations and educational programs leading to a career goal).
5. Choosing how to spend a period of time (what to do next week, month, year, etc. This type of career decision often encompasses several other types of career decisions.)

Whatever decision you make - do it! Don't wait for your employer or something external to trigger your response. If you need career counselling - get it and spend some time deciding what you want to do with the rest of your life.

Are you ready for a promotion?

Companies shouldn't promote employees simply because they've done well in their present position, but only if they can handle a higher level of responsibility. Employers will ask themselves the following questions before considering you for a promotion. See if you're ready:

Are you competent in your present position?

a) If you're not a solid performer in your present position, were you in the wrong position to begin with?
b) Would you excel in the new position, because you'll be able to use your transferrable skills? Or,
c) Is it possible that you're not ready for a promotion?
d) How well have you prepared yourself for the next promotional level?
e) Do you really know the responsibilities of the new position you're aiming for?
f) Will you need more training to prepare you for that promotional opportunity?

Dealing with Difficult Situations

Have you shown your employer that you're serious?

Have you gone through career counselling, decided where you want to go and shown your employer you're serious about your ambitions? If necessary, have you registered in courses that will help you progress in your chosen career?

Can you communicate effectively?

If you can't get along with co-workers, clients and bosses, you'll likely stay where you are and not be considered for a promotion. You'll be communicating with others for the rest of your life and will be living with a life-long handicap unless you make this one of your primary goals. Take public speaking courses so you can say what you want to say, when you want to say it.

Are you a long-term investment?

Companies may be reluctant to hire you if they perceive you're a job-jumper. They'll want to recoup any money they spend on training for you, so they'll be looking for stability on your part. Let your employer know that you're serious about your career choice.

Are you a good role model?

If you had your choice, would you be willing to work for someone like yourself? What faults do you have? Are you prepared to work on your faults and improve them? Do others respect you and accept your ideas as valid (or do you have to fight all the way to get your ideas accepted)? If the latter is the case, you may need to work on your interpersonal skills.

Will you be supervising others?

If you've never supervised others before, make sure you obtain supervisory training *before* asking for a promotion. Get the training and put yourself ahead of some of your competitors who want the same promotional opportunities.

Are you ready to be a supervisor?

Some people never make good supervisors. For instance, if you're the top salesperson for your department, think twice before accepting a supervisory position. You require a new set of pre-

Dealing with Difficult Situations

requisites if you're a supervisor. Typically, sales people hate paperwork and sales supervisors have to do a lot of paperwork. Sales people love dealing with a variety of people, having challenges and meeting sales quotas. Sales supervisors may find themselves tied to an office or a desk and may miss the lively interaction with their clients.

Choosing the right career for you is very important, not only when your work life begins, but later on in life as well. Remaining flexible is a must, for success.

The rewards of choosing the right career

Those who work at a suitable career find life tremendously stimulating. Somehow they find that their work generates its own momentum, which brings extraordinary satisfaction to the person. These fortunate people can't wait to get up in the morning and start their days running. Mondays for these individuals, are outstanding. Those with this attitude towards work, find they have a much better chance of progressing within their chosen careers.

On the other hand, some have difficulty making decisions and wait for outside forces to initiate changes in their lives. I always say, *'The only thing you get by fence-sitting is slivers.'* If you're one of these fence-sitters, remember that your indecisiveness can raise your stress level considerably. You can probably recall a time when you waited and waited before making a decision and can likely recall the relief you felt when you finally got off the fence and made a decision. So, get off that fence and start making decision about where you want to go with your life! There are answers to this dilemma, but you must be willing to invest time, effort and dedication to turn things around.

Many people go through the 'blahs' when they reach thirty-five or forty. They make such comments as, *'Is this all there is?'* They've probably reached many of their personal and career goals and find life very dull and uninteresting. This likely happens because they haven't had another goal on the 'back burner' ready to kick in when they came close to achieving their present goal.

Some workers are forced into setting career goals because they've been let go from a position (either laid off or fired). For some, this becomes a true blessing in disguise, because they're forced to look at their lives and make serious plans about where they want to go. For some, it might be the first time they've really asked themselves what they want to do with their career lives.

Goal setting takes a lot of effort, dedication and time, but *it's worth it!* If it takes two years for you to decide where you want to go, that's okay, as long as you're steadily working towards finding the right career for you. Don't attempt something unless you really want to succeed at it. There are too many competitors out there - people who know where they want to go and how they're going to get there.

The big question for many is how to find their ideal career. Most find this when they obtain professional career counselling. I find that those with the mid-life career blahs can feel frustrated and depressed, but as soon as they find a new channel for their abilities and talents, their outlook improves immediately. You might consider looking at the career counselling service we offer by going to: www.dealingwithdifficultpeople.info/unique-career-counselling-service

Overlooked for a promotion

Consider this situation. There's a promotional position in your company that you've applied for because you believe you're well qualified for it. You submit your resume for consideration and learn that someone else has been hired for the position. You *know* this person is less qualified than you, so you're upset. What steps should you take? How should you approach this situation? Is it too late to do something about it? No, it isn't. But simply complaining to the hiring supervisor or saying, *'How come you hired somebody who's less qualified than I?'* is not likely to work.

Instead, phone the supervisor who was in charge of hiring and ask for fifteen minutes of his time (we'll assume that it's a man). If he asks why, explain that it's important for you to obtain some information regarding the position. He'll have his guard up, but if you're persistent he'll see you. He expects you to attack him and will be on the defensive, even before you enter the room. So your approach has to be more subtle. (The hard-nosed approach of most labour negotiations won't work in this situation.)

You could start by being honest and admitting you're upset. Say, *'I think you know I was really looking forward to being accepted for this position and it has upset me that I wasn't chosen. Can you help me determine what I'm missing in my background that's keeping me from being promoted?'*

Dealing with Difficult Situations

He'll feel he's somewhat off the hook because you're discussing your failings, not questioning the decision. If he says, *'The other person was just better qualified than you,'* your response should be, *'Could you be more specific about the qualifications that are necessary for the job?'* After he has pointed out the qualifications, paraphrase what he has said and add, *'I have that kind of experience - in fact, I have more than you've said is necessary for that position, so I guess that isn't the problem.'*

He'll have to admit you're right. *'No, I guess not. You have seven years' experience in that area.'* (You know that George, who got the job, has only five years' experience. Don't throw this at the supervisor - store this information for later.)

Next you ask, *'What other kinds of qualifications were necessary for this position?'*

He may suggest some additional type of knowledge or experience and your reply might be: *'I don't think that's a problem either.'* Here you would give further facts showing that you have these qualifications as well (assuming you do). In short, keep giving factual reasons why you don't think his explanation eliminates you as a candidate. He'll try to pull out some plausible reason why you didn't get the job and he won't be able to do it.

At the end of the interview, you say something like, *'Well, I don't know where this leaves me, because it appears that, from what you've just told me, I was the best qualified for the job. As you stated, as far as experience is concerned, I needed five years' experience and I have seven. I know George only has five. As far as education goes, I have ... and I know George has only ... I'm still at a loss to know why he got the job and I didn't. What do we do now?'*

You've put this person on the spot. You've presented your facts in such a way that it can't be denied that you're right.

Many would say that all you've done is make the person angry. This may be so, but the supervisor will be angry because you're right and he's wrong. This may be the time to ask for an impartial person to be involved. If you're in a union environment, your steward could be called in to mediate. If it's a non-union environment, a representative of the Human Resources Department could be called in to solve the dilemma.

Dealing with Difficult Situations

Another choice could be to mark time and leave the meeting with this comment; *'Well, it's unfortunate that this happened. I really feel upset, because I should have been given the job. Can I count on you to see that I won't be overlooked for the next promotion?'*

This type of approach is low-key without being wishy-washy. You keep your cool - and your temper - but also give yourself a better chance of being treated fairly in the future. It might put the company in a very difficult position to demand that they pull back the promotion they have already offered to George. If George had been given a written job offer, he would be able to sue the company. You may have let the company off the hook. They may even recommend you for a promotion in another department. In fact, that's one of the things you can ask them to do.

Would you feel comfortable doing it this way? I hope so. It's a win/win situation.

Try to guard against being overlooked for a promotion in future by making sure your boss knows what kind of career plans you have. Ask him or her to watch for any promotional opportunities that might help you get where you want to go. Otherwise, no matter how good your qualifications are, you might be overlooked again. The oversight may be unintentional - the result of a certain type of conditioning.

You need to make sure your employer recognises that you're a candidate for promotion. You might also talk to people in the Human Resources Department. Explain that you're looking for a promotional opportunity and ask to be kept informed about any suitable positions.

PART 2

AT HOME

Dealing with Difficult Situations

CHAPTER 5

DIFFICULT SITUATIONS – COUPLES

Confused Messages

Men and women *do* communicate differently. It's not necessarily the words they use, but what their words and actions mean to them. Male and female approaches to situations differ in so many ways. These differences can accumulate until the couple wonder if they think and act alike under any circumstances.

Here's a situation that shows what often happens during communication between spouses. A couple has just returned from vacation and the wife is struggling to catch up with the family laundry, shopping and cleaning:

1. ***Husband's Intention:*** He wants to let his wife know that he recognises and appreciates the extra load she's been carrying. He considers what he might do, to communicate how much he appreciates her hard work:
   a. Buy her some flowers.
   b. Take her to dinner.
   c. Tell her how he feels.
   d. Be more helpful at home.
2. ***Husband's Action:*** He decides on (d) and puts a load of laundry in the washer.
3. ***Wife's Reaction:*** She sees him doing the laundry, doesn't realise his intentions and has to decide:
   a. Is he criticising her for not having the laundry done?
   b. Is he trying to tell her she shouldn't spend so much time on the phone?
   c. Is he trying to be helpful?
   d. Does he feel guilty about something?
4. ***Effect on Wife:*** She decides it's (a) and feels hurt and put down.
5. ***Wife Encodes:*** I'm not going to let him know that his actions have hurt me. Shall I:
   a. Say nothing.
   b. Say *'Thanks.'*
6. ***Wife's Action:*** She decides to say *'Thanks.'*

7. Effect on Husband: She understands and appreciates what I've done.

This is a classic situation where the husband's intention was positive and caring. However, the effect on his wife was the direct opposite of this. A much better approach would have been for him to back his actions up by telling how he feels (as shown in (c) husband's intentions). Using positive verbal feedback, he would have made sure his wife knew why he was helping her.

Male/Female Friendships

'My wife has such deep friendships with her girlfriends that I often feel left out. She also has lunch with men she works with. She insists that those relationships are necessary for her to succeed at her job - that they're just platonic relationships - no hormones involved at all. I've never had a platonic relationship with a woman in my life and can't understand why she needs this kind of friendship!'

There seem to be vast differences in the kinds of relationships/friendships that occur between men and those that occur exclusively between women. These differences are: Female friendship usually involves talking about feelings and personal lives. Back in your grandmother's era women called their best female friends, their girlfriends. After they disbursed their husbands and children in the morning, these girlfriends gathered at one home or another. They drank coffee, gossiped, shared recipes and secrets, cared for and relied on one another. This ceased the minute their husbands appeared on the scene. The man of the family won out over girlfriends.

Today women meet under different circumstances; in conference rooms and restaurants. There's less time for every-day exchanges and the topics are different. Instead of discussing recipes, they're more likely to discuss some professional crisis they're facing and the most recent fast-food ideas they can use to prepare for dinner.

What's changed this attitude in women? Because children often move far away from their childhood support group of siblings and parents, they find themselves facing problems their parents never experienced. Problems, such as how a woman can climb the corporate ladder; what she should wear to look successful; should she consider a common-law relationship; what about birth control and abortion; how to handle two-income family problems; how to balance work and home responsibilities. These are all faced by modern women in the workforce. This is where other female friends provide their input and expertise.

The experiences of the two generations have become so different in such a short time that women can't discuss these problems with their parents. If women really want to talk openly, having knowledgeable contemporaries is crucial. Factors that can have a negative effect on friendships, such as getting married, having a baby or getting divorced, are more easily overcome when they have established strong bonds beforehand. Women meet some of their closest friends at work and maintain those friendships long after they've moved to different companies. Because of their limited time, when women get together, they get right down to the nitty gritty issues. There isn't enough time for chit chat and conversations seem to deal with deep and meaningful topics.

Often, women turn to their female friends for emotional support. The turnaround is that these friendships (at times) can often be stronger and longer-lasting than those they share with their husbands. They're finding their friendships with other women to be the most intimate, profound and durable relationships in their lives. This is especially true where the husband has not learned to be truly intimate and open with his wife. For many women, these ties are also stronger than their family ties. Women no longer use friends as stand-ins for family. Instead, friends are becoming part of an extended family. Unexpectedly, these friendships result in stronger marriages, because husbands are no longer expected to meet their partner's emotional needs exclusively.

Men have had access to a system of friendships that women call the 'old boys' network' for centuries. They met in taverns, exclusive professional and social clubs (no women allowed). Men seldom worked in teams or networked with women. Men in the 'baby-boomer' era are less authoritarian and more team-oriented with women than older men in the workplace.

Male friendships used to revolve around activities. Within the past generation this has all changed. Do men benefit as well as woman from the new emphasis on friendships out of the family or all-male circle? Yes, mainly because it's now acceptable for them to have close female friends. The biggest change in friendships is that men and women have learned how to have solid, long-lasting platonic friendships. This is especially true with women who are employed in upper management of companies. It's a regular occurrence that she will have lunch or even dinner with male colleagues to discuss business and often strong friendships and mentoring occur.

Unfortunately, only one-third of single men (compared to three-quarters of single women) say they have a best friend. When men do, it's usually a friendship with a woman. Both men and women may suffer through crisis alone, if a strong network of friends and supporters is not available. Both need a strong support group to handle the rigors of daily living.

Emotional Abuse and Sniping

'My husband and I have fallen into the habit of sniping at each other and I'm tired of it. How can I convince him that this is detrimental to our relationship, to our children and is driving away our friends?'

This is a kind of emotional abuse couples occasionally or continually use on each other. Either spouse can suffer from this abuse. True emotional abuse involves a *constant* deluge of intimidating, sarcastic remarks, demanding, reprimanding, shouting, belittling or emotional blackmail. The more a marriage is in trouble, the more sniping there seems to be.

Sniping includes the following:

1. One partner is telling a story. The other spouse keeps interjecting with corrections to the story.
2. One partner makes disparaging comments related to the other's sex, forcing the partner to defend his/her gender. (i.e.: *'Men are such aggressive drivers. They act as if they own the road!'* or telling dumb-blonde jokes).
3. Start fights in public or in front of friends or family.
4. Play one-upmanship games or compete openly with their partners.
5. Something went wrong, so it has to be because of something the other partner has done (scapegoating and/or pass-the-buck). *'You're always doing ...'* Or, *'Because of you ...'*
6. Won't admit they're wrong even when they know they are.
7. Competitive - If their partner wins at a game they're playing, they become cranky or sulk.

Dealing with Difficult Situations

8. If a woman's partner wants some privacy or space, she follows him around asking, *'What's wrong?'* and won't take the explanation that he wants to be alone to think things out.
9. Set their partner up for disciplining the children by making comments such as, *'Wait until your Mother/Father gets home!'*
10. They hold grudges, pout or give others the silent treatment.
11. Make cutting or sarcastic remarks.
12. Make fun of how their partners look, what they wear or things they do.
13. They dig up old problems and indiscretions and can't seem to let go of past arguments.

These behaviours could be the result of boredom, the need to put their spouse down, a power struggle or all of these. They've likely fallen out of love and have lost all the fire and passion they may have had towards each other. It's a kind of disease that will seldom improve unless the couple takes action to stop it. Whatever the causes - it's a form of torture that gives bad 'vibes' to the other person and constantly picks away at their self-esteem level. Someone has to stop it or it will continue and probably escalate into divorce or violence. Counselling is often the only solution.

Emotional blackmail is where the abuser plays on the person's fear, guilt or compassion. They intend to constantly depreciate the person's self-esteem and self-confidence levels. The emotional abuser can be very unpredictable and prone to drastic mood swings.

For example: Friends of Sandra and Ben had observed drastic changes in their behaviour since their marriage five years ago. Sandra had been a bubbly, outgoing woman who desperately loved Ben and went out of her way to please him. Ben was very proud of his beautiful, successful wife and bragged about her to everyone.

By the end of their third year of marriage, she had become a quiet, apologetic person who tried so hard to please, that she gave up most of the activities she liked doing before her marriage. She slowly dropped all her old friends and became more and more withdrawn. Ben changed from being a polite, easy-going man, into one who became openly manipulative, belittling and judgmental of Sandra's accomplishments.

The signs were there - their marriage had become an emotionally abusive relationship. The abuse started slowly and gained

Dealing with Difficult Situations

momentum over time. Although this can be women emotionally abusing men, most victims of emotional abuse are women who believe they're responsible for their partner's or others' happiness and well-being. She believes her job is to fix relationships and she feels guilty if she can't.

More often than not, children in these relationships are also emotionally abused. They in turn, follow their role models and repeat the cycle in the next generation. Society needs to identify the signs of abuse and take steps to help both the abused and the abuser to change.

Equality

'I keep getting told that things are equal in the workplace for men and women who have the same talents and abilities. I don't believe that for a minute. Women - especially those with children - get a raw deal!'

In addition to the well-known problems working wives and mothers face - there is one that has far more serious consequences, because it begins in the home.

For example: Two employees (working for separate companies) are given the same situation to deal with. One is a woman; the other is a man. Both are married, have a son fourteen and a daughter nine. It's 2:00 pm. Because of an emergency, their boss tells them that it's necessary for them to leave on an 8:00 pm plane for an out-of-town meeting tomorrow. At work, this is identical for both employees. The difference occurs on the home front.

Male: Phones spouse tells her about his trip
Female: Phones spouse tells him about her trip;

Male: 6 pm wife serves <u>his</u> dinner;
Female: 6 pm eats dinner <u>she</u> has prepared.

Male: Wife helps pack his bag;
Female: Packs own suitcase;

Male: Wife checks list of items he's to take;
Female: Checks list of items she must take with her;

Male: Wife asks if he wants a ride to airport;
Female: She calls a cab so he can stay with the kids;

Dealing with Difficult Situations

They return from their trips the next evening at 8 pm. Both are exhausted and bone weary. Neither has eaten much since noon, (mouths are watering for a ham sandwich). They enter their front door:

Male: Wife greets him at the door with, *'Hi Hon!'* Gives him a kiss and asks about his trip; Children yell, *'Hi Dad!'*
Female: Husband watching TV yells, *'Hi Hon!'* Children meet their mother and describe what went wrong with their day.

Male: She hangs up <u>his</u> coat;
Female: She hangs up <u>her</u> coat;

Male: He flops into chair in living room explaining how tired he is;
Female: She flops into chair in living room explaining how tired she is;

Male: Wife asks if he's eaten yet;
Female: Asks, *'Have you guys eaten yet?'*

Male: Wife makes him a ham sandwich and tea;
Female: Makes herself tea and a ham sandwich. Her son sees it and asks her to make him one too; followed soon after by her daughter. Her husband leaves the TV to ask for one too. No ham left - she has tea and toast;

Male: Wife unpacks <u>his</u> suitcase, finds a spilled bottle of after shave. Wife washes contents of his suitcase.
Female: Unpacks <u>her</u> suitcase, finds a spilled bottle of hand cream. She washes the contents of her suitcase.

Male: Wife goes to bed, feels amorous towards him, but knows how tired he is. She covers him up and lets him sleep.
Female: Husband goes to bed, feels amorous towards wife and starts making advances. She mumbles, *'I'm too tired tonight.'* She's shocked by his next comment, *'I told you this job would be too much for you!'*

This scenario points out the inequities between the home pressures of men and women. Men's lives are made so much easier, because they usually come home to a caring, nurturing, empathetic partner. This partner is called a ***wife***. It's unfortunate that although many men are learning how to nurture, most women don't have this luxury! If they did, half their frustrations and the feeling that there's

Dealing with Difficult Situations

'something missing in their lives' would dissipate and there'd be true equality at home.

Breadwinner/child and home-care roles

'My husband 'helps out' around the home, but doesn't do his share. We both work, but I think I'm being short-changed - doing far more than half the home and child-care responsibilities.'

Traditionally a man's job was to be **The Breadwinner**. The woman's job was **Home and Child Care**. Now that women are sharing the breadwinner duties, they believe that men should share the home and childcare duties as well. Many working wives wonder how they can keep up with their double workload. Employed women still spend an average of two and a half hours a day to a man's one hour a day doing chores around the home.

When a wife asks for more help, often the reply from her husband is *'What do you mean - I help you around the house!'* This is the same husband who 'helps' by taking the garbage out once a week. In reality, he's not 'helping his wife;' he's helping himself; simply doing part of his share.

It's possible that one or both of them don't have time to do their share of the home, yard and child-care tasks. The person in this position should hire someone to do their portion of the work or pay other members of the family to do it. The person requiring the help pays the salary of the helper - regardless of whether it's the husband or the wife.

In the past, when women stayed at home with their children, the children seldom, if ever, helped out around the home; that simply wasn't their job. Presently, in many homes, when mothers work away from the home - everyone pitches in. This builds responsibility and teamwork in the children that prepares them for future responsibilities.

Men are learning that nurturing doesn't have to be an exclusively feminine trait, but can be a very masculine characteristic as well. These are the husbands who see their wives come dragging home from work and say, *'Had a tough day? How about a cup of tea?'* Or, *'Do you want half an hour to yourself while I fix dinner?'*

Dealing with Difficult Situations

The two-career couple – Can their marriage survive?

'Before our marriage, my husband promised that he would do his share of the household chores and that when we had children, he would also do his share. When we were first married he did help around the house and made a stab at looking after our daughter, but he's stopped helping out now that I'm back at work. He seems resentful that I'm climbing the corporate ladder and is trying to force me to have another child. It looks like he's hoping I'll quit work. Economically, we can't afford this and I'm not ready to sacrifice my career by having another child right now.'

As women earn more money and take on more responsibility at work, they also participate more actively in decision-making at home. Their husbands see themselves losing the privileges and power their fathers had been given without question. And they rebel. Men, who before marriage, had enthusiastically agreed to an egalitarian marriage, discover that they don't like their new lifestyle. They defend themselves by saying they lose patience when they see their wives put their boss's needs before their own. They openly admit that the main thing they want from their wives isn't intellectual stimulation. What they want is affirmation of their maleness and that they're the boss in their relationship.

Regardless of the husband's age, income or educational level, a wife's employment seems to have a negative impact on men's mental health. As their wives become more and more successful, many become afraid their independent wives will abandon them.

After several years of trying it out, many men feel that it's time to get back to a more traditional style of living. This is the time when some of their wives are soaring ahead in their careers and are reluctant to take time off to be a 'wife' and have children. Instead of complaining openly about their discomfort, men turn their attention to holding back their wives' careers. It's during this time that many husbands start neglecting their share of the home responsibilities, doing less and less and rebel if the wife suggests getting outside help. Somehow, they think a woman demonstrates her love for her family by doing household tasks and caring for their children.

The women become more and more frustrated as they try to fight fatigue, find solutions to their husband's resentment and their own guilt feelings. They find they have to switch their assertiveness on

Dealing with Difficult Situations

and off as they enter their two environments. Women admit their jobs interfere with their personal time with their families - but don't know how to change things.

While struggling to make a two career family work, both men and women suffer, but women are more overwhelmed by their load. Soon, the physical toll of working, maintaining a home and taking care of children wears them out. Some drop their housekeeping standards because there simply isn't enough time or energy left to live up to their former standards.

After several years of climbing the ladder, many women are reluctant to leave work to have children. Persuading their wives to concentrate on motherhood becomes the ideal way for many husbands to retain their manhood. Fatigue causes a few women to retreat to full-time domesticity. Many women holler 'uncle' and succumb to this, letting their husbands dominate their marriages, but are soon back to work after their maternity leave is over because of economic realities.

The women who haven't thrown in the towel, fight to avoid being dominated by their husbands and to maintain equality in their marriages. They acknowledge that they're angry and why, turning it on their husbands - fighting fire with fire. Each of them hopes to force the other to see their viewpoint by expressing their anger verbally, sexually and even physically. The more the husbands criticise their wives, the more frustrated their wives become. Most of the men admit that what they want from their wives is that they pay more attention to them - to be closer and more loving. They reject feminist values and their wives' hostility towards them for not helping out more.

Husbands lament that they get their wives' leftover time and attention, feel as if they are at the bottom of the list of their wives' priorities and yet they still refuse to help out more at home. They maintain that their wives' jobs come first; that their wives have lost their femininity; that they've stopped being wives and mothers and are now workaholics. And they fight back by helping even less. Sometimes, because they're so angry, men begin to experience sexual impotence. Others resort to drugs and alcohol or decide they've had enough and look for satisfaction and love in another partner.

Dealing with Difficult Situations

There are no pat answers to this dilemma, but unless the couple openly and honestly discuss what's happening to them behind the scenes - or receive family counselling, the marriage will continue to be a battle ground for supremacy, hurting not only each other but their children as well.

Getting help at home

'You've said that everyone should help out at home, but that's easier said than done!'

If your family won't help around the home, try the following strategies for getting them to share the household responsibilities:

1. Write down *all* the chores that need doing around the house and yard. Include everything. Make a copy for each member old enough to read.
2. Call a family conference.
3. At the family conference, ask all members to volunteer to do some of the chores. Fill in the chores you feel comfortable handling and have your spouse add his as well.
4. The remaining chores are then assigned. (And don't let it be 'dear old Mom or Dad' who takes them on; Mom and Dad don't have time either!) Even two-year-olds should have chores, such as:
    a. picking up their toys;
    b. putting their dirty clothes in the clothes hamper;
    c. helping with the dusting, making shelves and drawers neat or tidying shoes in a closet
5. Make sure your family knows you're counting on them to do the job right the first time. Explain that you don't want to have to nag them to get their chores done and ask: *'Can I count on you to do these chores?'* Get a commitment from each of them. Then, like a supervisor, follow up and make sure they do the chores properly. Decide what the consequences will be if they don't follow-through.
6. Give rewards. Signs of love and appreciation are necessary. Adults are normally rewarded for work well done - children should be too. You might put a monetary value on the chores the children are expected to do (in the form of an allowance) and deduct money for each breach of duty. Special family treats could be arranged for exceptional work. Let your children help decide what these special family treats involve.

Dealing with Difficult Situations

7. Keep track of work completed. Make sure each child knows when duties are expected to be done. If they're constantly saying, *'I don't have time,'* help them plan their time, but don't do the chores yourself.
8. Make sure children have the training they need to fulfil their obligations.
9. Avoid power struggles. If children won't give you their word that they will do a task, ask them why. Acknowledge their reason and reply, *'I know that taking out the garbage is not exactly a chore you like, but someone has to do it. Who do you think should be doing it?'* Be willing to negotiate, but be firm and reasonable. If you are, the chore will usually be done.
10. For particularly unpleasant tasks, have a rotation system in which all family members capable of doing the chore take a turn.

Home Time Management

Life runs smoothly at the office - but why does it fall apart at home? Where's the gas bill? When is Sally's next dentist appointment? What groceries do I have to pick up on my way home from work?

When you have a dual lifestyle - balancing career and home duties - it's usually the home front that does you in. Learn to use business techniques at home as well.

Planning is essential to getting your homemaking chores under control. Use lists for everything: groceries, things that need doing around the home and yard. (And who's expected to do them). Set priorities. Is it really more important to have a spotless house or yard or to spend an hour teaching Sally how to knit or to show Billy how to throw a football? Your lists should be divided into:

> ***Have to - Priority As***
> ***Need to - Priority Bs***
> ***Hope to - Priority Cs***
> ***Forget it - Priority Ds***

Don't forget about time for yourself. This is the area that's usually low on the list of priorities, but in reality should be near the top. Unless you feel good about yourself and what you're doing, you will be the sacrificial lamb who gives and gives to others, but seldom put your own wishes first.

Dealing with Difficult Situations

In order to be more effective in dealing with all aspects of their lives, wise parents learn that they must be 'selfish' and do special things for themselves. Putting yourself first is ***not*** a sin - it's a necessity (providing you don't take it to excess).

Delegate jobs to your family and follow up. That's the essential ingredient of delegation - follow-up. This is done to ensure that the job is being done properly, to give praise for a job well done and help in improving the quality of the performance. Have a plan set up as to what you will do if the job is not done. Be consistent with discipline and fair to all members of your family.

Use the Swiss Cheese Approach to family chores as well. Wallpapering the kitchen takes planning and can be done with 'instant tasks.' When cooking, make multiple batches - it takes just a little longer to make meals for four days than just for one. Utilise your freezer as much as possible. Stop wasting your time picking up groceries every second day - make fewer trips.

Some leave most of the family chores until the weekend, but find that their family doesn't have time to do things together. One man decided to correct this and did the shopping on Thursday evening. His wife did a batch of wash every day until it was all done. This eliminated the six batches usually done on Saturday, which tied her to her home unless she did it all at once at a laundromat.

Hire a student to do those jobs that pile up - cut the grass, paint the fence, shovel the driveway, help with the spring cleaning. In the summer, consider hiring a 'Mother's helper' so baby-sitting and home care can be accomplished at the same time. Have emergency phone numbers ready. Leave 'chore lists' for your children - make them feel part of the 'team' - that they're contributing something to the family unit. Plan treats to reward good performance.

Parents face common challenges:

- How to make the most of the time they have with their children when time is a premium? And;
- How can they make sure their children get the love and attention they need when parents are away from home eight hours plus a day?

A conscious, planned effort must be made. Both parents need to find time for the following:

1. Individual time with each child where they can have 'special' time with the parent. This can be 10 - 15 minutes each day and a set time on the weekend.
2. Keep track of your children's 'other lives' - at the baby-sitter, the day care, kindergarten, school, sports and artistic activities etc.
3. Learn about special events at school and take time to attend. Make it a responsibility of your children to keep you informed.
4. Practice effective listening - try not to be judgemental. Don't make contact times with your children an inquisition. 'Hear' what your children are <u>not</u> saying - watch their body language.
5. By effective time planning, you can eliminate unnecessary steps when completing tasks that will give you more time with your family.
6. Prioritise things you have to do, remembering that your children should hold a high priority for your home time.
7. Enlist children's help or ask for their presence when you're doing chores, so you can 'chat.'
8. Plan special outings that comply with individual needs. At a family conference, have each member state the special things they like to do as a family. Try to utilise this list when planning special outings.
9. Learn to be aware of your own stress level - don't over-react to minor incidences with your children. If you've had a bad day, explain this to your children and ask if you can talk to them later (give a specific time - whenever is best). Don't put them off too long - do follow-up on things they need to discuss with you.
10. Don't feel guilty when you need 'private time.' Honour your children's need for privacy too.

Guilt Giving

'My parents are always trying to make me feel guilty about things I do or don't do. They do the same thing to each other. How should we be dealing with these accusations?'

Some of their guilt-ridden statements are:

'I spent all day cooking this meal and it takes you fifteen minutes to eat it. The least you could do is help clear the table.'

'You never call me any more.'

Dealing with Difficult Situations

'It's 3:00 am. How come you're so late? Do you want me to have a heart attack?'

'If you loved me you'd ...'

'What will the neighbours think?'

'Do you want Grandma and Grandpa to think you have bad manners? Get busy and write those thank-you cards.'

'How can I believe you now, when you lied to me the last time you did this?'

'How can you just sit there watching your stupid football game when there's so much to do around here?'

'I work night and day to bring home my paycheque and you reward me by ...'

'I stayed with your mother because of you kids.'

Handle guilt feelings by dealing with the issue. First, you would identify which comments or statements were guilt laden. Then you'd respond by letting the manipulator know that you're aware of the manipulation. In the last example, the father was trying to lay guilt on his children because he stayed in an unhappy marriage. His son handled his father's attempt to make him feel guilty by replying, *'You've just tried to make me feel responsible for how you feel because you stayed with Mom. Why do you feel I was responsible for that decision?'*

The father retaliated with explanations about why he stayed. The son repeated his comment, *'Why do you feel I was responsible for **your** decision?'* The father finally had to admit that he had to take full responsibility for his actions, not his children.

Sally's parents always expected her to become a teacher and made it clear that her choice to become an accountant was wrong. Sally needs to accept that she can choose to do or be something other than what others may expect or want her to be. It's nice to have others' approval, but not at the risk of her feelings of self-worth. She has the right to choose how she lives (providing she's not breaking the laws of the land). However, she also must be ready to take the consequences of her behaviour and choices.

Dealing with Difficult Situations

When others try to shove you around emotionally, you should state how you feel. When others disapprove of what you do, it has nothing to do with what or who you are as a person. Keep in mind that ultimately you're responsible for your emotions. You have the right to stand up for your rights and needs (even with your parents and people in positions of authority).

CHAPTER 6

DIFFICULT SITUATIONS - WIVES

Moody

'How should I deal with my wife who's so moody and negative that I've found myself becoming very negative myself.'

Could she be going through menopause or suffering from PMS (pre-menstrual tension)? If so, encourage her to see her doctor to obtain relief.

If it's not this, it's possible she has turned into a negative thinker who might also be a whiner, complainer and bellyacher. These people are experts at giving you reasons why it's wrong to enjoy life. These wet blankets intend to take the pleasure out of life for themselves and others. They berate those who seem to enjoy life and encourage others to take life 'more seriously.' It's hard for others to enjoy life in such a rigid environment.

Use feedback to explain what her behaviour is doing to those around her. Encourage her to concentrate on what's good about life, rather than what's bad. Ask her permission for you to show her by some sign that 'she's doing it again!' Suggest that she take an assertiveness or positive-thinking course to change her approach to life. Life is too short to spend it grumbling.

Those who have mood swings (are up one hour, down the next - up one day, down the next) probably allow others' behaviour and actions to affect their day. It appears that she has fallen into this habit.

Every day we're faced with negative situations that cause negative emotions. Look at all the emotions others try to give us: we feel anxious, ashamed, confused, depressed, disappointed, embarrassed, hopeless, helpless, manipulated, frustrated, hesitant, humiliated, foolish, ignored, inferior, insecure, intimidated, jealous, nervous, rejected, resentful, restricted, sad, silly, stupid, suspicious, tense, troubled, uncomfortable, uneasy, upset, victimised or worried. No wonder we have problems remaining positive thinkers!

Most of us react to these negative stimuli. Someone throws an angry remark at us, a friend makes a hurting comment or a parent tries to

Dealing with Difficult Situations

make us feel guilty - and we react accordingly. Does your wife maintain control over her emotions and reactions under those circumstances or does she react automatically to the negative stimulus from others and retaliate, feel hurt or feel guilty?

It's the little annoyances that ruin things, so if she can learn how to handle the little annoyances, she'll have more energy and stamina to handle the really tough ones and become a more positive thinking person.

If she believes that outside circumstances cause unhappiness and that she has no control over this unhappiness - she's wrong. Outside forces and events cannot be harmful unless *she **allows them to affect her**.* Happiness comes largely from within a person. While external events may irritate or annoy her, she still has control over how she responds to each negative situation.

Does she blame others for how she feels? When she makes comments such as, *'He always makes me feel so inferior.'* Or, *'She makes me so mad when she ...'* Or, her own self-talk says, *'You goofed again. How dumb can you be? Won't you ever learn?'* she's allowing others (and herself) to ruin her day. By allowing herself to feel badly about situations or take on guilt she doesn't deserve, she's giving **herself** a bad day. She's going to gain nothing by blaming others for the way she feels.

What happens to her self-esteem level when she's not in control during these negative situations? Does it stay intact or is it bruised by the other person's negative actions? This is what keeps her off-balance. When she feels in control of situations, she'll feel as if both her feet remain firmly planted on the ground. But, if she reacts badly to someone's negative behaviour, she may find herself losing that control.

How can she make this happen? She'd learn how to turn negative situations off and not let them affect her emotionally. If she allows herself to absorb the negative feeling, she'll have to get rid of the feeling somehow - so she mustn't let it 'in.' Because she's probably been on 'automatic pilot' when reacting to negative situations in the past, this technique may take considerable practice before it becomes automatic - but it will be worth it! Why don't you pass this technique on to her and see the difference?

Dealing with Difficult Situations

Unwarranted fears

'My wife is a very timid person who seems to be afraid of everything. She did have a terrible childhood and I've tried to make sure that our marriage makes her feel secure, but I cringe whenever I see the fear in her eyes. How can I help her get over her constant state of worry?'

Start by having patience with her. She's not doing this on purpose to make you angry or upset. Have her identify the worst thing that could happen to her if her fear became a reality. Ask her what the chances are of her fear becoming a reality. If you haven't suggested that she receive professional counselling; please do so. Many people who've had terrible childhoods need to have counselling, so they can leave their past behind and start life with a clean slate and more confidence. Most laypeople don't have the skills or the expertise to do this on their own.

Your main focus should be to support her as she goes through her counselling. The counsellor may require you to take counselling as well, so you can understand the process and why she acts the way she does. This way you can be more supportive to your wife's needs.

These people often use cop-out phrases to bind them to the past using such phrases as:

- *'If only I were younger - taller - slimmer - more attractive ...'*
- *'I should have done this years ago.'*
- *'I should have been more careful.'*
- *'I was supposed to ... am trying to ... ought to ... have to ... need to ... can't ... or must do ...'*
- *'I can't change the way I am because ...'*
- *'The trouble with ...'*
- *'S/he made me ...'*
- *'You always ...'*
- *'You never ...'*

Whenever possible, encourage her to eliminate these phrases from her vocabulary unless she's willing to do something constructive about her comments. If these unwarranted fears are keeping her from doing the activities she wishes to do or have become overwhelming, it's time for her to seek professional help.

The fear victim is so ruled by anxiety and the fear that it arouses, that she avoids the situation and thus avoids facing the issue. She believes that dangerous or fearsome situations are cause for great concern, so she must continually think about them. Some people suffer from such problems as claustrophobia, agoraphobia, fear of heights, snakes, spiders, bees, the dark, being alone and of the unknown. This is irrational, because worry or anxiety:

a) Prevents an objective evaluation of the chance of a dangerous event;
b) Will often keep the person from dealing with it effectively if it *should* occur;
c) May contribute to making it happen;
d) Cannot possibly prevent inevitable events; and
e) Makes many dreaded events appear worse than they are.

Potential dangers are not as catastrophic as they appear. Anxiety does not prevent them but may increase them. Worrying may be more harmful than the feared events. A university study showed that, of the events people fear;

> 40 per cent never happen.
> 30 per cent happened in the past.
> 22 per cent are needless, petty or small.
> 8 per cent are real, but divided into:
> > Those the person could solve.
> > Those the person can't solve.

Everyone must love me!

'The other day I came home from work to find my wife in tears. She had knocked over a bottle of soft drink at the supermarket and it had shattered all over the items on the shelves. When an employee was asked to clean up the mess, he gave my wife dirty looks - didn't say anything - just gave her dirty looks. This devastated her and caused her outburst at home. Why does she overreact to these kinds of situations?'

Her goal in life is likely to have everyone - spouse, children, boss, friends, shop-keepers and even the person who comes to the door selling magazines, think she's the greatest. She hasn't learned that she can't please all the people, all the time, so feels fully responsible and guilty if a person shows they don't like her. This is irrational, because it's an unattainable goal.

Have her start by identifying when others are using her. Help her find ways to handle those situations. Praise her when she stands up for herself and constantly remind her that she can't please everybody all the time.

For the incident she's just experienced at the supermarket - explain that the employee over-reacted. She didn't break the bottle on purpose - and yet she accepted the guilt he was sending her. Help her understand that she shouldn't let others give her a good or a bad day. Encourage her to control how she responds - to remind herself that she is over-reacting - instead of allowing herself to absorb the negative feelings. Suggest that she picture you when these types of situations happen and ask herself how *you* would react should you be faced by such an incident. Tell her she has your full support and confidence that she can handle things in the future.

Guilt

'My wife is forever bringing up every mistake I've made in the past. It irks me that she will not forgive me for mistakes I've made. Most of these mistakes are minor ones, but she has the memory of an elephant and pulls them out whenever we have an argument. Why does she do this?'

Remind her that you can't change the past despite how she feels about it. Let her know how unfair you feel she is being to constantly bring up your mistakes from the past. It's important that when you did make a mistake that you admitted it (many people find it difficult to do say the magic words *'I made a mistake.'*) This is a powerful tool to use to fight people who love bringing up your failings. *'You're right. I didn't do a good job of fixing the kitchen cupboards. I've learned a lot by that experience and that mistake won't be repeated.'*

Don't allow yourself to be re-infected by her guilt. When she brings up the past say, *'Why are you bringing that up again? What has that to do with what we're discussing?'*

We live in a guilt-ridden society. We allow others to make us feel guilty. And as if other's criticism isn't bad enough, we all seem to

Dealing with Difficult Situations

have a little twerp inside us who loves to criticise. This voice makes such comments as, *'You goofed again! Can't you do anything right?'*

We feel guilty if we can't understand what someone's saying on the phone or we feel guilty because we make mistakes or identify things we've done in the past that we're not proud of. Instead of wallowing in guilt - learn from the experience. If an apology is needed to remove the guilt - then apologise.

As long as you have given a situation your best effort - that's all you can expect of yourself. For some reason society has taught us to feel guilty because we make mistakes. If you made a mistake - recognise that it's just that - a mistake and simply don't do it again. Mistakes are to learn from and should not make us feel as if *we are* a failure. Stop being hypercritical and start using positive reinforcement. *'I'm proud of the way I painted that room!'*

When others try to make you feel guilty, stop and identify what their comments really mean. Analyse whether there is some truth to their comments and then act accordingly. Recognise when others are attempting to manipulate you by trying to make you feel guilty. You can't change the past despite how you or they feel about it.

It's also a sad fact that in everyday life, we receive ninety-eight per cent criticism and only two per cent praise. Let's say you've worked very hard painting the bathroom and are very proud of your accomplishment. You wait patiently for recognition from members of your family. Is recognition likely to come? In many instances - *no* - that's not the case. What you're more likely to hear about, is a small portion of the task you did wrong (*'You missed this spot,'* or *'The paint ran here.'*)

Unfortunately, if someone criticises us, we may automatically accept the comments without question. This allows the one giving criticism to control how we feel about ourselves. This obviously can seriously affect our self-confidence level.

Then we may get the feeling that we *did* do a poor job and accept the guilt feelings that accompany the criticism. Learn to evaluate the relevancy of other people's comments. Are your guilt feelings warranted? Could you be responding negatively because that's the way you've always responded in the past? Re-evaluate the situation. What type of job do you feel you did? Were you originally pleased? Why aren't you pleased now?

Dealing with Difficult Situations

If you're the receiver of criticism (whether it's constructive or destructive) you may still feel like responding defensively. Before allowing your defence mechanism to kick in, consider the following:

1. Control your thoughts and behaviour. Keep in mind there may be some truth to the criticism.
2. If the criticism is valid - apologise. Let the person know what steps you'll take to correct the behaviour or problem. Strive not to repeat this failure or cause the problem in the future. Leave feelings of guilt behind. Don't let the criticism overwhelm you and affect the rest of your day. Instead, learn from your mistakes.
3. When others criticise you, don't immediately feel you must retaliate. Instead, listen carefully to their comments.
4. Ask for specifics if the criticism is vague. For instance, the person says, *'I don't like your attitude.'* This is very vague, so ask the person for specifics. (Watch your tone of voice). Don't make your comments accusatory, otherwise the person will become defensive).
   'What is it about my attitude that concerns you?'
   'Well, you made some nasty comments to Patricia when she was visiting us. I know you don't agree with everything she says, but I feel you should be courteous to her because she's my friend.'
   Now you have something specific you can correct.
5. Confirm your understanding of the problem (using paraphrasing).

Don't climb into a shell when others criticise you for something. We often set up this kind of defence mechanism in ourselves. If something or someone hurts us (especially someone we're close to) we're likely to withdraw and 'lick our wounds.' This can double the negative effects of the problem.

Handle guilt with facts - don't let your emotions get in the way. For instance, a stay at home neighbour asked Audra, a working single mother, *'Why aren't you staying at home with your children?'*

'Do you think I'd be a better mother if I stayed at home with my children and went on welfare rather than go to work to support my family?'

'Well, not really - but I still think your children need you to be there for them.'

'That wouldn't be practical in my case. I can't help but wonder why you're trying to make me feel guilty about my decision to return to work.'

When others try to shove you around emotionally, you should state how you feel. When others disapprove of what you do, it has nothing to do with what or who you are as a person. You have the right to stand up for your rights and needs, just as they have the right to stand up for theirs. Your task is to find the middle ground between pleasing others and pleasing yourself.

Stealing from work

'My wife Cheryl works in an office. She occasionally brings coloured pencils, paperclips, pens, felts, lined paper and staples home from work. Our children have watched and commented to me about her stealing. I know I've got to talk to my wife about her stealing from work. What should I say to her that won't sound like preaching?'

Explain how you feel about it. For instance, phone her at work and say, *'Cheryl, I need to talk to you today, because of something that concerns me. I watched Judy the other day when you came home from work with some lined paper. This afternoon, she asked me if it was okay to take items from school the way you take some from work. I suggested she talk to you about this when you come home. I wanted to warn you about this before she approaches you. You probably haven't realised how she perceives what you're doing. She wants to know if it's all right to steal - because that's exactly what this is. How do you think you'll approach this?'*

This will prepare Cheryl for the situation and make her look closely at the example she's setting for your children. Between you, decide a rational course of action and what she should tell your children about what she's been doing.

There was a time when thefts from inventory only affected industries that had 'attractive' types of inventory. Increasingly, all types of inventory are becoming subject to theft - not only completed assemblies, but parts and even raw materials are also being stolen. Some employees go far beyond a few pencils. It's not that they're kleptomaniacs, but rather, it's to get back at management. Some of these people will steal quantities far in excess of what they could ever use. To some extent, it's their way of getting around the rules and back at those in positions of authority. Usually the employee who constantly steals is a poor employee - not only because of his or thieving - but for other reasons as well. It's not just that s/he has a low regard for company property, but frequently s/he also thinks little of the company for which s/he works.

It's not economically justifiable to lock everything up, nor is it possible to catch all the culprits, but if management removes some of the temptations, they will have fewer losses. Having only one or more people in charge of office supplies can cut down on pilfering. Having employees sign for stationery and equipment is another. The employee who takes home a few coloured pencils so that his or her child can complete a colouring book is setting a bad example in attitude. Make sure you make this clear to your wife.

Wife Sexually Harassed at Work

'My wife came home from work the other day very upset and crying. I spent the evening trying to find out what had happened to her at work. At first she said, 'I'll handle it.' But as the evening progressed, she still didn't settle down. I insisted that she tell me what was wrong.

'I'm being sexually harassed at work!' she finally explained. My first impulse was to go to work with her the next day and punch the guy in the nose!

'That's what I was afraid you'd want to do! What I need are solutions to the problem, not more problems to worry about. That's why I didn't want to tell you about this in the first place.'

With that, we sat down and determined the alternatives open to her. I wanted her to quit her job the next day, but she was adamant that she loved her job and nobody was going to force her to leave it.

We decided that the best alternative would be to call the Equal Employment Opportunities Commission in our area to learn what her rights were and how to handle her situation. The next day, my wife called her office and said she was ill (she really couldn't work that day).

The Equal Employment Opportunities Commission advised us that she should document everything that had happened; try to find witnesses

Dealing with Difficult Situations

to the actions and whether this man had harassed other women before. She was to send copies of this documentation to the man who harassed her, her supervisor and his manager. By law, if those senior people 'turned the other cheek' and ignored her plight, she could charge them with harassment as well. Their silence would mean that they condoned the sexual harassment. Because of their senior positions, they're legally obliged to step in and do something to stop the harassment.

We followed the Commission's advice. She confronted the man, he apologised and she obtained his assurance that he would not harass her in the future.'

I discuss sexual harassment at several of my seminars by explaining what sexual harassment is, what victims can do about it and where they can go to complain formally. One of the primary harassment complaints is the telling of dirty jokes. In classes where there are both male and female participants, I often receive comments such as, *'Why should men have to 'clean up their act' just because women are now working in a male-dominated field? They're the ones invading our turf, so **they** should have to abide by our rules - not theirs!'*

My normal response to this comment is, *'I know it's difficult to change your conversational patterns because of this change in the workplace. I'd like to ask all of you who object to cleaning up your language, whether you use this type of language at home?'* Most agree that they don't use that kind of language at home. *'Then why do you think it's acceptable in a professional place of business?'*

My next question to them is, *'Do any of you have daughters and how old are they?'* Usually a few hands go up. To those, I ask, *'When they're old enough to work, say seventeen, what would you do if you learned that someone she works with was sexually harassing her? What would you do if it was your sister, your girlfriend, your wife or your mother being harassed?'*

A common answer is, *'I'd punch him in the nose!'* My next comment is, *'Let's turn this around. How do you think the boyfriends, husbands and fathers of the women you're sexually harassing feel about **your** actions? Why do you feel it's acceptable to treat any women that way?'*

This usually puts the situation into a clearer light. They suddenly realise that if they'd like to *'punch someone in the nose'* if someone

Dealing with Difficult Situations

harassed their wife, sweetheart, daughter or mother, then maybe the female they're harassing has a father, husband or boyfriend who might be thinking about doing the very same thing to them! Many of them did not know what could be termed as being Sexual Harassment behaviour. These would be:

Verbal:

- Telling dirty jokes with sexual connotations;
- Asking for sexual favours;
- Comments about one's sexual anatomy;
- Pursuing an unwanted relationship;
- Unwanted compliments with sexual overtones; or
- Condescension or paternalism that undermines self-respect.

Visual:
- Staring at someone's sexual anatomy;
- Holding uncomfortably long eye contact ;
- Giving sexual messages;
- Flirting non-verbally; or
- Pornographic pictures.

Physical:
- Unwanted touching and making physical contact; or
- Standing too close.

This could be a man harassing a woman (the most common complaint) a woman harassing a man, a man harassing another man or a woman harassing another woman. For example, if I (a female) told offensive jokes and refused to stop telling them, another woman could charge me with sexual harassment (female charging another female). The same holds true of a male colleague who could also charge me with sexual harassment if he objects to my lewd jokes (male charging a female).

Want some Peace and Quiet!

'When I get home from work I'm exhausted and all I want is a bit of quiet time before I'm bombarded with my kids and my wife's chatter. But, you guessed it - I'm attacked as soon as I get through the door with all their problems and things that happened to them during

Dealing with Difficult Situations

their day. How can I convince them that I need this space when I first get home from work?

The way to start is by communicating your wishes. Call a family conference where you explain how important it is for you to have a 'time-out' period when you get home from work. Explain what you need and when you'll be ready to deal with their issues. Use family conferences to discuss any problems that occur that affect the entire family.

Battle of the Sexes

'When I get home from work, my stay-at-home wife goes on and on about what happened to her during the day. I keep waiting for a 'punch line' or something interesting I can relate to and be interested in, but I find she talks about mundane things such as the new detergent she tried that day.'

One particular day, she spent a considerable time explaining to her husband about her day. Nothing of any significance happened and her husband stated, *'What's your point?'*

The wife felt devastated that her husband thought what she did all day was insignificant. He on the other hand, wondered where she was going with her comments and waited for the punch line (which never came). He felt disappointed because she wasted his time by talking about issues that were unimportant to him.

It might help to understand the needs your wife might have. To her, which detergent she's using *is* important. The problem is likely that you have different expectations of what you need from each other. When a woman marries, she expects her husband to be her best friend. Men don't know what kind of talk women want; don't miss it when it isn't there and they misread each other's body language. Men's communication focuses on the significance of the information given, while women's focus on inter-relationships. When women get together they talk about personal matters - situations that happen at home and at work. Men are more likely to talk about sports, politics, business matters and other topics, but stay clear of talking about their personal life.

In female to male communication, the woman asks most of the questions. Women see questions as a way to continue a conversation, while men view questions as requests for information.

Dealing with Difficult Situations

Men therefore, are less likely to ask personal questions. They believe that if she wants to tell him something - she'll tell him. Men often think questions show intrusion, while women believe they express interest and intimacy.

Another habit that gives women the impression men aren't listening is that they switch topics more often. Women talk at length about one topic - men jump from topic to topic. When women talk to each other, they often overlap each other's conversations, finish each other's sentences and anticipate what the other is about to say. If women do this while conversing with men, many men view this as an interruption - that it's rude and displays a lack of attention to what they've been saying.

When a woman expresses her point of view, her female listeners usually express agreement and support, whereas men point out the other side of the issue. Women see this as disloyalty and a refusal to offer support to their ideas. Women use talk to establish rapport. They prefer other points of view expressed as suggestions and inquiries rather than as direct challenges or arguments. Men are more comfortable with an oppositional model. A discussion becomes a debate: a conversation becomes a competitive sport.

Women use the pronouns *'you'* and *'we'* much more than men. Men are more likely to stick to facts and opinions. This comes across to women as authoritarian, not comprehending that it illustrates the masculine form of communicating rather than a show of supremacy.

Women often phrase their comments to sound as if they are questions. *'Our meeting is at ... three?'* This rising inflection at the end of a sentence is an implied question and leaves the listener with the impression that she's uncertain of what she's saying. A woman at a community club board meeting said, *'Ummm, I'd like to say something. This may sound dumb - it's just a thought - but maybe before we discuss program strategies, we should figure out our goals. I mean, I don't know what you think, but it sounds logical to me ...'* Her ideas were ignored by the male members.

Women make more listening noises like, *'uh-huh ...'* to encourage the other person. Men expect silent attention from their listener and interpret a stream of listener noise as overreaction or impatience on the part of their female listener. Men also believe these noises mean the woman agrees with him, when she may not agree with him at all. Because men don't make as many listening noises, women assume they're not really listening. Men are less likely to make non-verbal signs of listening either and many continue doing whatever they were doing before the conversation began. Women are more likely to nod their head more, give direct eye contact and stop whatever else they may have been doing when the conversation began.

Wife wants more intimacy

'My wife hardly talks to me any more. She's mad at me because I won't talk about what's `inside' me - that I keep too much to myself and don't share my feelings with her. She tells me that she wants more intimacy, but I don't understand exactly what she wants from me?'

Intimacy involves having complete trust in another person. Intimacy is obtained by 'letting it all hang out' and allowing others to know what's happening inside you. This involves revealing how you *really* feel about what the other person does and considers the other person's feelings when communicating with them. This involves a considerable amount of empathy. By revealing your true self, the other person can almost know how you'll react to situations. If they care about you, they'll try to stay clear of those they know will upset you. They'll automatically protect you from situations that might unnerve or upset you and find ways around difficult situations so you won't feel hurt.

When we look at relationships that survive, we find that the couple are good friends and treat each other with respect. They share values and trust one another implicitly. Trust is the foundation of any relationship and without it - a couple won't feel safe about revealing their inner selves. If they don't feel safe, they can't be vulnerable. If they're not vulnerable, they can't be intimate.

The ability of allowing people to see the 'real you' may be overshadowed by the fear that others may use this weapon against you in the future. Is this what's holding you back from being intimate with your wife? Unless you establish this trust, true intimacy will not occur.

If you observe people getting to know each other (of the same or mixed genders) there are several steps they take to get to the stage where they reach intimacy.

One person reveals trusting information. The second person accepts that trust and reveals similar information. As the trust grows between these people, they enlarge their trust and reveal more and more. This could be almost instantaneous or could take months to occur, depending on the comfort zone of the participants. But, this feeling of intimacy could suddenly end, if one person does something that the other sees as a betrayal of that trust. To many couples, the ultimate betrayal is infidelity or the threat of infidelity.

In marriage, women use talk to create intimacy, where they openly express their feelings and thoughts. Men use touch to create intimacy (use non-verbal communication) and use talk to maintain independence. Men are on guard to protect themselves from put-downs or others who might want to push them around.

Most women are comfortable admitting negative feelings, but society has almost forbidden men to admit to these perceived weaknesses. Therefore, this limits their options for expressing their feelings. Society says they're allowed to show happiness and anger but are not allowed to show any feelings between those two emotions. Therefore, when men feel anxious, disappointed, jealous, sad, hurt, rejected, stupid, intimidated, insecure, ashamed or ignored, their outward appearance can show misleading verbal and non-verbal signs of anger. This ambiguous behaviour confuses women and adds to the male/female communication gap. On the other hand, when some women get angry, they end up in tears. This gives men the impression that she's feeling hurt, rather than angry, which adds to men's confusion.

Many women complain that the men in their lives don't share their thoughts and feelings with them. They feel that their men don't trust them, by not letting them know what their feelings are. This male vulnerability keeps many men and women from sharing true intimacy. The husband would have to examine what he was *really* feeling at the time and put those feelings into words. For this process to work, men require enormous trust in their partners.

Some men take the chance and confide their innermost feelings to their wives, but unfortunately, their wives don't keep that information to themselves, so the husbands lose trust in their wives. Women should be very careful not to reveal their husband's confidential admissions about their feelings to others - especially with their female friends.

Dealing with Difficult Situations

If men give others (especially their wives) the weaponry and reveal their weaknesses, many men fear that the knowledge could be used against them in the future - so they clam up and resist verbal intimacy. Is this the situation in your case? Have you trusted her with private information and she's not kept that confidence? If this is what she's done, explain how betrayed you felt about her revealing your most inner secrets with others - that this is the reason for your lack of intimacy.

When men feel upset about something, most need time and privacy to mull over the situation. They see their wives' insistence on sharing the problem as interference to this process. If their wives persist, they feel they're nagging and pull further into themselves. This leads to even more frustration.

Wives should back off, letting their husbands know they're there when they're ready to talk about their problem. Instead of giving into their husband's initial desire to push her away from him, the husband should try to understand that his wife needs to 'make everything right.'

She Mumbles

'My wife mumbles. How do I deal with her when she mumbles, then picks fights with me because she says I have a hearing problem? I know there's nothing wrong with my hearing, because I only have this problem with her.'

Many people *do* mumble. They fail to a-r-t-i-c-u-l-a-t-e their words, so their words run together. Watch when she communicates with others. Do others have problems understanding her too? Ask her to record some of her conversations so she too will see that she mumbles.

If mumblers have problems being understood, it certainly seems worthwhile for them to take steps to improve this skill. Otherwise they're allowing themselves to remain handicapped in the most important communication skill of all - speaking. They can improve this by joining Toastmasters or Toastmistress clubs or by taking public speaking courses. They'll learn breath control, how to project their voices and how to speak clearly and sequentially when they talk.

Dealing with Difficult Situations

Has High Pitched Voice

'My wife has a high pitched voice that rises even more when she's excited, angry or upset. It's got so I hate the sound of her voice.'

Start by gently explaining how her voice affects you. If her voice bothers you, it likely bothers others as well. If she doesn't believe you - have her ask her friends whether her voice is grating. You might suggest that she record a normal conversation and replay it to show her how high pitched her voice is.

If she agrees that it requires work - she can have elocution or speech lessons that will help her learn how to modulate the pitch of her voice.

Because many of my seminars run for three full days, I spent several months lowering the pitch of my voice so it would be more pleasant to listen to. It has now become my normal voice. She can do the same, if she wants to spend the effort to change it. The choice is hers.

Misunderstandings

'My wife and I are forever misunderstanding each other. I listen carefully to what she says but I'm at a loss to understand what's gone wrong'

This couple were travelling to another city. The wife was thirsty, so asked her husband, *'Would you like to stop for a break?'*

He answered, *'No, I'm not ready for one yet,'* so they didn't stop.

The result was the wife became annoyed with him because she felt that he didn't consider her wishes. This is what caused his confusion. Unfortunately, the husband didn't see that his wife had wanted to stop to fulfil her own needs. She should have been more direct and explained more clearly, *'I'm thirsty. Please stop at the next restaurant.'*

Women use talking as a way of giving support and nurturing. Men use conversation to either achieve the upper hand or to prevent other people from pushing them around. She should have stated clearly what she wanted from him.

Dealing with Difficult Situations

Can't read maps

'I get so annoyed with my wife when she reads a map. Instead of reading it the right way, she turns it right around.'

This difference in reading maps occurs because of the left brain/right brain differences between men and women. Most men are better at conceptualising space and distance than women and have more ability in visualising objects in three dimensions. To ease her understanding of the direction she must go, she will turn the map according to the direction the car is facing and will direct her husband to turn left or right accordingly. As long as her method works – why complain?

I Need Solutions - Not Emotional Support

'My wife doesn't help me when I'm sick.'

Her husband had complained that he didn't feel like getting out of bed, that he didn't feel very well. His wife stroked his brow and gave him sympathy. He became upset because she didn't seem interested in making him feel better. She gave emotional support: he wanted solutions.

I Never Get My Way!

*'Why do I always have to do what **he** wants to do?'*

She had said, *'I want to go to a movie tonight. What do you want to do?'* Or *'The basement is a real mess. What do you say we clean it this weekend?'*

Her husband interpreted her comments as commands, resisted her telling him what to do, feels manipulated, so responded resentfully. She thinks she's made suggestions and presents her requests as ideas, not demands. He would respond much better if she had made straightforward requests - not suggestions. *'I think it's about time we saw a movie.'* And, *'This weekend, we should clean the basement.'*

My Wife's a Nag!

'My wife is a nag. How do I stop her from nagging me?'

Men complain that women nag and are too emotional. In men, stressful situations trigger a fast rise in his heart rate and blood pressure (fight or flight response). When he feels that surge in blood pressure at the anticipation of an argument, his body and brain react in self-preservation. Women's nurturing peacekeeping nature is more likely to choose a way through the conflict using compromise or negotiation.

It's also possible that the wife nags because she doesn't think her husband was listening to her when she spoke on a topic earlier. She believes this because he doesn't make listening noises, does not look her in the eye when she's speaking, interrupts her more often and doesn't show non-verbally that he's paying attention to her, so she repeats what she's said earlier. He thinks of this as 'nagging.'

All of these conflicting views of situations iron themselves out during a marriage (providing the couple have the patience to see things though). So whenever you don't understand why others are doing or saying something, ask them why they're doing so. If they react emotionally, ask them to explain what they're feeling at the time and what triggered the reaction. It's only through the effort of both spouses that these situations can be ironed out.

Indecisive

'My wife is very indecisive and has a terrible time taking action when she needs to make important decisions. She asks all her friends to help her make important decisions and if she gets conflicting advice, she's even worse. She wavers between several choices or changes her course of action three or four times before making even a tentative decision. Her behaviour is driving me mad!'

Start out by letting her know how upset you are when she acts indecisively. Remember that this type of person has a terrible time making decisions and are compelled to ask everyone they meet to help them make decisions. They seek the perfect solution and are on edge if they can't find one. Once they make a decision, they discover a flaw in it and change their minds again. They're wishy washy and inconsistent, swaying back and forth between choices.

They bury their head in the sand hoping that if they put off making a decision long enough the problem will go away or someone else will make the choice for them. They're very consistent in their inability to make a decision and assume they won't make the right choice. Even the simplest of errors will lower their sense of self-worth. Some may use delaying tactics to get even with others.

Dealing with Difficult Situations

If she must make decisions, have her write down all her choices and solutions. Have her identify the pros and cons for each choice - then encourage her to make a decision and write down the steps she'll take to make it happen. If she comes to you asking for your advice, stop yourself from answering automatically. Instead, ask her, *'What do you think you should do?'* Eventually she will see that she's capable of making decisions for herself. Give her deadlines for each decision that you expect her to meet. Don't weaken and make the decision for her. Make her do it.

Worrier

'My wife is a worrier. She jumps to conclusions and makes assumptions rather than ask for more information about the true situation.'

Worriers bottle up their negative feelings, seeing only the dark side of every issue and expect the worst. These worry warts mull over the situation, until they convince themselves that things will go wrong. Some worry to the state where they're stressed to the limit and can't cope at all. Watch for her body language signals of withdrawal from you that could indicate an unexpressed hurt feeling.

Give her constant feedback on what she accomplishes. Explain you're concerned because she's become a negative thinker and you want to help her overcome that negative habit. Have some sort of signal you can use to let her know that she's worrying needlessly - again. Have patience - it may take a long time for her to overcome this and she may remain a worrier all her life. It's part of her personality to think of the worst scenario rather than look forward to a more pleasant one.

Dependent

'My wife is smothering me! She's so dependent on me that it's making me want to stay away from our home. She waits all day for me to come home and monopolises my time so much that I have no privacy whatsoever. I've told her repeatedly that she's smothering me and have asked her for some `space,' but she won't listen to me. What do I have to do, threaten to leave her before she hears me?'

This is a form of passive behaviour. Dependent people believe that they should be dependent on others and must have someone stronger on whom to rely. While we all depend on others somewhat, there's no reason to encourage dependency, for it leads to loss of independence, individualism and self-expression. The dependent person is at the mercy of those who protect them. Dependency causes greater dependency, failure to learn and insecurity, since one is at the mercy of those on whom one depends.

She fails to do things for herself or learn new skills and suffers from insecurity when her defenders are not available. She should strive for independence and responsibility and learn to refuse to accept help just because others offer it. Taking risks - which could possibly result in failure - are still worth trying. Failing is not a catastrophe.

Most dependent adults grew up in homes where the parents taught their children to be dependent and to lean on them. Women from these homes usually switch their dependency to their husbands when they marry. This is an almost automatic response. If she had lived on her own before her marriage, she'd likely have lost her dependent nature.

Your wife needs encouragement from you to see that she has an independent life of her own. Unfortunately, she went right from her parent's home into your marriage. Her passive behaviour keeps her from attempting independent action. Try sending her to assertiveness training or buy her some books on the topic. You might suggest that she get a job outside the home to help her make independent decisions.

When she asks you for help in deciding - stop yourself from automatically stepping in to help. Instead ask her, *'What do you think you should do?'* Nine times out of ten, she'll know what she should do - she just wants confirmation. When she realises that she knew what to do all along, she'll see that she can make more decisions by herself.

CHAPTER 7

DIFFICULT SITUATIONS – HUSBANDS

The Silent Treatment

'My husband has the habit of sulking and giving me the silent treatment when he's miffed about something. How can I get him to communicate with me when we have disagreements, instead of clamming up or saying 'Whatever you say, dear.' This infuriates me and causes even more difficulty with our communication.'

Sulking or 'the silent treatment' is a form of indirect aggression. Ignoring others or giving them the silent treatment by refusing to discuss issues with them is manipulative and unfair to the recipient. This negative reaction is a no-win situation for both parties. Often the person giving the silent treatment wins the battle, but prolongs the war. If they don't settle issues (and remove the 'blips' that have accumulated on both their screens of annoyance) the issue will resurface later.

This isn't to say that people can't walk away from an argument until they've calmed down, but they must return within a reasonable length of time and resolve the situation with the other person. Let your husband know that his actions are 'dirty pool' and an act of indirect aggression. Explain that it's important for everyone to discuss and resolve annoying situations immediately so they don't accumulate and end up causing a major blow-up later.

When I discuss the silent treatment at my seminars, I ask for input from my participants on whether they believe men or women use the silent treatment more. The consensus is that women use it far more than men. The explanations are that traditionally, women were not supposed to argue, so they gained the upper hand by refusing to talk about an issue. Later, when women felt more comfortable expressing their opposing opinions, they found they were still using this tactic. When asked why they continued doing this, their reply was often, *'He never listens to me, so why should I bother expressing my opinion!'*

The assumption by women that, *'He never listens to me,'* stems from the differences in male-female communication styles. Women face each other directly with eyes anchored on each other's faces when conversing. Men sit at angles to each other and look elsewhere in the room - periodically glancing at each other and often mirror each other's body movements. Men's tendency to face away from them when conversing and because he appears to be staring at a spot on the wall instead of giving eye contact and looking at them, gives women the impression that the men aren't listening to them, when in fact they are. However, many men admit that they do 'tune out' if the woman appears to be 'nagging.'

This doesn't mean that men don't use the silent treatment themselves. On the contrary, almost 45 per cent of the silent treatment occurs when men refuse to talk about what's really going on. In modern society, studies show that men and women use the 'silent treatment' just about equally and both deserve a rap on the knuckles to encourage them not to use this manipulative ploy. For example, a wife notices that her husband is uncommunicative, usually a sign that something's wrong.

She says, *'What's the matter, dear?'*

'Nothing.' he replies.

'I can see there is. Won't you let me in on what's happening?'

'I told you, I don't want to talk about it!'

This just puts the man on a bigger island of aloneness. Not only has he refused the well-intentioned help offered to him, but he's compounded his problems by pushing his wife away from him. This is likely because their problem involves the need to explain feelings which he may believe is a sign of weakness and be reluctant to reveal this possibility to others.

Use of Humour

'When we're out in public, my husband is constantly embarrassing me by his stabs at humour. Most of this is aimed against women and I've got to the stage where I'm ready to tell him that I'll walk away from him and go home if he does it again. Why does he do this?'

This is a form of 'sniping.' Make him realise that you're deadly serious about this. Explain how you feel when he uses that kind of sarcasm, *'When you make jokes about women, you force me into the position of having to defend my gender. This is mean, cruel and destructive to our relationship. How would you feel if I constantly ran down men by telling jokes about them? If you continue to do this I will ...'*

Men have a distorted sense of humour. Yes I know, declarations of this kind can get me into hot water, but there's no avoiding the truth.

Often the widest division between who's in on the joke and who's left out is between men and women because they don't necessarily find the same situations funny. Women often wonder why men don't think *their* jokes are funny and other times wonder what men are laughing at.

Men's humour often relates to the sexuality or sexual parts of the opposite sex. These include obscene or hostile jokes (with an intention of aggressiveness, satire or defence) cynical jokes (critical and blasphemous) and sceptical jokes. These jokes mention forbidden subjects, engage in offensive or childish behaviour, slip beyond bounds of good taste and often violate moral taboos. This type of joking has hostile elements (similar to the rough-and-tumble horseplay and shoving of young boys) that are used to vent aggression. In this way, men's comedy feels more personal and insidious to women, who see the verbal blows as 'below the belt' and not fair.

Men's humour also pokes fun at social conventions; and some accuse women of not laughing at a good joke. Often what the women are hearing is not funny, but rather hostility and sarcasm disguised as humour. When it comes to humour, men give and women receive most of the time.

Women are more likely to console, rather than laugh at anyone considered a 'victim.' This is one of the reasons certain forms of slapstick comedy appeal far less to women than to men. Men are more prone to like slapstick comedy (such as the Three Stooges poking each other in the eye) that many women don't find the least bit funny.

Young boys get more pleasure in hostile humour than girls. At an early age, boys choose aggressive cartoons as the funnier ones. Even at the age of three, boys are more likely to act silly, make faces and horse around than girls. They practice this on each other from childhood.

Women are more likely to joke about the powerful, not the pitiful, concentrate on big issues and question the way the world is put together. They traditionally use self-deprecating humour even if it erodes their self-esteem. It's not threatening for a woman to joke, if she's only joking about herself or other women. However, if she tells a joke about the male power aristocracy in front of a member of that group, the man may feel threatened and angry.

Female humour shows a refusal to take authority seriously and women are less likely to look up to their supervisors than men. Women's humour directs some of its most effective material at men, questioning their authority and showing a certain amount of disdain. Women see the 'rules of the game' in business as mainly childish games that only 'boys' would consider playing. In this way, women's comedy can be more ominous than men's.

Women are more likely to conjure up an image that is well known to others such as, *'Remember how Tim Allen on the Home Improvement Show did ...'* Her communication says, *'I have an image in my mind. Do you have the same picture?'*

Non-Verbal Communication

'My husband constantly confuses me because of the ambiguous way he communicates with others. What he says verbally often differs widely from what his body language is telling me. For instance he's being treated for a very painful back injury and the pain he's suffering shows plainly on his face. However, when I question him about the pain, he replies that it 'Isn't too bad.' Should I believe his verbal or nonverbal communication?'

We 'hear' what people say partly through what their body language, tone of voice, etc., tell us. If you have to decide whether to believe a person's verbal communication or his/her non-verbal communication - I always opt for the non-verbal. I've found that only con artists and compulsive liars can lie consistently without having their body language give them away. This is because they've told their lies so often that they actually believe the lies they're telling.

Explain what you've observed and ask him to be more honest in his answers about his health. Let him know that there's no disgrace in being in pain and it's all right (in fact necessary) for him to share his situation with you. Tell him how shut out you feel because he isn't being honest with you.

Dealing with Difficult Situations

Being able to interpret non-verbal signals is probably one of the best assets anyone can have. If you want to be a good communicator, it's essential to be aware of and try to understand non-verbal signals. However, don't jump to conclusions by judging only one body-language signal. It's the combination of body language signals that point to what the person is really saying non-verbally.

A common body-language signal is seen when we place our hand on the arm or shoulder of an upset person. We shake hands with people, which originally meant that we were extending our empty weapon hand to show that we came as a friend. Now, it can mean that we're giving our word, that the exchange to follow is above board and that we're trustworthy or can simply mean *'Hello. Glad to meet you.'*

We get clues that a person is annoyed, impatient, anxious or upset when we see them tapping their fingers. If they shift their weight from one foot to another, the person has either been standing too long or they're becoming impatient. When they frown, it could mean that they don't understand what's being said or they might disagree with what's being said. The clenched jaw (more noticeable in men) shows they're upset, angry or anxious.

Rapid or abrupt speech may signal an upset, worried, excited, anxious or angry person. If they raise the volume of their voice, they could be nervous or angry. The woman who raises the pitch of her voice and the man who drops the pitch of his voice are both showing that they're nervous or angry. Jumpy body movements indicate nervousness, anxiety, fatigue or anger.

A flushed face could identify that they're embarrassed, excited, angry or that they're feeling hot. It could also show that they have high blood pressure or they're going through menopause. You'd have to look for other non-verbal signals to confirm which was the case.

Arms across the chest could mean they feel defensive, physically awkward or physically cold (for example, if they're a patient forced to sit in a cold room in a skimpy examination gown!) Men who wish to show their power, will straddle a chair. Others will put their feet up on a desk and won't remove them when someone comes into the room. Power-hungry people take up more space on couches or benches than is their due.

A slumped posture could mean that the person is tired, relaxed or depressed. The person who shrugs could be indifferent or doesn't

Dealing with Difficult Situations

know the answer to a situation. Those who avoid eye contact could be shy, bored or could be because of their cultural background. This behaviour is often misinterpreted as a sign of shifty behaviour or showing a lack of self-confidence, when the cause may be something quite different. They may live in a culture that regards eye contact with the elderly or those in positions of authority as disrespectful.

People who lack assurance, show this by their body language. Their posture shows defeat, there's little eye contact, their voices are soft, they wear a fixed smile and they take up as little space as possible (pull all their 'ends' in).

Is reading a person's body language full-proof? No, because it's often the combination of several signals that point the way to what they're really saying. Learning to understand the signals takes practice, but once learned it's one of the most valuable communication skills you can have. Read everything you can about body language and start practising!

Rush Hour Traffic

'I hate rush-hour traffic!'

Byron drives home from work, feeling pretty tired from a stressful day at work and finds himself fuming because the traffic is backed up *again*. It feels as if he spends half his life waiting in traffic to get home. He finally gets home, strides through the living room past his children and slams his bedroom door. He's allowed the traffic jam to upset him. And it doesn't stop there.

What happened to his two children who were sitting in the lounge room watching TV when he strode by? They're likely wondering what *they* did to make Dad so upset. This puts them on edge, so they snap at each other during dinner. You can see how Byron's bad mood has a domino effect on his family.

Byron knows he's likely to face traffic jams on the way home - it happens three out of five times - so why has he allowed himself to become so upset? When he was driving home, he had the choice of five ways to react.

He could:

Dealing with Difficult Situations

- Try leaving work half an hour later. This may get him home just ten minutes later than now, but with far less harassment because the rush hour would be over.
- Vary his work hours (either earlier or later) to stop the negatives he receives now.
- Buy some DVDs that have calming music and listen to them while he's driving home.
- Allow himself more time to drive home.
- Allow himself to get upset during rush-hour traffic.

The choice is his.

Can't Say 'No'

'My husband gets himself in trouble when others ask him to do something for them. He wants to say 'No,' but seems to end up saying 'Yes' instead and over-commits himself which eventually causes serious problems for him.'

If he has trouble saying *'No'* to requests, each step forward can help him learn when and how to say *'No'* comfortably and effectively. Suggest that he try the following:

Step 1: Identify a situation where he's said *'Yes'* inappropriately.

Step 2: Identify the reasons why he said, *'Yes.'* Was he concerned that he had to say *'Yes'* otherwise he might injure the relationship or look bad to the person? Was he worried about the other person's feelings?

Step 3: Help him prepare himself for the next occasion so he'll prevent the situation from happening again.

Step 4: Encourage him to practice his new response with you. Rehearsing with you or another uninvolved person might help him have the confidence he needs to carry his plan to completion.

Encourage him to know what *he* wants, before he decides to say *'Yes,'* and not allow himself to feel compelled to return a favour from a friend.

Workaholic Husband

'My husband has been a workaholic for years, but the situation's getting worse. Our children and I never see him any more and he's always tired. There's no need for him to work as hard as he does. We

could manage on much less financially than we do now, but he won't listen to me when I tell him this. What causes him to work so hard and why won't he listen to me when I tell him what's happening to our family?'

To admit that we're workaholics seems like a black mark on our character. However, it's never weak to realise that our life is out of balance and that perhaps our priorities need re-adjustment. Society has taught us that we can never work too hard. Work defines our character and consumes about fifty to sixty per cent of most adult's lives. The first most common question asked when people meet is

'What do you do?' It's a social nicety or acceptable protocol. When people spend too much time on leisure activities, society does raise an eyebrow, but cheer on those who spend weekends in the office rather than at the lake.

Workaholism can manifest itself in children, teenagers and those in their early adult years, but it usually occurs more to those in their forties and fifties. Work addiction usually happens to middle-class people who are seldom driven to overwork by economic need. Some workaholics gradually become emotionally crippled and addicted to control and power in a compulsive drive to gain approval and success.

Like any other addiction, workaholism can harm not only one's health and family, but can cause severe anxiety and depression. We all want acceptance and respect for the work we do. However, many people find themselves caught up in a compulsive drive towards success and approval. Many don't even realise this is happening, until a major crisis like a divorce or heart attack occurs.

Some workaholics come from dysfunctional families whose pattern of behaviour and interaction with others have been affected by some form of addiction (alcohol, drugs, food or perfectionism). As adults, they pride themselves on being free of any addiction. *'That will never happen to me!'* is a familiar statement. Family members of workaholics can become co-dependents and can fall into the trap of supporting the addiction, as they try to 'keep the peace.'

Most people assume that all workaholics are unhappy, but that's not always true. Another school of thought takes a different view, that contrary to public opinion, some workaholics aren't slaves to their work - they're doing exactly what they want to do. They're happy

Dealing with Difficult Situations

doing exactly what they love to do - work - and they can't get enough of it.

However, there are three basic kinds of workaholics:

- Those who work because they truly love to work - love their jobs - work hard and long because they receive pleasure from doing so. They're under stress but seldom suffer from *dis*tress.
- Those who're motivated not by enthusiasm, but by such things as competitive feelings, job pressures, budget cuts, financial problems, family or relationship problems. They are under stress and suffer from *dis*tress.
- Those who work because they feel driven to do so (compulsive behaviour). Their stress becomes *dis*tress and they suffer because of it.

It sounds as if your husband fits into the third group. These workaholics normally fear failure; of being thought of as lazy; that others will find out that they aren't as good as they think they are or they're slipping in their ability level. Typical signs for those in the second and third categories:

- Are always working, but are resentful about it - often bringing home work in the evening and on weekends;
- Suffer from nervous disorders;
- Don't eat or exercise right;
- Seldom spend time with their family;
- Never take time off from work when they're ill. (They're the ones who pass on the flu bug to the rest of the staff because they *do* come in when they shouldn't); and
- Don't know how to relax, to play or simply 'goof-off,' and often (erroneously) use competitive sports to 'relax.'

Some workaholics are addicts who use work as their drug of choice. More bad news is that workaholics are hellish to work with, are demanding and not very effective. They can be emotional cripples wired into power and control. Obsession drives them in their often fruitless search for perfection, approval and success. They're always running, always busy - even when on vacation. Characteristically work addicts hate taking vacations, unless they can combine holiday and business. Just sitting on a beach doing nothing makes them nervous. They keep wondering why the phone doesn't ring and often take a cellular telephone and their answering machine with them on vacation, *'So they won't miss any messages.'*

Have a serious talk with your husband. Don't let him leave your talk without explaining why he's working so hard. Make sure he knows the effect his behaviour is having on your family. A very simple question to ask him, which might shock him into realistically looking at what he's doing is, *'Suppose our doctor told you that you had only six months to live. What would you be doing during those six months?'*

He likely would say that he'd spend more time with his family, travel or anything other than working harder. This reality check might jump-start him on the road to changing his priorities. If that doesn't work, you may have to identify some of the consequences that could happen should his behaviour not change (be ready for this before your meeting). Marriage counselling might be warranted, especially if he admits that he's working to get away from his family situation.

All three types of workaholics unfortunately, can pressure themselves so long and so hard that they suffer from what used to be called a nervous breakdown. The more modern terminology for this ailment is burnout.

To check for signs of burnout, ask him the following questions:

Does he feel:

- Down or depressed much of the time?
- There's no hope for improvement in his circumstances?
- That no one cares?
- Constantly complains?
- Intense pressure or competition at work?
- That no matter what he does, it won't be enough?
- Fears that he's going under any day now? Or,
- Has trouble eating and/or sleeping properly?

If he feels even two or three of these, he could be in trouble. He needs a complete rest from all of life's pressures and should be under medical care. Help him identify activities he can drop or delegate to someone else. It's not likely he can reduce his stress at work unless he can work fewer hours or go on stress leave.

Could you or your children help more at home? Families that work together as a team can be a great help to those approaching burnout. See that the situation does not repeat itself in the future, because workaholics tend to revert to old bad behaviours.

Forgetful or negligent

'My husband conveniently 'forgets' things. His usual comment is, 'Sorry, I forgot.' Or 'I thought you were looking after that!' Or, 'I didn't know you wanted me to stop at the store for milk!' Is he really forgetting all those things or is this his way of manipulating himself out of doing things?'

This is passive resistant behaviour. Those displaying this trait expect others to remind them of what they should do, deadlines they must meet and who's responsible for doing what. Deal with his actions by asking him for verbal and written commitments (if necessary). This trait is especially destructive in a work situation.

Explain that it isn't your responsibility to remind him of appointments or activities he's supposed to attend. Give him a calendar for his own use where he can put down important dates and activities. If he asks you, *'When am I supposed to take David to his hockey practice?'* ask him to look on the calendar. If he neglected to write it down, suggest he ask his son or call to confirm the time. Stop running interference for him. He's setting a poor role model for your children, who will probably pick up his bad habit and use the same tactics on others.

Blasted from our Bedroom

'My husband snores so loud that I can't even be on the same floor as he is, let alone sleep in the same bed as he does. This still doesn't give me a good sleep because I keep reading about sleep apnoea and the danger he might be in if he has it. What can I do to make him realise that we have a serious problem.'

Take heart. Snoring has noble origins that go back to prehistoric days. For those who have to put up with snorers, this knowledge probably won't make up for the hours of sleep they've missed. Nor will it make up to the snorers who've been elbowed, yelled at and even kicked out of their own beds. A recent study suggests that we shouldn't hit a snoring man, because:

Dealing with Difficult Situations

a) He might hit back!

b) In his own way he may be protecting you!

That roof-jarring commotion may be the remains of an ancient protective device that's outlived its use. Some believe that male hormones may be the culprit, for men snore far more and far louder than most women. In addition, snoring occurs during a person's period of deepest sleep, when their conscious mind is least aware of its surroundings and when the snorer is most vulnerable.

But pray tell, why do men snore so much louder than women? Well, there is an explanation. When our human ancestors left the safety of the jungle and ventured onto the materialising tundra some five million years ago - sleep proved to be one of man's most defenceless times of the day. So nature stepped in and provided men with a unique defence mechanism. It enabled men to utter the earth-shattering noises they practice nightly. By mimicking the sounds of their most common predators (the carnivorous nocturnal cats and hyenas) early man could broadcast throughout the night: *'Hear me roar! Leave us alone or you'll have to contend with a mighty warrior!'*

That knowledge probably isn't going to help modern men and women (except to give them a chuckle or two). So what is one to do to stop the din and bring peace to homes once again? Many resort to unusual treatments such as taping a tennis ball between the snorer's shoulder blades. Others give a sharp elbow to shock the person into retreating from the offensive object. Some resort to taping their mouths so they can't breathe through their mouths or resort to sleeping sitting up by piling up to six pillows behind them. Most of these remedies provide only temporary relief.

Then what works? Have him start with a thorough medical. People who snore usually do so because there's an obstruction to the free flow of air in their breathing passages, often caused by excessive tissue in the uvula and soft palate near their throat. A laser treatment can eliminate snoring in most patients by using a technique that burns away tissue in the passages at the back of the mouth and nose, reshaping and reforming the openings which allows for greater airflow. After three to five ten-minute office visits under local anaesthesia, eighty-five to ninety per cent of patients given the laser treatment stop snoring. Most find the treatment an almost painless process.

Dealing with Difficult Situations

Far more serious than the snoring itself is 'sleep apnoea' which occasionally accompanies snoring. Often, this distinct, rhythmic form of snoring (four or five times in quick succession, then a twenty- to forty-second pause, then a new eruption) results from a blockage of the snorer's air passages. This can be caused when the person's tongue falls back in the mouth and their throat muscles relax. Many lack the ability to sleep and breathe regularly at the same time. Their snores are actually the brain rousing itself so their body is stimulated to gasp for air.

People with short, receding jaws are prone to this condition. Many sufferers have fat necks that narrow the throat passages even further. The first treatment prescribed in those cases is weight loss. There are also medications that promote regular breathing and small nasal masks worn by some patients. Put on at bedtime, the mask is connected by a tube to a miniature blower that forces air into the nose to keep breathing passages open.

A simple operation to cut away tissue lining at the back of the throat, remedies most cases. Extreme cases however may require a tracheotomy. (If he snores constantly or snores and feels good in the morning, he probably doesn't have apnoea).

Husband poor listener

'How do I deal with my husband's bad habit of making me repeat everything that I say? I use the same volume of voice when I repeat my message, so I know he wasn't listening to me the first time I spoke. Another habit he has is he never looks at me when I'm talking. This habit is really annoying me and is causing a drift in our relationship.'

She had explained to him about a difficulty she'd had in getting her car serviced. After she'd explained all the details she'd asked, *'What do you think I should have done?'*

He responded with *'What?'* showing that he had just 'tuned into' what she'd been saying.

She might have received more attention from him if she had started her conversation by explaining what she wanted from him. *'I need your opinion on how you think I should have dealt with a situation I faced today.'* Then she would have given him the background information about the problems she'd faced getting her car serviced.

Dealing with Difficult Situations

She should also discuss her concerns about his habit of not listening and explain how she feels when he 'tunes her out.'

As described earlier in this chapter, women face each other directly with eyes anchored on each other's faces when conversing. Boys and men sit at angles to each other and look elsewhere in the room - periodically glancing at each other. They often mirror each other's body movements. Men's tendency to face away from them when conversing, gives women the impression that the men aren't listening to them, when in fact they are. The only times men will really look at the person who's speaking for any length of time are if;

a. They're trying to evaluate whether the speaker is lying or not,
b) The speaker is hostile and they may have to take defensive action or
c) They're evaluating an attractive woman.

In the latter case, they'll glance over the woman's body while listening to her comments. This is highly distracting to the female speaker because his eyes mirror that he's not really listening to what she's saying, but rather sizing her up as a woman.

Another time they 'tune out' is when a woman nags them to do something. You'll have to determine whether you could be guilty of doing this by repeating your comments when you think he may not have been listening.

Explosive issues

'The other day, my husband and I were discussing the issue of abortion and we ended up in a shouting match and haven't spoken a civil word to each other since. How should I have handled this situation?'

There are many topics that fit into this group, where you're on one side of an issue and a relative, friend or acquaintance is decidedly on the opposite. When you find yourself in this kind of conversation (where neither party will budge) say, *'You're entitled to your opinion, the same as I am. Let's agree to disagree and not talk about this topic in the future.'*

If the person persists on discussing the topic, state, *'I'm firm in my decision that we should drop this topic because neither of us is*

Dealing with Difficult Situations

willing to compromise our opinions. Let's not talk about this any more.'

If the person still persists, use the stuck record, *'I've told you, I won't discuss this topic again.'* If necessary, ask them to account for their actions. *'Can you tell me why you brought up that issue again, when I've told you twice that I don't want to discuss this?'*

Make sure you use this technique only for exceptional situations, not as an excuse for situations where you simply want to win. Use it specifically for issues about values and morality.

We're Lost!

'Why won't men ask for directions when they're lost?'

The wife said, *'We're lost. Let's stop and ask someone for directions.'*

Husband, *'Let me have that map, I shouldn't have relied on you for directions.'*

In this case her husband spent the next half hour trying to learn where they are in relation to where he wanted to go. Why wouldn't he ask others for directions? He explained that he doesn't want anyone to know he's in trouble - he'd rather find his way out by himself. This way no one can get 'one up on him.'

If the woman was driving, she feels very comfortable asking others for directions and can't understand her husband's stubbornness in trying to do it on his own.

My Husband - The Expert

'Why does my husband always have to be the expert and give three or four solutions to my problems? It's getting so that I don't even discuss the difficult situations I've faced during the day because he's always got a better way of dealing with issues than I do.'

In a conversation with her husband the wife had explained her frustration at her inability to lose weight. She became upset when her husband listed five solutions to her problem.

When the woman discussed the problem she had with her husband, she expected to receive a sympathetic ear and listening noises such as, *'I see ...'* Or *'Uhm hmm ...'* Instead, the man believed she had

Dealing with Difficult Situations

identified her problem so he can help her solve it. Because he believed this, he made several suggestions about how she could solve her problem. His wife felt as if he was showing her that she couldn't handle the problem herself, so feels hurt.

When women have a complaint, they often look for emotional support (not solutions). When men hear a complaint, they feel challenged to come up with a solution.

What he should have said was, *'Do you want my help with this problem?'* before diving in with solutions. The man's intentions were good. Male communication dictates that when someone identifies a problem to them, they should identify solutions - not give sympathy.

Husband won't discuss his work

'When my husband gets home from work, he never discusses what happens to him during the day.'

At a recent seminar with both of men and women, I noticed that one man had been very talkative while his wife sat silently beside him. Towards the end of the evening, I mentioned that women frequently complain that their husbands don't talk to them. The man agreed with my comment and stated, *'She's the talker in our family.'* The audience burst out laughing, while the man looked puzzled and hurt.

'It's true,' he illuminated. *'When I come home from work, I have nothing to say. If she didn't keep the conversation going, we'd spend the whole evening in silence.'*

This situation points out the incongruity of the usual conversational styles of men and women. Men talk more than women in public situations and often talk less at home. This pattern has caused havoc in marriages. The solution is for both men and women to adjust and bridge the gap between their diverse conversational styles.

Unresolved Conflicts

'My wife and I are having more and more unresolved conflicts.'

The emotional roles men and women play out during arguments relate to the degree of power they feel within a relationship. Because women often find themselves in a subordinate role, they fall into the habit of restraining anger or expressing it in passive ways (such as whining, nagging or crying). Self-disclosure and discussing feelings

Dealing with Difficult Situations

are more comfortable for women. If these are not forthcoming from men, the women feel threatened.

Many arguments between couples start when a woman tries to start a discussion about a problem they face together. The man - at least at first - will likely try to avoid it. Once the discussion gets under way, men want to come up with a solution *fast*. Women however, want to discuss the problem, it's possible solutions and ramifications, before coming to a decision.

Women are more likely to see a conflict as stemming from within the relationship; men see conflict as coming from something outside of it. Most conflicts are about trust, power or intimacy. Women complain that their men withdraw from conflicts and don't share enough. Men and women who respond to conflicts defensively, stubbornly or who consistently withdraw, may do the most damage to their own and their partner's happiness. Those couples who never fight because they're afraid to rock the boat, may be unhappier in the long run than those who *do* fight.

In marriage, when friction arises, many women believe that the marriage is working fine as long as they can discuss their problems (which she feels builds intimacy). The men feel that the marriage isn't working if they constantly need to talk about it. He'd rather find a swift solution and go on to something else.

Won't Argue

'My husband hates conflict - in fact it's so bad that he remains mute or walks away from situations that must be dealt with. He doesn't defend himself, even if others wrongly accuse him of doing something.'

These people hate controversy, confrontation and arguing, so they remain silent. They're likeable people, but keep their ideas to themselves. This is their protection to keep others from discounting their ideas. Even when they're upset or angry, they refuse to criticise. They feel that they're not in control in confrontational situations, so keep their thoughts to themselves.

They keep quiet rather than state their disagreement. When aggravated, rather than show they're agitated, they respond with a grin that is more of a grimace. This nervous gesture signals their true feelings even though they may feel angry or hurt. They passively keep their feelings to themselves. No matter what happens; they

Dealing with Difficult Situations

grin. This ambiguous set of signals confuses others who instinctively know that something's wrong.

Use feedback to explain that you're aware of his displeasure. Ask open-ended questions. *'I can see you don't agree and welcome your suggestions. How do you see solving this problem?'* Wait for his reply. Don't let him shrug off his opinions as not being important.

If decision must be made, have him write down his ideas relating to an issue and if the issue is with you, set a time for you to discuss the controversial issue. Explain that you expect him to be honest and promise that you'll listen carefully to what he says. Don't let him leave your meeting without expressing his ideas or side of the situation.

Controlling Husband

'All our married life, my husband has taken care of our finances. Lately, I've become concerned, because statistics state that it's likely that he'll die before I do. I want him to explain everything to me, so I'll be prepared, but he keeps putting me off saying, 'I don't want you to worry about things like that!''

You must discuss your wishes with him and explain why you need to know the information. Make a list of all the things you need to know and discuss each item. Start by examining your bank accounts. Are there any outstanding loans? Learn where the accounts are and the amounts that are in each account.

Then list any investments you and your husband have made including superannuation funds held in both your names. Check over last year's income tax forms to determine what kind of income was made and list any other financial details you need to include. Be firm in your need to know this information.

No Will

'It's been twenty years since my husband and I prepared our wills. Since that time, our children have married and have children. I've been trying to get him to update our wills, but so far I haven't had much luck.'

Make an appointment with your lawyer to at least update your own will. Tell your husband about the appointment and suggest that he attend as well to update his own will.

Dealing with Difficult Situations

Makes all the decisions

'During our marriage, I've noticed more and more that my husband has taken over when major (and some minor) decisions are made. I want to have my say, but he ignores my wishes.'

Marriage is a partnership and it appears as if yours is failing in the equality area. Explain how important it is that you be given an equal opportunity when decisions are to be made. Start by itemising all the decisions that he has made in the last while where your wishes are not given fair attention.

Explain the consequences should this happen again and be ready to follow-through with those consequences.

Jealous Husband

'My husband is a very jealous man - not only relating to his relationship with me - but in other areas of his life. He's jealous when a co-worker gets a promotion and when one of our children graduated from college he sulked for days because he never had the chance to graduate himself. How can I explain how destructive his jealousy has become and stop it from happening again?'

He suffers from jealousy and resentment and cannot accept that others have earned whatever recognition or status they've achieved in life. He likely feels that others' achievements were obtained through 'luck' and that he's deprived because life hasn't been so kind to him. To put others down (and make himself feel more important) he tries to discredit others' accomplishments. He may even want revenge and even if the attack is unprovoked, he may vent his frustration on others with hostile acts.

Use feedback to identify what his actions are doing to those around him. Ask him to account for why he has such a jealous nature. Once he's admitted that he has a problem, let him know when his jealousy is rearing its ugly head again. It will help if you encourage him more and give lots of praise for his own authentic acts.

When that approval doesn't come - his jealousy surfaces. Show interest in him - his goals, ambitions and successes and downplay his perceived failures. He seems to desperately need this kind of approval. It's likely that he hasn't had much approval for most of his life and craves it from others.

Dealing with Difficult Situations

CHAPTER 8

DIFFICULT SITUATIONS - CHILDREN

Children in control

Have you observed parents saying, *'For the fourteenth time - you can't have a chocolate bar?'* Or heaven forbid, has this been *you* making that comment? Or are you a working parent who comes home from work - arms filled with groceries and have to navigate around school books, shoes, coats etc. to get past the door? Do you enter the kitchen that was spotless when you left that morning to find the counter covered with so much mess that there's no place to put the groceries? You place the grocery bags on the kitchen table and look around your messy kitchen and notice that the slices of bread from a new loaf of bread are slewed across the counter drying out, there's melting butter dripping from a container down the side of the counter and you observe an open jar of peanut butter with a knife protruding from it? Do you automatically shout at your children about the mess?

Or, do you follow everyone around at home picking up their belongings and putting them where they should be? Are you tired of doing this? Then it's time for you to learn a valuable parenting technique. This technique is used by the *Tough Love* group who are normally called in when pre-teens or teens get out of control and need a firm hand. But why wait until your children are in trouble? Instead, start when they're three or so with the 'three strikes - you're out' philosophy advocated by this group. This encourages children to understand the philosophy of taking responsibility for their actions and that there *will* be consequences if they act out or break family or communal rules. So how does one start? One starts by learning the technique of feedback.

To refresh your memory; the three steps in the process of feedback are as follows:

PROCESS OF FEEDBACK

a. Describe the problem or situation to the person causing the difficulty. Give examples.
b. Define what feelings or reactions their behaviour causes you (sadness, anger, anxiety, hurt or upset).

Dealing with Difficult Situations

c. Suggest a solution or ask them to provide one.

Most children will change undesired behaviour if it's brought to their attention in a kind, non-threatening way. But there are exceptions to the rule. Older children may not care what you think, feel it's not worth changing to suit you or have a habit that's hard to change. Others change their behaviour for a while, but slip back to doing it their old way. In either of these situations where the negative behaviour continues - further feedback steps are necessary.

FEEDBACK STEPS

1. Follow a. b. and c. steps from the Process of Feedback.
2. Second instance: repeat #1.
3. Third instance:
   (i) Ask the child to explain why s/he's still doing something that s/he knows annoys you (the child must be mature enough to understand this).
   (ii) Explain the consequences if the behaviour or situation happens again.
4. Follow-through with the consequences.

If the child is under four or five years of age you would leave out 3 (i) because the child would not have the reasoning power to answer that question. But if the child is older than that, it will make them think about why they were still doing something that they ***know*** annoys you. This will often stop the cycle or at least initiate a conversation to identify why their unacceptable behaviour is still occurring.

Start using this technique with three-year-olds. Let's say you're tired of picking up Johnnie's toys every night. Enlist Johnnie's help to complete this task. Say, *'Johnnie, it's bed time. Time to pick up your toys.'* Johnnie ignores you and continues to play with his toys. Repeat, *'Johnnie, it's bed time. Time to pick up your toys.'* Johnnie ignores you and continues to play with his toys. Using the 'three strikes and you're out' technique, you say, *'Johnnie, it's time to pick up your toys. If you don't pick them up, I will have to put them in a plastic bag and you won't be able to play with them for a month.'* If Johnnie doesn't pick up his toys, follow through with the consequences.

It's important that you consider the consequences carefully. The consequences must match the situation. For instance, if you come

Dealing with Difficult Situations

home to a messy kitchen every night, instead of shouting at your brood, call a family conference and say, *'I'm tired when I get home from work at night and am very upset when I come home to such a messy kitchen. I expect each of you to clean up after yourselves. If you don't in the future, I'll have no choice but to start removing privileges.'* You would then stop driving your children to their events such as ballet or music lessons or to sporting activities. For teenagers, you could have them make their own meals or do their own washing and ironing (which they are fully capable of doing anyway).

If you're tired of picking up after your children, call a family conference and say, *'I've been after all of you for months to pick up your things and put them where they belong. From now on, if I find things lying around, I'll put them in a box and have an auction to sell them to the highest bidder. Even if one of these items is a school book or a 'game boy' the owner will have to bid for it.'* This will convince your children that you mean what you say and they will not want a sibling to be able to bid for their game boy. Never threaten consequences unless you're willing and able to carry out the consequences. Make sure your spouse uses the same tactic - both must give a united front and grandparents must not interfere (as they're prone to do, stating that you're too hard on your children).

The result - no more shouting matches with your children where you find yourself stating, *'For the fourteenth time, you can't have a chocolate bar!'*

Don't Mess With Mom

[Someone sent me the following e-mail
and I chuckled when I read it:]

My son came home from school one day with a smirk upon his face.
He decided he was smart enough, to put me in my place.

*'Guess what I learned in Civics Two that's taught by Mr. Wright?
It's all about the laws today, the 'Children's Bill of Rights.'
It says I need not clean my room, don't have to cut my hair.
No one can tell me what to think or speak or what to wear.*

*I have freedom from religion and regardless what you say,
I don't have to bow my head and I sure don't have to pray.*

Dealing with Difficult Situations

I can wear earrings if I want and pierce my tongue and nose.
I can read and watch just what I like and get tattoos from head to toes.

And if you ever spank me, I'll charge you with a crime.
I'll back up all my charges, with the marks on my behind.
Don't you ever touch me, my body's only for my use, not for your hugs and kisses - that's just more child abuse.

Don't preach about your morals, like your Mother did to you.
That's nothing more than mind control and it's illegal too!
Mom, I have these children's rights, so you can't influence me
or I'll call Children's Services Division, better known as C.S.D.

Of course my first instinct was, to toss him out the door.
But the chance to teach him a lesson made me think a little more.
I mulled it over carefully. I couldn't let this go.
A smile crept upon my face; he's messing with a pro.

Next day I took him shopping at the local Goodwill Store.
I told him, 'Pick out all you want, there's shirts and pants galore.
I've called and checked with C.S.D. who said they didn't care
if I bought you K-Mart shoes instead of Nike Airs.

And I've cancelled that appointment to take your driver's test.
The C.S.D. is unconcerned so I'll decide what's best.'

I said, 'No time to stop and eat or pick up stuff to munch.
Tomorrow you can start to learn to make your own sack lunch.
Just save the raging appetite and wait till dinner time.
We're having liver and onions - a favourite dish of mine.'

He asked, 'Can I rent a movie to watch on my DVD?'
'Sorry, but I sold your TV for new car tires for me.
I also rented out your room - you'll take the couch instead.
All the C.S.D. requires is a roof for over your head.

Your clothing won't be trendy now and I'll choose what we eat.
That allowance that you used to get, will buy me something neat.
I'm selling off your jet ski, dirt-bike and roller blades.
Check out the 'Parents Bill of Rights,' it's in effect today!

Dealing with Difficult Situations

Hey hot shot, are you crying and why are you on your knees? Are you asking God and me to help you out, instead of C.S.D.?'

'Can't you do anything right?'

When children are young, they depend on their care-givers to either make them feel good or bad about themselves. Most parents and caregivers are nurturing and loving and want their children to feel cherished. Unfortunately, some caregivers don't realise the devastation destructive criticism causes to the fragile ego of a child. As they mature, everything in their lives may be based on their earlier experiences, values and biases.

Children's self-esteem level is strongly influenced by how they're criticised. Constructive criticism talks about a child's behaviour. One form of destructive criticism is to label the child, rather than discuss the child's behaviour. Destructive criticism is exactly that - destructive. It eats away at the psyche of the child until the child loses his or her self-respect.

For example, *'Benny, you're the sloppiest child I know.'* That's labelling Benny and is a form of emotional abuse.

'Benny, that's the third time you've spilled your milk!' This discusses Benny's behaviour. Benny can change his behaviour, but doesn't really understand how he can stop being sloppy, careless, dumb or stupid.

Many parents label their children so often that they grow up with 'negative tapes' that they replay throughout their lives. Many never rid themselves of these negative tapes. Others need extensive therapy to erase them.

I conduct seminars that help participants raise their self-esteem and self-confidence levels. I remember one seminar where I observed one of the participants. This man was about thirty-five years of age, tall and handsome, well dressed and looked as if he had his 'act' together. During the seminar when I discussed negative tapes and asked the participants to search their past to determine if they had any negative tapes running around in their heads, he sat thoughtfully for quite some time. Then his eyes lit up and he wrote something on his notepad. Our next step was to determine what impact those negative tapes had on their lives and the activities those tapes had

Dealing with Difficult Situations

kept them from attempting. He started writing and filled an entire page of his notebook.

At the end of the session, he told me his story. When he was thirteen, he grew fifteen centimetres (6 inches) in six months. Now we all know what happens to children who grow that fast - they become like German Shepherd puppies - awkward, un-coordinated, lose their manual dexterity and balance. Most children would outgrow this awkwardness. Unfortunately he was not allowed to outgrow this stage because everyone – his parents, siblings, his friends, gym teacher and even his soccer coach - kept reminding him how awkward, clutzy and un-co-ordinated he was. When he was fifteen, he was six feet three inches tall - a perfect candidate for what sport? You guessed it - basketball. But did he try out for basketball? No. Why? Because he believed he was awkward, un-coordinated and clutzy.

When it was time to date and dance with girls - he didn't try that either - because he was un-coordinated. Fix cars? No - that took manual dexterity. Learn how to use a computer? No again - that also took manual dexterity.

On his list were things he had not attempted to do for twenty-two years because he felt he would fail in any attempts he made! And all because of the negative tape that had been placed in his brain when he was a vulnerable teenager. What a shame. Was he still that awkward teenager? Of course not - but in his brain he still was. I asked him, *'Now that you know about this negative tape, what are you going to do?'*

'I'm going to try all the things on my list - starting with learning how to play basketball!'

So, if you catch yourself labelling anyone (especially a child) - apologise immediately. Say, *'I'm sorry. You didn't deserve that remark. What I meant to say was ...'* Then discuss the behaviour that offended you.

Not as smart as your brother

I grew up thinking I was a dummy who had a bad memory. In school I was one year behind my brother. He was a hard act to follow. He never seemed to study and always got in the high 90s on all his tests and exams. I struggled for years trying to keep up, but never seemed able to get any higher than the low 80 percent level. It didn't help that my teachers kept saying, *'You're not like your brother are you?'* I always felt I had a bad memory and that I was a failure at school.

Years later, when I owned a successful training business, I mentioned these feelings to my parents. My mother said, *'You weren't trying to keep up with him were you?'*

I replied, *'Of course I was – he was my role model.'*

'Didn't you know that he was born with a special gift?'

'And you didn't give it to me?' I laughed as I responded.

She also laughed and said, *'Didn't you know that your brother was born with a photographic memory? He can tell you what page a certain paragraph is on in a book he read three weeks ago!'*

'No, I never figured that out. I always felt as if I didn't have a good memory.'

'What do you mean? Look at all the information you have to remember when you're presenting a training seminar and look how successful you are!'

All of a sudden, my memory was fine and I was able to remove that negative tape from my brain!'

Destructive Criticism

Here are examples of constructive and destructive criticism parents and caregivers use on vulnerable children:

Destructive criticism: *'You're not as smart as your brother, are you?'*
Constructive criticism: *'You really excel at sports. Could you try a little harder to get better grades?'*

Destructive criticism: *'Can't you do anything right?'*
Constructive criticism: *'You know you can do better than this. Look at how well you did on your last test.'*

Destructive criticism: *'What a clutz you are. That's the third time you have done that wrong.'*
Constructive criticism: *'You seem to be having problems with this project. Is there anything that I can do to help you?'*

Dealing with Difficult Situations

Destructive criticism: *'You ought to know better.'*
Constructive criticism: *'Jim, you're far too old to be pulling stunts like that. Can you tell me why you're doing this?'*

Destructive criticism: *'You're a naughty girl.'*
Constructive criticism: *'Jill, don't write on the wall!'*

Destructive criticism: *'You're a bad boy.'*
Constructive criticism: *'Billy, I have just cleaned the house. Please pick up your belongings and put them away.'*

Destructive criticism: *'You're so inconsiderate!'*
Constructive criticism: *'I won't allow that kind of behaviour. Please apologise to Bob for not sharing the toys.'*

Destructive criticism: *'Jenny, you're the sloppiest child I know!'*
Constructive criticism: *'Jenny, please be more careful with your paint set. They leave stains when you spill them.'*

Destructive criticism: *'Sometimes I wish I never had kids!'*
Constructive criticism: *'You have been very noisy this afternoon. Please go to your room so you can have some quiet time before dinner.'*

Destructive criticism: *'Mary, this is a D. How dumb can you be?'*
Constructive criticism: *'Mary, let's talk about your report card. I am concerned about the D you got in math.'*

Destructive criticism: *'Must you always look like a slob?'*
Constructive criticism: *'Lennie, please go back to your room and put on a clean outfit.'*

Destructive criticism: *'What a spoilt brat you are!'*
Constructive criticism: *'Jim, we can't tolerate that kind of behaviour. You're not to throw toys in the house.'*

These destructive criticism messages are all put-downs and are almost impossible for the child to deal with. They're coming from a person in a position of power. This (as should be expected) puts these children on the defensive and gives them negative feelings about themselves. Most of these comments label the child and give them guilt feelings for not being what the powerful adults want them to be.

Labels are very destructive. For instance, how can Jenny 'unbad' herself? Because the parent hasn't defined the specific behaviour

Dealing with Difficult Situations

Jenny's used, she really doesn't know how to start improving herself. Jenny's parents have put negative tapes in her head that may stay there until she's mature enough to realise the tapes are no longer true. But look at the damage that it's done to Jenny in the meantime!

If you identify that children are receiving negative tapes from other authority figures, step in immediately to correct the problem. All parents should occasionally sit in during their children's school classes to determine whether their teachers are using labels to criticise their students. The parents should speak to the teacher if they identify destructive criticism and if necessary talk to the principal of the school. Watch for the kind of criticism given by babysitters and day care workers and correct your children if you catch them criticising others improperly.

Compulsive behaviour

'I believe my grandson suffers from obsessive-compulsive behaviour. He does actions over and over. Just washing his hands is terrible to watch. You would think he was a surgeon scrubbing up for an operation. He washes before meals, after meals, when he comes home from school and after doing his homework. Although he's only eight, his room is immaculate with everything in its place. He has a fit if other children come into his bedroom or play with his toys. If they do, he spends considerable time washing his toys.

I've mentioned my concerns to my son and his wife, but they say that he's just a clean boy. I think it's far more than that and think he should be receiving psychiatric help. What should I know about this illness?'

Your grandson sounds as if he desperately needs help. His rituals are compulsions to him. He needs order and symmetry in everything he sees and does and will panic if he can't have that symmetry. I normally don't encourage grandparents to step in, but in this case it appears as if the parents are turning a blind eye to their child's problem.

If you're able to determine the name of your grandson's doctor, make an appointment to discuss your concerns. It's unusual that his school has not noticed this problem. You might contact the school counsellor, explain your concerns and ask him/her to observe your grandson's actions at school. Both the doctor and the counsellor should be warned not to tell your son and his wife that you've talked

Dealing with Difficult Situations

with them regarding your concerns. One book that can help you with this disorder is *'The Boy Who Couldn't Stop Washing'* by Dr. Judith Rapoport.

Low self-esteem

'My daughter mopes around the house saying she's a failure at everything. She has few friends, refuses to try anything new and is starting to fail at school. Her lethargic, negative, attitude is starting to rub off on the rest of the family. There's constant bickering at the dinner table.'

'My son has gone through a tremendous growth-spurt and is about five inches taller than his classmates. He takes a ribbing, because his weight hasn't caught up and he's quite gangly and under-nourished looking. How can we help him through this difficult time?'

'My daughter is fine dealing with her classmates, but becomes a shy, awkward, backward teen when she interacts with boys. Our baseball team will be going to another city on a chaperoned bus for a game. A girlfriend of one of the players invited her to accompany the team. She refuses to go, stating 'What would I say? I'll probably make a fool of myself. No I can't go' How can I help her be more comfortable in situations with mixed groups?'

Teens no longer seek the approval of their parents and teachers; they seek the approval of their peer group. Surveys taken in junior and senior high schools reveal that teenagers' main focus in life is often their relationships with their friends. Most teenagers suffer from low self-esteem at least part of their teen years. To them, everyone is more popular, better-looking, dresses better or are smarter. They're too tall or short, early or late bloomers have acne and other skin problems, are too heavy, thin or believe they're dumb. They wonder how they're going to turn out (a frightening prospect when their bodies are doing such unusual things to them). Many peer at themselves in the mirror, trying to picture the finished product and seldom come up with an answer unless they strongly resemble a parent. Because early bloomers look older, society often treats them as if they *are* older (when they're not ready for that role).

Many parents make the serious mistake of comparing siblings in a family, causing bad feelings for all concerned. Just because Jane is an 'A' student, don't expect Roland to be. As long as Roland is

Dealing with Difficult Situations

giving his best effort, that's all his parents should expect. Accept him as he is. Parents who aren't sports conscious, might completely miss the fact that Roland is the star basketball player for his team and make light of this accomplishment. No wonder Roland is mad at his family. The only ones who fully appreciate him are his basketball team mates and those who follow basketball at school.

As parents, we have to understand how important it is to help our children know they have the right to state their wants and needs. Children who have developed a strong sense of their own value by the time they attend pre-school, will normally get along well with other children. Respect your children's strengths and abilities. Praise their successes. They'll probably try to deny their successes because most teens are embarrassed by any public attention they receive from parents. Secretly, they're very pleased at the recognition.

Everyone has a special ability or two. Help your teens cultivate theirs and identify the areas where they're likely to succeed. For instance, *'Marge, you did so well at learning how to play the piano that I think you'd probably do well with an electronic keyboard. Would you like to try one to see if you like it?'* Or, *'Jim, you love basketball so much, have you considered contacting the YMCA to see if they're looking for basketball coaches for summer camp?'*

Neglected children

'Both my husband and I work to make ends meet, but feel we're neglecting our children. We spend so much time at work and doing chores around the home that we don't have much quality time left for our children.'

Many families have little time to spend with each other or their children. Everything piles up and they find themselves rushed off their feet. The answer to this is to get everyone in the household involved in completing chores. It's not just husbands who require encouragement to help out at home. Some children believe that Mom should make their beds, clear their dishes off the table and cater to their every need. Children who grow up believing that while they're children, they're on this earth to have nothing but fun - are deprived on one of life's important learning experiences.

If they do, they're only breeding dependent, often demanding children who expect a 'free ride' through life. Many of these children end up depending on external events to make them happy.

Dealing with Difficult Situations

These children seldom achieve the exhilarating feeling of independence that comes from knowing they can do whatever is necessary to succeed.

***Parents should never do for children
what they can do for themselves.***

Couples who share parenting and household duties cope better than couples who follow traditional practices. Their children become part of the 'team;' become responsible for their actions and take part in the smooth running of the home. Both parents can help make this happen.

Lying

'How can I tell when my children are lying to me?'

Let's face it. Your children have lied to you in the past and will likely do so in the future. The usual reasoning behind lying is to avoid punishment for a wrongdoing and in later life, because of peer pressure. The older the child becomes, the more convincing liars they become and the more likely they are to think that lying is okay. By the age of twelve, they no longer consider lying as always being wrong and most adolescents become accomplished liars.

Having respect for parents, helps children resist peer pressure somewhat, but peer influence increases as they grow older. It's hard for parents to fight the pressure exerted if their child gets in with a bad crowd. If necessary, they may have to change the child's school or send him or her away for a summer with relatives to remove them from the bad influence.

Lying peaks at age fourteen, when teenagers become more secure. Parents are likely to deal with them as independent people so the power struggle lessens and the teens learn the high consequences of getting caught. The smarter the child - the less they cheat, possibly because they realise that the consequences of getting caught, might not be worth taking the chance.

What parents do about lying determines whether their children lie often and seriously. Younger children can learn from moral tales about people who lie. For instance (if they're sports buffs) explain that because Ben Johnson was charged with taking steroids many people don't trust him now. Describe how the more they lie, the

Dealing with Difficult Situations

fewer people will trust them and the more they'll question their honesty. Identify the differences between little lies that save people's feelings and the lies that betray trust.

How can you tell if your children are lying? Watch their body language. When children are proud of what they've accomplished, they're open with their body language. When they feel guilty or suspicious, they hide their hands either in their pockets or behind their back. If you accuse them of something, they'll likely give you an incredulous look and reply, *'Who me?'* To try to make you believe them more, they'll actually put their hand on their chest (a non-verbal sign of honesty).

Don't get in the habit of assuming your children are lying. It's better to be misled than disbelieve them when they're telling the truth.

When you do catch a child telling a lie, give separate discipline for the lie and the offence, making sure the punishment suits the crime. Explain that it's their lying you don't like, not them (deal with their behaviour - not with them as individuals). Try to determine why the child is lying. Could there be an underlying cause? Show them by example by admitting your mistakes, then show how you deal with and correct your mistakes. Look for other signals of lying such as:

- Avoiding eye contact (usually they look down);
- Blinking rapidly;
- Twitching and swallowing repeatedly;
- Clearing their throat and often wetting their lips;
- Covering their mouth when speaking;
- Shrugging;
- Rubbing their nose;
- Scratching their head while talking;
- Putting their hand to their throat;
- Rubbing the back of their neck (especially prevalent in males who are lying).

If you see these signs, you have a good indication that they're lying. One sign alone doesn't necessarily mean they're lying; it's usually a combination of these. Most people who lie can't back up their lies with facts. So when in doubt, ask for facts.

Dealing with Difficult Situations

Tattle Tale

'My son is forever tattling on the other children at his day care. How can I explain that this will keep him from having friends and shouldn't be done unless the action of the other child is really serious?'

Tattling or snitching often occurs due to jealousy or to pay others back for some perceived wrong. He's trying to discredit others, so he looks better to others. Use feedback to explain your displeasure at his actions. Make sure you praise him for his accomplishments and that you're unhappy about his using this tactic to bring attention to himself.

Tattling is a kind of power play; a way children try to make others look bad. The common targets of tattling are sisters and brothers, because tattling is part of sibling rivalry. It's a method children use to ally themselves with their parents. They expect appreciation, rewards, extra love and attention.

Toddlers may sound as if they're becoming tattle-tales, but they may just be giving their parents information they think they should have. At this stage there's seldom malice intended by their tattling. For tattling:

1. Explain to the child that they're tattling and how you feel about this. The child must understand the difference between tattling about unimportant matters and describing important facts, such as another child needing help. Your child must know s/he can come to you if s/he's really frightened about something another child is doing. This could be running into the street without looking to see if cars are coming or others are playing with matches.
2. Try not to pay attention to tattling, but don't ignore the child.
3. Don't assume the tattler is right and punish the person they tattled on. Investigate carefully before acting; otherwise the tattler will believe that you've condoned his/her behaviour.

Pretends he's sick

'What do I do when my son pretends he's sick? He's been missing a lot of school lately.'

Dealing with Difficult Situations

Children who complain regularly of illness might be unconsciously using their bodies to express unhappiness at what's happening in their life or as a way of expressing stress. Or it could be a way of drawing attention to other problems. They may copy symptoms they've seen their friends or other family members use to gain extra attention.

Does your child pretend to be sick just before it's time for his soccer games? Or does it happen in the middle of the night (which could be legitimate illness or could identify that he's afraid of the dark)?

Look carefully at the times you believe your child is faking illness. Is it early in the morning and possibly he doesn't want to go to school? Is it only on rainy or cloudy days? (Could he be afraid of lightening or thunder?) Is it when he faces having a test at school? Does it happen on the two days a week you do volunteer work way from your home? (He wants you to stay home, so you'll be there when he comes home from school?)

If your doctor has already ruled out physical reasons and the child still complains of illness, reassure him that you want to find out what's causing his illness, rather than tell him that you know he's faking his sickness. Talk about the feelings he's experiencing when he complains of pains. Ask about school work, how he's getting along with his friends and anything else you think could be causing the difficulty. This may encourage him to talk about the hidden problems he didn't feel free discussing with you earlier.

When he's healthy give him extra attention and show you value his company by spending time with him. If the illness persists and the doctor has ruled out physical illness, it might help to have the child (and often family members) see a counsellor.

On the other hand, some mothers miss their children far more than the children miss them and suffer more separation anxiety. When they're accustomed to being the centre of their child's world, it can become lonely for parents to be on the fringe of their children's lives.

Some children miss school because of complaints such as headaches and stomach upsets. What frightens many of them isn't school, but leaving their mothers, who depend on them for companionship and comfort. These parents may urge their children to go to school, but their non-verbal behaviour shows that they're still wanted at home. They worry constantly about the youngsters' health and keep them at

Dealing with Difficult Situations

home for the least sniffle. Often professional counselling is necessary to break the cycle.

To ensure this doesn't happen; parents must have other interests besides their children. This is where good friends, hobbies and a challenging lifestyle are the best defence against the parent's loneliness.

Falling behind in School

'My daughter Rachel is falling behind in school. She's in grade two and just doesn't seem to be able to pick up the lessons. What should I do?'

The first step is to talk to her teacher and I'm sure you've done that. You may need to provide a tutor or do some work with her at home to see that she can keep up. Another is to teach her a technique that I wish every parent and teacher would explain to children and that is the skill of paraphrasing. Can you imagine how frustrating it is for a child to have a teacher give instructions on how to do something and the child doesn't understand the instructions? Most children just watch others to see how they are to complete an assignment, but think how much better it would be if they could check it out themselves instead of relying on others?

Using paraphrasing, the child would say to the teacher, *'Do you mean that you want us to ...?'* That way she could check to see if what the teacher said and what she understood were the same.

For some reason schools do not teach students this technique so it may rest on you - the parent, to show your children how it works. Using paraphrasing, a person checks out what the other person is saying using such phrases as, *'I want to make sure I understand your instructions. You want me to ...?'* Or, *'Do you mean that ...?'* This way there are no misunderstandings. It's an excellent tool that they will use throughout their lives to improve their communication skills with others.

Dealing with Tantrums

'My son is four and still has temper tantrums. Some little disappointment happens and he's stamping his foot and screaming.'

When children lose their tempers and express their anger in inappropriate ways, it's important to look beyond the outburst to

Dealing with Difficult Situations

detect what caused it. You'll notice that behind every outburst is some negative feeling the child has to cope with. Help them learn how to cope with their negative feelings. For instance, if you told him to go to bed and he resorted to a tantrum, you might find that he was in the middle of an important game with his older brother (he was winning). This doesn't mean you give in to the tantrum. Instead explain that if he had told you about the importance of the game, instead of screaming at you, you might have allowed him to finish the game. Point out that everyone has to deal with occasional embarrassing or frustrating situations.

Because he had a tantrum (instead of explaining his need to finish the game) he'll have to go to bed without a bedtime story (or any other withdrawal of privileges).

Never reward unacceptable behaviour with privileges.

If your son has tantrums in public - remove him immediately. Explain that in the future, he will have to stay with a babysitter and miss special excursions because of his behaviour. This tactic is especially effective if there are other well-behaved children who will accompany the parents while the errant child stays home with a babysitter. This way, the errant child will receive isolation - the opposite of what s/he was hoping to obtain by having tantrums.

The Terrible Two's

'My two-year-old is very bright, but still can't put sentences together. She's prone to having tantrums especially when she doesn't get her way.'

She's going through the 'terrible two's.' This is a very frustrating time for toddlers. They try and try to communicate with us, but we don't understand what they're trying to tell us.

I compare this inability to communicate to an adult who has had a stroke that affects his/her speech. How frustrating this must be for both these individuals!

Parents need to spend more time and effort to understand what their toddlers are trying to communicate. This extra effort will reap many benefits - a happier toddler and an end to the tantrums caused by the toddler's communication frustrations.

Dealing with Difficult Situations

Battling Children

'When should parents step in to break up arguments between two children?'

Try to get your children to solve their own differences unless they've become physically or emotionally aggressive towards one another. If that happens, separate them and take steps to stop the behaviour from happening in the future. Look behind the behaviour to see why they're acting the way they are. Do they feel left out? Aggressive behaviour is often the way children express damaged feelings, because they don't know any other way to express their frustration.

Dealing with bullies

'My seven-year-old son has changed behaviour drastically in the past month. He's gone from being a well-adjusted happy boy, to one whose behaviour swings between throwing tantrums and withdrawal. How can we investigate this without making matters worse?'

Talk about the behaviour he's displaying and ask him (in a non-threatening way) what's happening. *'It's not like you to have tantrums and get angry this way. What happened to make you so angry?'*

Do the same for his symptoms of withdrawal. You might find that he's facing serious problems either at school or with his peer group. These behaviours can often be a sign that someone at school is bullying the child. The suppressed anxiety and anger at his predicament could be demonstrated as tantrums at home. This is likely an environment where he feels safer in expressing his anxiety, frustration and anger. Knowing you care about him, will start you both on the way to solving his problem.

If he clams up, talk to his teacher and even his friends about his behaviour so you'll know what hidden problems exist for your son. Don't let the situation slide or his behaviour is likely to worsen. Consider getting professional counselling if the above attempts do not correct the behaviour.

'My son throws toys, has tantrums and is generally a tyrant. My friends have stopped bringing their children over, because he's so violent with them. I'm afraid he's turning into a bully.'

Dealing with Difficult Situations

Most children have temper tantrums to get attention or to express frustration. This is why the 'terrible twos' is often the time when children start resorting to tantrums. Parents must let the child know that their behaviour is unacceptable. The child should be sent to isolation (the opposite of what they had hoped to get by their tirade) and told they can come out when they are ready to behave properly. Do not send them to their bedroom but another area because they may associate their bedroom with punishment and balk at going to bed. After they have calmed down, talk to them about their behaviour and find out what was behind their explosion.

If parents observe their child displaying hurt or angry feelings by wilful destruction or excessive anger towards others, the child is possibly a bully. Children display this tendency by throwing things, breaking another's toys or hitting or biting others. It's important to analyse what's behind the child's destructive behaviour. When a child takes delight in torturing animals or other children or if bullying shows up in early life, it's a sure sign that professional help is needed. If children's behaviour is not dealt with before they enter the school system, their destructive pattern may escalate until others (teachers) insist that they obtain professional help.

When children's destruction of an item is deliberate, you can help them handle the results by stressing the rights of others. To start, the child should apologise to the person s/he hurt or whose property was destroyed. Then, identify the costs of repairing the broken item. Children should replace or fix whatever they break. Give a value to tasks they can perform around the house or yard, so they can pay for the damages they've caused. (This is one strong argument in favour of regular allowances for work performed).

'My eight-year-old son is anxious and unhappy. He complains of tummy aches with no medical cause, resists going to school and his grades are dropping. He's having nightmares and cries at the slightest incident. He finally explained that a boy at school was pushing and shoving him and trying to make him fight. How can I help him deal with bullies?'

Bullies get a kick out of upsetting others and beating them up. Their victims are often quiet, suffer in silence and don't seek help. Bullies are visible, so they usually get counselling, but their victims are the unseen problem.

Dealing with Difficult Situations

Start by having a discussion with your son's teachers. If the teacher is un-cooperative, speak to the principal. Many elementary schools help these bullied children by offering special clinics for them. They act out 'bully' parts where they're subjected to name-calling and teasing, so they can learn effective measures when dealing with aggressive playmates. Often the role-playing situations are from problems experienced by one of the group members.

The classes concentrate on building the self-esteem level of children which helps them send the message that *'I'm not someone you can easily victimise.'* It becomes easier for them to tell other students to stop teasing them or walk away from threatening situations without feeling like a failure.

Another approach is to speak to the bully's parents. Unfortunately, children who are bullies often come from dysfunctional homes and their parents may not cooperate and help solve this problem.

One Canadian city is having police officers speak at schools explaining the consequences of bullying. They also address the students about the unacceptability of standing by when they observe bullying - that they must stop it or at least report it. No longer is it acceptable to either bully or stand by and watch it happening.

Students who get into fights at school sign a contract with the police officer, the school and the parents that they will straighten out, otherwise they'll be charged by the police. Others sign contracts that they will do their homework, behave at home and write a paper about being assertive without being violent.

One last resort for parents is to contemplate getting the police involved by lodging assault charges against the bully. Often having a police officer reprimand the bully will result in positive changes in the bully's behaviour. Do everything you can, before resorting to changing schools for your child.

Monkey see - Monkey do

'So many children I see today don't seem to have the everyday manners I expect in children. Don't parents give their children the basics anymore?'

It's unfortunate, but many of us save our everyday manners for strangers, but don't use them with the important people in our lives - our family members. Some families treat each other badly.

Unfortunately, this sets the stage for children's actions with others. Sharing and caring for each other takes a nosedive when families stop using common courtesy and everyday manners with each other.

Why don't they treat family members with the same courtesy they give to their friends or even strangers? They drift into it - because of bad habits, familiarity and an uncaring attitude. The idea, *'My family will like me no matter how I act,'* becomes their behaviour pattern. Unless they identify and correct this negative habit, it will just continue unabated. The family will likely grow apart.

Stay together for our children

'My wife and I are always battling, but we've decided to stay together until our children are older.'

Couples who stay together 'because of the children' are often surprised by the reaction of their children when they finally decide to split up. Their children wonder why their parents stayed together as long as they did because their lack of common courtesy to each other has been missing long before the break-up was made official.

Children, teens and young adults are strongly affected by how their parents treat each other. They're more upset by non-verbal expressions of anger such as sarcasm and the silent treatment than was originally thought. Children watch how their parents show their anger and how they act when and after they fight.

Unresolved anger bothers children and they're very quick to pick up tension between their parents. Children as young as nine months old sense when their parents are fighting and become distressed.

Arguments that parents haven't resolved during a confrontation, sit there like time bombs and children wait anxiously for them to erupt again.

Arguments that express anger in a physical way using hitting and pushing are far more damaging and hard to forget for most children. They learn that hitting and pushing during arguments are acceptable so they use this behaviour on their friends and schoolmates. This behaviour results in additional problems.

Children need to know that arguments have their place. Parents need to show obvious signs that an argument is solved and be willing to negotiate or compromise. Arguments that conclude with parents apologising to each other, help children understand that all arguments aren't wrong. This kind of argument doesn't have a lasting effect on children. They learn that arguments are all right if they're solved peacefully and end with no winners or losers.

Over-reacting to behaviour

'Sometimes I lash out at my children without thinking.'

Unfortunately, parents make comments in the heat of the moment, little realising that their comments can seriously damage their children. Picture a situation where a child has tripped, fallen down and broke a household item in the process. Yelling at the child for breaking the item is double punishment if s/he hurt him or herself during the fall. Those who bawl out a child under these conditions should practice the following:

1. It's imperative that you comfort the child and deal with the broken article later. When it's time to discuss the broken item, don't speak on impulse. If necessary, walk away for a minute or take yourself away mentally for a moment and think of something other than the problem. Count to ten.
2. Don't use physical violence as a form of discipline.
3. Develop responses to familiar problems and strive to use them. If the child balks, consider giving firm consequences should they not do what you ask them to do and make sure you follow-through with action.
4. Concentrate on your child's positive behaviour. Most children want to please, but if the only way they perceive they can get your attention is to be bad, that's what you'll get from them. Try talking calmly about the situation. If that doesn't work, rather than yelling or hitting them, give them isolation for their bad behaviour or start removing privileges.
5. Use humour whenever possible to control your anger. For example picture yourself tossing an imaginary cream pie in your child's face if s/he does something to make you angry. This will defuse your anger and keep your objectivity. Don't say or do something you'll regret later.

Divorce

'My wife and I have decided to separate and divorce. How are we going to explain to our children that we've decided to end our marriage?'

Dealing with Difficult Situations

Whenever possible, both parents should break the news to their children. The sooner the better, rather than take the chance that they'll hear about it from someone else. Keep your comments short to lessen the anxiety.

Make sure they know they're not the cause of the divorce. It's important for parents to realise the way children think. Children somehow believe that they're responsible for all the good and bad situations that happen around them. Parents might have to initiate this subject, because sometimes their children haven't even formulated the idea in their minds enough to .talk about it. It may just be a feeling they have, that somehow they were responsible.

When asked why you don't love each other any more, keep your antagonism to each other out of your answers. You might say, *'We fight too much.'* Or, *'We aren't happy living together any more.'* Watch that you don't reinforce the idea that you don't love each other any more; otherwise your children might feel that you could stop loving them as well.

Summer vacation blues

'In two weeks, my family is leaving on a two-week vacation. It will be a five-hour drive until we arrive at a cottage we've rented. If it's anything like last year, the children will start whining five minutes after they get in the car and will spend much of the time at the cabin stating, 'What can I do?' How am I going to survive the holidays?'

As any parent will agree, driving is not the challenge - driving with children is! Close quarters (being within arm's reach of siblings) the confinement itself (lack of movement) and the boredom of having to sit and 'do nothing' can add up to a horrifying experience for all involved. Add a pet to this scene and there's chaos.

Many parents (passengers only) resort to taking tranquilisers and wish they had the nerve to give some to their offspring as well. Some plan their trip so their young children sleep through it.

So how can children survive after the many new games (bought specially for this trip) have run their course? Have the youngest and oldest pair up, rather than having rivals sit together. Try playing a game called auto bingo that provides an element of surprise depending on what's happening outside the car window. This is where points are given to the first child who spots:

Dealing with Difficult Situations

- A red car, a blue station wagon, a car with four people in it, one with three people
- The first cow, horse, sheep
- A barn, haystack, farmer, etc.
- Each child counts a particular colour of vehicle for 15 minutes.

The one who counts the most - wins a prize. Make a list before leaving on the trip or compile it while in transit. Each child will have a copy of the list and will get extra points for special items such as spotting a police car, an ambulance or fire truck. This activity never gets mundane because the scenery keeps changing.

Before leaving, involve the children in planning the trip. An older child could sit in front with the driver and help navigate. Chart rest and food stops as you go. Consider packing a picnic basket for a quick roadside lunch break. Leave sharp-edged, hard and heavy toys at home or in the boot - they can be dangerous in small places.

As you reach certain points on the highway, introduce new games. Take books, games, pens, paper, colouring books, crayons and snack treats for when they start to get restless. Building toys can keep small hands busy as can hand-held video games. Magnetic doodle boards can provide hours of fun. Teenagers can listen to their favourite music and younger children can listen to books on audio tape or DVD movies with their own headphones. If you have a portable recorder, buy an inexpensive microphone and tape your children singing along with music from the car radio.

Pack soccer balls or other action sports equipment for active play at rest stops. Be aware of the need for youngsters to stop for a bathroom break within a half-hour to an hour after eating. Keep wet tissues or a damp cloth wrapped in plastic for sticky fingers. And don't forget litter bags.

When you reach the cabin and your children ask, *'What can we do?'* brainstorm with them to see what alternatives they can devise. Weeks before leaving on your trip, start listing alternatives you can suggest and make sure you have the necessary items for projects. For younger children, empty egg boxes, pipe cleaners, pompoms, bits of felt, glue, eyes, childproof scissors and other innovative items can be used imaginatively to make any number of creatures. Use this opportunity to teach your children how to knit, crochet, macramé, tie knots, whittle and carve wood. Make Christmas wreaths from pinecone, nut and shells found nearby.

Dealing with Difficult Situations

Get other children in the area of your cabin involved. Have them dress up in old clothes and put on a play. Another pleaser is to tie a rope to the trunk of a tree, with someone holding the other end. Have the children see how high they can jump as you raise the rope - giving prizes to all participants. Then, reverse the process and have them go under the rope doing the limbo (fun to do to music).

For older children, tie a rope to a strong branch of a tree (with knots every eight to 12 inches) and see who can climb the highest, the quickest. Have them wear gloves for this activity. Place an inexpensive double blow-up mattress (or old mattress that can be lugged out of the cabin) under the rope so they won't hurt themselves if they fall.

Be creative - encourage your children to be creative and vacations can be fun. However, don't plan *everything* for them. Leave lots of 'hanging around' time so they can make their own fun at their own pace, with their own friends.

There are usually three stages to summer vacation for children. Each stage has its own unique qualities:

Stage 1: When school is over and they need to wind down, but still need a structured environment. It's an ideal time to register them for camp so they can run off their excess energy. If this isn't possible, children may welcome the chance of participating in swimming, art or computer lessons.

Stage 2: This is a quieter time, about the middle of their holiday. Families should plan their holiday time for this stage if possible. This time should not be over-scheduled, giving the children time to adjust to the slower timing. You'll have to think of projects for them to do, but you won't likely have to keep them amused, especially if there are other children around.

Stage 3: This is the final week or two of their holidays where getting ready for school is of primary interest. By this time they should be rested and ready to get back into the groove and daily schedule of the fall, so encourage a faster pace.

Mother/Daughter Relationships

'My relationship with my daughter keeps running hot and cold. One minute we're soul-mates and the other adversaries and at war. What's going on besides hormones being out of whack?'

Dealing with Difficult Situations

Throughout history, there's been a love/hate relationship between most mothers and daughters. When the daughter is an infant their relationship is close and constant because of the defencelessness of the child. But as the child becomes more and more independent, subtle changes occur. Bystanders often observe, but miss the meaning behind these changes.

From the time little girls are as young as two or three, many are aware of the power they have over one of the more powerful people in their lives - their fathers. They learn to be very manipulative in finding ways around being criticised or punished for their wrongdoings. They become 'Daddy's little girl.' Some will use this power against their male siblings. Because Daddy thinks she can do no wrong, when they're in conflicts with their brothers they can usually count on their fathers to see their side of the story.

Some little girls are jealous of the attention their fathers pay to their mothers and will express this in many ways. In the middle of the night, they steal into their parents' beds and park themselves between the couple. When the parents are watching television, they climb up between them. If the father and mother are having a conversation, they climb on their laps and make constant efforts to divert their fathers' attention from their mothers. They accomplish this by asking their fathers to help them with something (anything). Often mothers are put into the unenviable situation of wondering if they're becoming jealous of their own daughters.

When they reach their early teens many become boy crazy and today's girls are encouraged to go to extremes to 'get their man.' Many are starved for male affection (absent fathers). Peer pressure and the image of romance permeate life for these budding women. Their hormones are out of whack; one minute they feel very grown up and the next they feel like helpless little girls. Society shows them that being grown up includes having a boyfriend, but boys their age, aren't interested in girls. Having sympathetic mothers during this period can help these budding women.

During their teenage years, most daughters become adversaries, not only of their mothers, but their fathers as well. They buck authority and believe that their parents (and especially their fathers) live in the dark ages.

Mothers can keep the bond strong if they empathise with their daughters and let them in on the excitement of what's in store for them. They also need to help them keep both feet on the ground if they shirk their daily responsibilities at school and home. If not handled correctly, this can alienate the mother and daughter.

When my daughter was in her mid-teens, I made an effort to know where she was going. She balked at telling me because she often didn't know herself. She couldn't understand why I left precise information about where I would be, especially when I was out of town. When a family emergency required her to contact me without delay, she related afterward that she doesn't know what she would have done if she couldn't reach me immediately. Then it hit home to her, that I wasn't controlling where she went, but simply wanted to know where she was in case of emergency so I could reach her. After that time, she changed her attitude about why I wanted to know where she was.

If their mothers are single parents, some daughters compete with their mother for the attention of the men in their lives. Some show a distinct sensuality around men (especially their mother's dates). These nymphets flirt outrageously with the men. If they're older teenagers, they may feel a sense of power if they detect a flash of interest in the eyes of their mother's dates. These men are not oblivious to the teen's sensuality and confirm this by stating to their mothers *'You're going to have to lock that one up soon.'* Thankfully, as soon as the teens assure themselves that they're seen as desirable, most find other activities to be more important, such as going to a movie with their friends.

When daughters grow up and find their own mates, the closeness rekindles between mother and daughter. Suddenly, their little girls are now women - women who need to know the skills that will keep their men happy - and Mom is there to provide it. And when the daughters produce their own offspring - the closeness increases tenfold. Their mothers become doting grandmothers who are available to step in to relieve them of their sometimes overwhelming motherhood responsibilities. This is the time when the daughters start to fully appreciate the sacrifices their mothers have made for them during their lifetime and the cycle repeats itself.

Daughter's Dating

'My daughter has just started dating and I realise that I'm terrified to let her go out. I remember all the feelings I had when I was a

Dealing with Difficult Situations

young man. How can I let her go out knowing she has a good chance of being coerced or forced into going beyond where she wants or should go sexually?'

This is the time that fathers panic. When their daughters start dating, many fathers find that they're terrified about letting her go out. They remember the feelings they had when they were young men and **know** that most young men are focusing on one thing - sex, sex and more sex.

Hopefully, at an early age you've established a communication line between you and your daughter. If the groundwork's in place, communication will continue, though there will be major changes in your child's need for privacy. Continue to empathise (major ingredient to communication) and put yourself in her place. Don't force on her, the values you had as a teenager. Life has changed and parents must change with the times.

Most parents (fathers especially) are tempted to 'grill' their daughter's dates to decide for themselves whether the young man is suitable and trustworthy. They'll ask questions such as: *'Where did you and my daughter meet? What school do you go to? What grade are you in? What do you hope to be when you graduate?'*

Nowadays, many daughters simply don't bring their dates home because of this fear. Most young daters meet at a fast-food restaurant and then go wherever they decide to go, either as a couple or as part of a group. This terrifies most parents, because they don't know where their daughters are or with whom. It's often the mothers who step in and smooth over the waters between father and daughter and allow her more freedom and set the ground rules.

Parents of boys are mainly afraid that some young gal will coerce their son into sex, get pregnant and he'll have to marry her!

Encourage your daughter to invite her dates to your home for dinner and make (or buy) something they'd likely order themselves, such as pizza. Don't start grilling him. Instead, treat him as you would any of your adult friends. Discuss something of interest that happened to you at work, what's going on at sports arena or anything else that won't seem like a grill session. He'll likely open up on his own to answer your unspoken questions such as: where he and your daughter met, what school he goes to, what grade he's in, what he hopes to be when he graduates, etc. The first meeting will decide for him whether he's comfortable being in your home. The more comfortable he is, the more open he will be about his background, morals and values.

Watch you don't set too many rules and regulations - this just makes teens feel as if you don't trust **them**. Do, however, quietly explain your concern for their safety, what to watch out for in relationships. When the opportunity arises, ask your teen questions about what they'd do if ... Identify what you feel are possible dangerous situations they may face. For example, being out with a date who's too drunk to drive (or too drunk herself); her date's getting too friendly and she wants a ride home or any other potentially dangerous situation. Make sure your teens know you won't lecture them - that you're there to help them out of difficult situations should they occur. The only rule you really should enforce is when your teen is due home, but be prepared to extend the normal curfew under special situations.

Sloppiness

'I've tried unsuccessfully to get my thirteen-year-old son to pick up his belongings when he comes home from school. I always know where he is by following the trail of clothes, books, shoes and food wrappers. He's been retaliating and calling me a 'nag' and the battle's on. I work all day and waste my valuable time either walking around his mess or cleaning up after her him.'

When she learned the skill of feedback, her approach changed to: *'Martin, I work hard every day and I get very annoyed at your actions. To be specific, I'm tired of nagging you to pick up your belongings every day. I've reminded you Monday, Tuesday and this is Wednesday ... Can you tell me why you're still doing something that you know annoys me?'*

Martin hummed and hawed, then said, *'Get off my back Mom!'*

His mother replied, *'Well the situation can't remain the way it is. Because we all live in this house, we all have certain responsibilities. One of your responsibilities from now on, is to pick up after yourself. I see two solutions to this. I'll take everything I find lying around and put it in a garbage bag and not let you have anything in it for a month or I'll take some of your privileges away from you.'*

Dealing with Difficult Situations

'What privileges?'

'Well, you need me to drive you to your soccer practices twice a week. I simply won't drive you any more.'

'Okay, I get your point. If I pick up after myself, you'll still drive me to my soccer practices, right?'

'Right. I know I can count on you to do your part around here.'

Martin started being more considerate and his mother stopped nagging him. She realised she hadn't given him responsibilities suitable to his age group and still pictured him as a younger child. She also realised that she'd had little, if any, time for herself.

Spends too much on clothes

'My son keeps after me to let him spend far too much money on his clothes. I can't understand the difference between buying a sweatshirt for ten dollars and one that costs sixty dollars (except the name on it). What's happening to teens these days that they have to be clones of each other? I simply can't afford sixty dollars for a sweat shirt.'

There's a great deal of competition in the teen scene. If one person has designer sweatshirts, so do all his friends. If his friends have a mobile phone, of course he wants one too. This is part of growing up.

Parents who know this situation is coming, should decide what they will and will not pay for, *before* speaking with their children. This way, teens aren't likely to pit one parent against the other. Discourage them from nagging you. Do, however, listen carefully to what they say - so you're not missing important messages. Tell them what you're willing to do. If they wish to buy something more expensive, they'll have to earn the money themselves.

Answer their plea, *'Everybody else can do this ... has that ... is able to ...'* with, *'We're talking about what you can do ... what you can have ... and what you're able to ... not everybody else.'* Then, tell them what you're willing to do or have them do. Set a good example by explaining items you'd like to have, but can't afford. Let them know that you too, have pangs of envy about what you want, but have to be realistic on what you can and can't have.

Let your teen help with problem-solving. When you feel you can't afford that expensive sweatshirt, have him join you to brainstorm how he might earn the money to buy one. Having a garage sale worked for one family and everyone ended up buying something they needed out of the proceeds from the sale of their unwanted belongings. Be creative - there are solutions.

Boy Crazy

'I'm a single mother. My daughter is only fourteen, but she spends most of her time mooning about boys. Isn't she too young to be concentrating all her efforts on that?'

Today's girls are frequently starved for male affection (absentee fathers). Try your best to make sure there's a suitable mature male in her life who can provide the role model she needs. Be careful to ensure that this male can be trusted to help her through this difficult period of her life. This can be a friend of the family, one of your own brothers or a significant other in your life. The latter is not suggested if you know the man is only going to be on the scene temporarily.

Girls in their early teens are faced with peer pressure and the image of romance permeates life for these budding women. Their hormones are often out of whack; one minute they feel very grown up and the next they feel like helpless little girls. Society shows them that being a grown up includes having a boyfriend. Boys their own age are often not interested in girls, which encourages them to seek (or be sought after) by older boys. They're seldom prepared to handle the sexual pressures that boys of sixteen or seventeen may place upon them.

Let her have romantic ideas, but watch that she doesn't lose touch with reality. Talk about how her life is changing. Let her know what's in store for her, but also help her to keep both feet on the ground if she's shirking her home or school responsibilities.

Daughter wants contraceptive

'My daughter came to me the other day and asked me if she could have birth control pills. I told her I had to think about it and would give her my decision next week. I don't know what to do. If I give her permission to get birth control pills, aren't I condoning and encouraging her to be promiscuous? On the other hand, if I don't

Dealing with Difficult Situations

approve and she has sex anyway, she may end up pregnant. What's the answer?'

There's no pat answer to this question. Both boys and girls need to know that sex is an adult activity. It's for grown-ups - for people who have the morals to decide whether to have a family, the ability to support one and the wisdom not to use their bodies for the sole purpose of gaining attention and affection from others.

By all means, have a heart-to-heart talk with your daughter. Make sure you explain all the aspects of the situation and that you hesitate to give her permission because it will look as if you're encouraging her to have sex. Point out all your concerns including your fear that she will be exposed to sexually transmitted diseases (prepare by getting pamphlets explaining what these are). Ask her why she feels she is ready for sex. Explain that if she has to sleep with a boy to keep him - then he's not worth having.

If she still feels she wants the pills, give permission, but urge her to be cautious and to always use a condom.

Double Standard

'My daughter came to me the other day with the comment, `Why does society still have a double standard? I'm an eighteen-year-old teen. I have sexual urges too and get turned on by my boyfriend. Why does society insist that I'm not supposed to have sexual feelings?' How should I deal with this?'

Many teens find themselves torn between remaining true to the values their parents have instilled in them and gaining peer acceptance by going along with questionable activity. Added to this are raging hormones that are urging them to have sex. Keeping out of trouble, yet keeping friends, takes self-confidence and skill.

Society's values have not kept up with the reality of present-day life. For centuries, society has had a double standard for males and females. Girls, more than boys receive mixed messages from modern society. On one hand they're told they shouldn't mess around and on the other they're assaulted by advertising that gives a clear message that sex paves the road to happiness. The media inundates young women with images of women as sexual playthings.

Encourage her not to get upset about others' beliefs and to recognise that it's natural for her to have sexual urges. However, this doesn't

Dealing with Difficult Situations

mean she has to act on those urges. Provide her with the information she needs to choose the route she will take. She alone should make the final choice.

Another single mother was not only distressed, but very offended by a situation both she and her daughter faced when they were dating. She identified the problem this way, *'A while ago I noticed that my very attractive 22 year-old daughter Barbara, was dating only occasionally. Mainly, she went out with her best friend, Karen. They usually joined a mixed group, but seldom did either young woman go out alone on a date.*

I questioned Barbara about this and she admitted she was reluctant to go out alone with men because of the problems she faced. She explained that part of her reluctance was because of the terror her friend Karen had towards dating. Twice, Karen had been the victim of date rape - when she was seventeen and again two months ago when she was twenty-three.

'How did this happen?' I asked. Karen had told Barbara that she'd liked the two men and didn't want to lose them by making them mad at her for demanding that *'No'* meant *'No.'* She hoped that they'd listen to her when she rebuffed their advances. Unfortunately, both men pushed her further and further sexually until they refused to stop. Karen said she felt dirty and soiled after they coerced her into having sex she didn't want. She hadn't pressed charges, but didn't see the men again.

My daughter Barbara, on the other hand, <u>had</u> insisted several times that *'No'* meant *'No,'* and found that this ended most of her relationships with men. She decided that it just wasn't worth the hassles, so socialised exclusively in groups instead.

'This phenomenon still amazes me. I'm a single mom and have run into exactly the same problem - but with men who should know better. You'd think that as men mature and their raging hormones have dissipated, that they'd be less inclined to push a woman further than she wants to go. Too many men have the mistaken opinion that what feels good to them, must automatically feel good to women.

I've had to drop several of these `octopi' because they simply didn't hear me when I asked them to stop touching me sexually. Some seemed to have an invisible cord that went from their mouths to their hands. Even a simple good-night kiss resulted in one or both hands

Dealing with Difficult Situations

automatically landing on my breasts or crotch. Others started more serious advancement on the second or third date and acted as if there was something wrong with me, because I wouldn't get into bed with them. They didn't consider that if I had sex with them on the third date that I'd probably do so with all the men I dated. How could they want me sexually with the AIDs scare, if they considered that?

If a man's hugs and cuddles progresses to intimate sexual touching before I have a chance to really know him, I retreat, rather than let him come closer. If they would only back off, they'd find that, like most people, I like to be held and cuddled and would probably want sex if not forced into it. The more they push, the more I run away.'

These men have not learned the difference between sensual friendship and sexual lust. Sensual friendship is when a couple hold hands, hug, stroke the other person's hair and cuddle while watching television. Most people are starved for this type of touching. Unfortunately society encourages the myth that touching between couples is always a prelude to sexual intercourse.

Men who insist on sex before the woman is ready, are on a power trip and want their wishes to supersede those of their `weaker' partner. These men often turn out to be wife and child beaters. You and your daughter will have to be patient. There are many fine men who do not fit this mould who are worth waiting for.

Secretive

'My son has been very secretive lately and accuses me of butting into his affairs - that he wants more privacy. I need to know what's going on in his life. How can I make him know that I respect his privacy, but need to have certain information to ensure his safety?'

Teenagers' obsession with privacy can make parents uneasy. Their closed bedroom doors, carefully guarded school possessions make many parents feel rejected and not trusted by their adolescents. This secrecy increases the fear that their children are hiding something.

Parents should treat their adolescent daughters and sons as they would want to be treated. This means no snooping into their affairs, reading their personal mail or journals. Your trust in them breeds their trust in you. The only exception to this is if you seriously feel they're using drugs or have stolen property. They must know that their right to privacy doesn't include the right to involve their family in illegal activities.

Jealousy and Envy

'There's such a vast difference between my two teenage daughters. My older daughter, Sharon, is very jealous of her sister Sarah because of her close relationship with her boyfriend and her popularity at school. Sharon is rather plain and has never had a boyfriend whereas Sarah is a lovely girl who attracts boys to herself by her outgoing and pleasant personality. Sharon is very awkward when she communicates with others and holds people at a distance from her. I accept my daughters as they are but am concerned because Sharon is filled with jealousy and envy against her sister and is starting to act out accordingly.'

Sharon is probably not aware of why she repels others. Start by having her describe to you why she thinks her sister is so popular and why she doesn't think she is. You will need to work with her to show her how her behaviour either invites or repels others. Ask her how she thinks others feel when she acts certain ways and why others respond differently when they're around Sarah. Be sure to praise Sharon about areas of her life where she excels. Her low self-esteem has come from somewhere - as her parent it's necessary for you to determine where those feelings originated. Could it be from her choice of friends? Could it be from put-downs she's suffered from at school?

Don't let her put you off if she refuses to discuss the issue with you. I wouldn't suggest you be so forceful, if she didn't have such a negative reaction to Sarah's positive behaviour. This shows she's confused about what she should be doing to obtain approval from others. Use 'what if' situations to describe how others might feel in different situations. Use situations where you've observed Sharon repelling others to make your point.

CHAPTER 9

DIFFICULT SITUATIONS - SENIORS

I want to stay in my home!

'I live in the home my husband and I shared for more than thirty years. He's gone now. Lately I've needed more help with daily chores. What worries me, is that several of my friends have fallen and I'm deathly afraid that I'll fall too. I dread losing my independence, but fear it's inevitable that I move into a nursing home.'

That's not necessarily true. Although many seniors require some help with bathing, dressing, walking, eating and using the toilet, this doesn't appear to be the case with you. Major studies have repeatedly shown that exercise programs can significantly make elderly people of all ages more fit and improve their balance. At age sixty, loss of muscle strength begins to occur. Exercises that involve weights can reduce this loss. It can increase muscle size and helps with balance, climbing stairs, getting out of bed and rising from a chair.

Usually home is where the heart is, so if you can manage, I encourage you to stay in your own home, If you require more help and don't want to involve your family, consider hiring a part-time aide who can do your heavier chores and shopping. Another solution is to share your home with another senior. This way you'll have someone available should you fall or become ill. This will also lessen the need for your family to become involved on a day-to-day basis.

Always keep in mind, that the more you can do for yourself, the more independence you'll keep. A good exercise program should be first on your 'to do' list to make sure you keep active enough to keep your independence. Another key to proper health and independence is maintaining an active lifestyle. Get out socially and live it up!

Alzheimer's Disease

'I'm sure my neighbour (who lives alone) has Alzheimer's Disease. She seems to have a 'blank' look about her and has started to shuffle when she walks. Just last year, she participated in aquasize classes,

Dealing with Difficult Situations

baked for the neighbourhood kids and was very active in the community. But lately, I've noticed that she mainly stays at home.

The last time I visited her, I noticed how dishevelled she looked and how untidy her home now appears. She has a dog and I heard him howling with the cold when we had our last blizzard. I had to go over and ring her doorbell to ask her to take him in. I'm concerned about her welfare. Could she possibly have Alzheimer's Disease or is she just getting old? How can I help her if she does have Alzheimer's Disease?'

Doctor's still can't determine completely whether a person has Alzheimer's Disease until the person dies. They can guess, but they don't know for sure until an autopsy is completed. But there are many signs they watch for that point in that direction. For instance, people suffering from Alzheimer's disease have difficulty communicating with others. They may not be able to make themselves understood or they don't understand what others are saying. They may become angry or defensive if they can't find the words to respond to others' questions.

Some forget within seconds, information they might have understood at the time it was spoken. Others might understand what others say if they're right in front of them, but fail to understand what others say when speaking to them on the telephone. Some can read words, but fail to understand the meaning of the words. Those who were very articulate or had the ability to put words to paper suddenly don't know how to find the words and even if they find the words, they forget how to write them down.

Another serious problem surfaces when they lose their sense of direction. Many become lost even in their own neighbourhoods or homes. The route they took to the corner store is suddenly unfamiliar to them. They forget where their bedroom fits into the layout of their homes. They try to put cakes into the dishwasher to bake, milk into the cupboard and sugar into the fridge. (We've all done the last two, but with Alzheimer's patients, this can be part of the overall pattern - not just an isolated incident).

Some become dangerous to themselves and others. One woman who lived in an apartment was forced to obtain her neighbour's help because she had become lost in her apartment when she had got up at night to use the bathroom. Somehow she had gone through the door to her apartment and it had locked behind her.

Dealing with Difficult Situations

Twice another senior almost set his apartment on fire, first by leaving something on the stove, then when he dropped a lighted cigarette on the couch. Thankfully, someone had been visiting him at the time.

Alzheimer's patients often live in the past and think their sons (who may resemble their fathers) are their long-departed husbands and talk to them as if they are. Others lose things and can become very agitated because they believe someone has stolen them. After one woman was diagnosed, her family packed up her belongings and found money hidden all over the apartment. Their mother had insisted that others had been stealing from her.

In this woman's cupboard were fifteen boxes of tea. The local grocer stated that every time she came into the store, she purchased tea (because she forgot that she had already bought some the day before). Unfortunately, many who deal with those suffering from the disease; forget that they may understand more than they let on. Be careful that you don't talk about them as if they aren't there.

If the above symptoms describe your neighbour, she may be in serious trouble and may not be able to protect or help herself. Do your best to see that she gets the help she needs by contacting her family, her doctor or any other person who may have a vested interest in her welfare. If there isn't anyone close to her, contact your local Alzheimer's Society or Mental Health Clinic to obtain an assessment of her condition.

After all I've done for you!

'My wife is trying to make our children feel guilty because she feels they don't do enough for her or spend enough time with her. She acts as if our children owe her a huge slice of their life because of `everything she's done for them.' Do our children really owe her that much? I think my children are hard pressed with demands from their careers, their partners and their children without having to take on the burden of looking after her needs too. What can I say to her to make her lighten up?'

Some parents have long memories and bring up events that happened years ago or try to transfer their responsibility to you or try to obtain pity from you by attempting to make you feel guilty. They make comments such as:

Dealing with Difficult Situations

'If you loved me more, you'd come over to see me more often.'

This son should reply by saying, *'Mom, why are you trying to make me feel guilty? You know I have too busy a schedule to see you more than once a week.'*

Grandparents might have considerable time on their hands and don't understand how little time their own children have to share with them. Their grown children often have no choice but to dole out their time in small doses while they're busy building their own family unit and caring for their own children.

Children do not 'owe' their parents anything. If parents did a good job of raising their children to be responsible adults, the children will give gladly of their time, effort and energy. The old expression: *'What comes around goes around'* is often true. Encourage her to put herself in her children's place. Your wife might have considerable time on her hands, so doesn't understand how little time your children have to share with her. If she's able, her best contribution could be to help her children occasionally with their load.

Soon your grandchildren will be grown up and your children can spend more time, energy and effort on not only their own needs, but yours as well. Studies show that nurturing parents who give because they want to give (not for what they expect back) will likely breed the same loving and caring attitude in their children. But children are individuals too. Some are very nurturing in nature - others aren't. Parents can't expect the same kind of caring from all their children. Instead of encouraging her to complain about how little she receives, encourage her to help your children more and see if the situation doesn't improve.

Dealing with Retirement

'My husband will be retiring soon. I feel he hasn't prepared himself enough to adapt to the drastic changes this will make in our lives. He lives for his work and isn't the handyman type who could keep himself busy around the home. I'm also concerned that he'll be underfoot and will need me to be with him constantly when I'm not at work. I have a busy life and don't want him to depend on me to keep him busy throughout the day. Is there anything I can do to make the transition better for him?'

Dealing with Difficult Situations

Retirement can be a difficult transition for some seniors. For others, it is seen as being the reward for years of hard work. The latter type is just waiting for retirement so they can do the things that are really important to them.

If you understand what happens during the transition, you can help your husband deal with the many changes he will face. Many retired people (especially those who equate their worth with how much they earn or how much work they do) may face a lowered level of self-esteem. Your husband may miss having something to get up for, something that makes him feel productive. Encouraging him to keep active and productive can be the best advice you can give him.

What are his hobbies? Does he like any particular sport - golfing or fishing? Could he get involved in community work – be a volunteer with Crime Stoppers, the Red Cross, Neighbourhood watch etc.? Could he continue working part-time as a consultant (if he's a businessman) or continue fixing cars (if that was his former occupation)? What spin-off interests could he delve into? For instance if he was an accountant, could he learn more about investments so you could be investing your money more wisely?

Statistics now prove that men can retire earlier and with fewer cares than women can, because 70 per cent of men and only 51 per cent of women have pension plans. Working women don't plan to retire or retire as early as men do, unless they're married and their husbands have a good income. This is because women traditionally enter the work force later than men and have built up less in their pension funds.

An emerging trend shows that when husbands retire, many of their wives decide to stay in the workforce. The women's reasons for doing so, relate to money (or lack of it) continued family medical and pension benefits, their own job satisfaction and a sense of identity. Their husbands may have been in the workforce for 45 years, but many wives are five to fifteen years younger than their spouses and have only worked for 20 or 25 years. The average woman now spends 35 years of her adult life working either part- or full-time before retirement. Many of these women simply aren't ready to retire. Women who marry older men or marry for a second time may still be in the middle of their career paths when their husbands retire.

Divorced women spend three more years in the work force than married or widowed women. This shows that women usually come out of a divorce worse off economically than men. Widows can collect from their husband's pension fund as well as from their own. Unfortunately, pension funds are not as kind to divorced women. They end up with just their own pension fund to count on, even though in their marriage, they may have stayed at home and cared for their children for many years. Many are exempt from receiving benefits from their ex-spouse's pension fund. The Canadian government corrected this inequity for those who obtained a divorce after the year 1977, but women who divorced before that date, don't receive any portion of their ex-husband's pension.

Many husbands object to the reversal of traditional roles where they're the homemaker and their wives are the breadwinners. This can affect the man's ego and power struggles often occur. Couples who are approaching this milestone in their lives should look carefully at the upheaval this might cause in their relationship. They need to take steps to lessen the perceived problems - before retirement! Have a serious talk with your husband so you can discuss these issues and resolve any potential problems *before* they happen.

Building Security

'An elderly couple live in a high-rise condominium building and they find that when they enter the building, others try to 'piggy-back' and get in without a key. This violates the security practices in their building. As the wife is small and elderly, she doesn't know whether she should take the chance of endangering herself by confronting them or whether she should just say nothing.'

If the person looks like the sort she could deal with, she should explain to them that she can't let others into the building - that it's a breach of the security rules of the building. Ask them to buzz their party on the intercom if they want to visit someone in the building.

If the person or persons appear menacing, she should go immediately to her resident manager. If these people take a lift, she should watch to see which floor they go to, so she has an idea where they've gone in the building. If the resident manager isn't there and she feels the people might be in the building for criminal reasons, she should call the police immediately.

Dealing with Difficult Situations

Dangerous Inaccessibility

'I had a frightening situation happen to me last month. I live in an apartment complex that has an intercom for entry into the building. Because youngsters played with the intercom during the night and bothered us so often, the management decided to have the main door to the building locked at 11:00 pm. This meant that if anyone wanted to visit someone in the building after that time, they couldn't contact them through the intercom. Instead, they'd have to phone their friends from a phone booth and their friends would have to come down and physically let them into the building.

This appeared to work well, until I became ill after midnight one night, while the rest of my family were away on holidays. I rang for an ambulance. They kept me on the line and became concerned when they found the ambulance drivers could not get into the building. It took over half an hour for them to gain entry to the building and this was only because a tenant came home and opened the door for them.

The day after, our building managers installed a lock box with a key to the building, just outside the main doors. Emergency services personnel were the only people with keys to this lock box so they could gain entry to our building after hours.'

For those of you who live in facilities that lock the main doors at night, you should consider this alternative in case of an emergency.

Heart Problems

'Last month my wife had a heart attack. She's home from the hospital now, but I find I don't sleep well at night. I haven't talked to her about it, but I'm afraid that I'll wake up one morning and find her dead in the bed beside me.'

This is understandable in those circumstances. Speak to her doctor to see how she's really doing and whether your fears are warranted. Take a CPR (coronary pulmonary resuscitation) course so you can act if she has another heart attack. Then if necessary, you can do your best to revive her.

If your wife is alone for a long time, you might get her an alert system that she wears around her neck that can summon help in

Dealing with Difficult Situations

seconds. This will not only make you feel better, but will make her feel as if she has more control if there is another emergency.

English as a second language

'My elderly neighbour is Chinese and comes from a decidedly different cultural background than me. I try hard to understand what he's saying, but I often can't understand him. He has the same problem understanding me. What can I do about this problem?'

Those whose second language is English, normally go through a complicated process until they become completely fluent in English:

Stage 1: They hear what you say in English.

Stage 2: They translate what you've said into their mother tongue.

Stage 3: They construct their answer in their own language.

Stage 4: They mentally translate it into English.

Stage 5: They give you a verbal reply in English.

You can see that this process takes time, so if you're conversing with someone whose second language is English, try to:

1. Use common language. You can't expect them to learn jargon or technical language right away.
2. Allow them time to go through the stages of interpretation to determine what you've said. The 'pregnant pause' between the end of your talking and the beginning of their answering, may be necessary for complete understanding on their part.
3. Watch their body language. If they give a helpless look or shrug their shoulders, you've lost them. Repeat what you said, trying different, more simplistic words.

Your neighbour also has a responsibility to try to lessen the problem. Encourage him to do his part by attending 'English as a Second Language' classes. Why not find out where they are held and see if he would be interested in attending a course.

Not important any more!

'My neighbour Bob has me concerned. His body language tells me that he's depressed. He shuffles along when I see him going to the store and I seldom see him working in the garden as he did before

his wife died. His spark for life seems to have gone out of him. Is there anything I can do to make him perk up?'

Just getting up in the morning is a chore for many seniors. The main cause is that they feel there's no meaning to their lives, they have nothing to get up for and have nothing to stimulate them into action. Depression is often the result.

When depression sets in, it triggers other responses. Suddenly people feel every ache and pain that can escalate into serious disabilities. Life takes on special meaning when seniors like what they're doing and have a good relationship with their friends and family. They seldom complain about their aches and pains.

Happy seniors are busy seniors. This mental and physical activity results in better mental and physical health that inevitably eliminates most of the daily aches and pains that plague many elderly. Society needs to give considerable effort towards keeping seniors active, happy and productive. Those employed in the recreational and travel areas will find their occupations becoming more and more valuable. This is due to the rising percentage of seniors who are truly living and enjoying their retirement.

Some seniors live in the past. They'll talk for hours about their childhood, but may not give the attention required to live in the present. Some believe that their past will always influence what happens in their future. They may use this as an excuse to avoid changing their behaviour. While it may be difficult to overcome past learning, it's not impossible. They need to realise that the past is important, but doesn't have to affect their future.

If life doesn't come up to their expectations, (because of lack of insight on their part) console them with the idea that it's never too late for conditions to change. Although some opportunities of youth may have passed, each phase of life brings its own compensations for those who seek them. Instead of dwelling on the past they need to concentrate their energy on building a better, happier life and making the most of the present moment.

Many people in this group state, *'I'm too old ... Not smart enough ... Not good at that.'* These people are stating, *'I'm a finished product in this area and I'm never going to be different.'*

Deal with this type of person by having a heart-to-heart talk with them identifying what you see them doing to themselves. Ask their

Dealing with Difficult Situations

permission to bring it to their attention when you hear them running themselves down or living in the past.

To help your neighbour with his negative feelings, suggest that he put a loose elastic band around his wrist and snap it (ouch) every time he catches himself using this type of destructive thinking. This negative reinforcement will keep him from dwelling on the past. By all means, encourage him not to hibernate - to get out, keep active and involved.

If you know he is good at something, ask his advice and suggest that others might want to have his help in that area. Do whatever you can to give him something to get up for in the morning.

Handling Grief

'My neighbour's wife passed away recently and her husband is having a terrible time adjusting to her death. Although he's in good physical shape, he's suffering emotionally. How can our family help him through this?'

Most of us don't know how to comfort a grieving friend. First pay attention to what your instincts say. If your first impulse is to phone or visit him, don't put it off by the fear that you might be intruding on his privacy. He'll probably appreciate your concern. Let him know how very sorry you are, but don't use phrases like, *'I know just how you feel,'* unless you've very recently lost a close loved one yourself.

Listen carefully to what he says. If he reveals that he doesn't know how he'll get through the days without his loved one - resist the desire to cheer him up or offer advice. What he requires right now is the opportunity of talking about his concerns - not on you providing answers.

Resist statement such as *'Don't feel that way.'* Or, *'This feeling is only temporary; the situation will improve with time.'* Many grieving people feel they should have done something to prevent the loved one's death, so there's an element of guilt. Telling him that his feelings are wrong, may only cause him to bury his feelings instead of resolving them.

People grieve, not only because a close friend or relative has died, but because of any serious loss. They grieve because a good friend moves away; they're laid off or fired from a job they love; they lose

Dealing with Difficult Situations

a limb, their eyesight or hearing; they have a financial disaster; a romantic relationship breaks up; they divorce or lose custody of their children. The pain can be intense, but no matter what the loss and the grieving process remains the same. The only part that changes is the degree of grief the person suffers.

The six stages of the grieving process can last varying lengths of time. These stages are:

- An overwhelming feeling of loss.
- Shock and denial *('This can't be happening to me!')*
- Emotional upheaval (mood-swings and depression).
- Withdrawal (lick their wounds in solitude).
- Understanding of loss (acceptance).
- Hope (things will get better).

Those suffering from grief may put up barricades to hide their feelings from others and may need reassuring words before they'll let others comfort them physically. For example: At a funeral, a close family friend tries to comfort the grieving widower. They try to give him a hug, but find him rigid and unresponsive and he appears to push them away. What's happening here? If you were offering condolences, you might feel hurt by this perceived sign of rejection. You wonder if you should pursue and keep offering your support or should you back off and let him grieve in private.

What's likely happening is he may feel too vulnerable to trust others with his feelings. He's afraid he'll 'fall apart' if he feels one *more* strong emotion. Therefore, he seems to repel others and physically push them away or remains rigid when others try to comfort him. If you're a close friend or relative, please don't give up; watch for non-verbal signs that he's ready for and needs comforting.

In later visits with him, try again to see if he's past his emotional upheaval. Watch his body language and reactions. If you perceive that he's still hurting and appears to need comforting, put your hand on his arm. If he doesn't pull away, put your hand on his shoulder. Again, if he doesn't pull away, attempt again to give him a hug expressing your wish to comfort him. When he's ready for comforting, he'll show you by his reactions. He may finally allow himself to sob and cry, knowing that there's someone else available to help him through his sorrow.

Some people may never allow others to comfort them physically - they're not comfortable with hugs and physical signs of affection. However, keep voicing your support and do all those little things that show how much you care about him. Just having your strength nearby might be what he needs to progress through the grieving process. Nobody should have to handle this transition alone. Be there when he needs you.

We're taking away your driver's licence!

'We're sorry, but we can't renew your driver's licence. Your peripheral vision and depth perception have deteriorated to a stage where it's unsafe for you to be driving.'

Dr. Teale had the distasteful task of informing a spirited, independent, seventy-two year old gentleman that his peripheral vision and depth perception had deteriorated to the stage where it was unsafe for him to drive. He had been contacted by George's daughter, who expressed her concerns that her father's ability to drive had diminished considerably in the last year. She had broached the topic with her father herself, but he had scoffed at her suggestion that he quit driving. His medical diagnosis confirmed that George's vision was not keen enough to enable him to drive.

How could Dr. Teale tell this highly independent man that he was going to have to be dependent on others for most of his transportation? He had been warned that George would be hostile and angry and might even refuse to comply.

'We're sorry, but we can't renew your driver's licence because you're not capable of driving any more!' This is the sentence that spells the loss of independence to many seniors. It's the final sign that they're really getting old. Many sink into a deep depression or become rebellious and refuse to comply.

Removal of driving privileges, for those who have had this valuable independence their entire adult lives, is comparable to putting them in jail. Many withdraw into themselves and become hermits, because they assert that, *'I'm not going to depend on others to get me around! I'd rather stay home!'*

I can't blame seniors for feeling despair when this happens. Being able to drive, spells independence and that independence was just removed from them. However, there are many ways seniors can deal

Dealing with Difficult Situations

with this. If they're handicapped, they could consider using a handi-bus. If they're mobile but don't have good bus service in their area, they could consider moving into a downtown condominium where they could take a bus to their destinations.

I always encourage the children of seniors who have lost this independence, to make gifts such as, *'This certificate is worth three trips to the shopping centre.'* Or, *'This entitles the bearer to one month of chauffeured driving to shopping and social events.'* In exchange, seniors could repay the favour by giving out certificates of their own stating, *'One free babysitting session.'* Or, *'One knit sweater for three rides.'* Or, *'One birdhouse for five rides.'*

Another choice is to have a charge account with a taxi company that you can use at your convenience. Try car-pooling to go shopping and visiting using a senior driver who still has his or her driver's licence. Be sure to pay your share.

I want to go to a deserted island!

'There are times when I'd like to go off to a desert island, rather than face all the problems I have with my children, their spouses, their children and step-children! I wish I could divorce them all!'

There have been some landmark cases that have allowed a child to divorce his or her parents or parents have given their children up for adoption, but most of us are 'stuck' with the relatives we're born with. Then, when we marry, we inherit all our new spouse's relatives! If our marriage breaks up, these relatives will likely remain part of our lives because of the children of our union. This is why it's so important to make that extra effort to get along with difficult relatives and in-laws.

Grandparents too, have had to adjust to the shift in traditional roles. They now have family units that include children, step-children, daughter and sons-in-law, their parents and step-parents and all the problems that accompany those relationships. With forty per cent of marriages ending in divorce, the role of grandparents is changing. Unfortunately, some grandparents lose contact with their grandchildren when the custodial parent moves away or an estranged son or daughter-in-law won't let the grandparents have access to their grandchildren.

Dealing with Difficult Situations

Other grandparents have the opposite and find themselves back in the parenting roll they felt was over when their children grew up. These grandparents find themselves in the middle of the dropping-off-and-picking-up routine when the custodial parent needs economical day care or after-school tending of their children. In many cultures, extended families are the norm and grandparents provide this care, whether the parents' divorce or stay together. However, in many modern societies, this just isn't an option, because of the distance between grandparents, their children and grandchildren or the grandparents themselves work during the day.

Step-Children

'I'm the parent of a child who has married a partner and now has step-children. I don't know how to deal with these children.'

Grandparents may find themselves in the middle, when their son or daughter re-marries and they find that they don't really like the new partner. More and more parents may find themselves contending with the new spouse's children (their step-grandchildren) as well as their own grandchildren. Staying impartial to the needs of all their grandchildren and step-grandchildren can be a substantial challenge.

Holidays are uniquely difficult for many grandparents of divorced or extended step-families. It's often situations that should be the happiest where trouble surfaces. Here are some tips on how to smooth the waters when family gatherings bring mixed family groups together in your home:

1. Keep your negative feelings of unease, jealousy (or whatever) in check.
2. Don't go overboard and try too hard. Because it takes a family group five years to click - don't expect miracles. Accept people for what they are, not what you wish they would be.
3. Be willing to compromise; bend with the needs of the entire group.
4. Try to determine the timing of visits long before the holidays.
5. Try to get to know the new members of your family. Remember to keep an open mind.
6. Have a toy or activity box that includes activities that will help amuse all the children during visits.

7. Find something to praise in each member (authentic only - there's always some endearing quality you should be able to identify).
8. Don't over-extend yourself - ask for other's help and be sure to acknowledge their help.
9. If the visit is an extended one - separate the group occasionally. Everyone needs 'private time.' Ensure that there is somewhere you and your visitors can go to have some time to themselves.
10. If arguments erupt between adult members of the family, give them time to settle their dispute (if possible in private, away from younger members of the family who may be traumatised by their arguing). If necessary step in and say, *'If you wish to argue, please do so elsewhere. You're disturbing me and I'm sure you're disturbing others as well.'* If they continue to argue, ask them to leave.

Undisciplined grandchildren

'I live with my son, his wife and three children. This became necessary when I broke my hip last year. I'm doing much better now and I've contemplated trying it on my own again. My present problem is trying to deal with my undisciplined grandchildren. They come into my bedroom without knocking and when I'm not there they ransack my room. They've broken several of my belongings, but don't seem to show any remorse. Last week at dinner, I decided to say something about it. I bawled them about for their destructiveness and forbade them to come into my room unless I invited them. My daughter-in-law has been very cool to me since then. Was I wrong to protect my belongings and to expect the children to respect others possessions?'

I can't blame you for guarding your possessions. I've felt the same way myself when parents bring unruly children into my home. If children spill their milk or break something accidentally, I'm the first to forgive them. But if it's wilful or careless behaviour, I speak up. If the children needed guidance and their parents don't provide it, you had every right to chastise them because they were rough with your possessions.

Speak to your daughter-in-law. Tell her exactly what happened. Stick to the facts and tell her what they broke, when and how. Then ask her what she thinks would be a solution to the children's disregard for the importance of respecting other's possessions.

You also might ask yourself if her coolness might not be a result of accumulated agitation because of other difficulties in your relationship with her. Have you tried to help out enough or have you 'helped' out too much (interfering with her 'space'). There could be underlying problems here and the only way to bring them to the surface is through open discussion. As a last resort, you could follow your plan and try it on your own again.

Clinging to son

'My wife accuses our son's wife of 'stealing her son' from her and that he doesn't spend enough time with her. I can see that he's spread so thin now with business and home responsibilities that he simply can't give her any more of his time. I've noticed that he seems to feel very guilty when she pouts and complains to him. How can I deal with this ongoing problem?'

Your son should straighten his backbone and talk to her himself. Your son should explain that his wife hasn't 'stolen' him from her; that his wife is his full-time partner and is simply taking her correct place at his side. If he won't do it, then it will be up to you to enlighten her.

You could add, *'When you complain about the length of time our son spends with you, he must feel stretched like an elastic band. From what I've observed of his responsibilities, that elastic band has been stretched as far as it can go. He has obligations to others both at work and at home that he must meet. This has no bearing on the time he spends with you. He has lots of love to go around and each love is different. For instance, he has his love for you, his love for his wife, his brothers and sisters, his children and his love for his friends. One does not overshadow the other and are all important people to him. If you keep smothering him, you'll just make his time constraints that much harder on him and he'll end up resenting your interference.'*

Either you or your son should consider giving your wife an itinerary of what he has to do (including driving Jimmy to hockey, Susie to Brownies) and how difficult it is to spend more time with her.

You can help by finding activities that will keep her occupied. It sounds as if she's channelling all her energies towards her grown children. This could be the real challenge and both you and your son would benefit if you both attack this problem.

Dealing with Difficult Situations

Whiners, Bellyachers and Complainers

'The woman in the room next to me in the nursing home is a negative-thinking person who is constantly complaining about something. I get tired of hearing her beefs, but because she lives so close, I have to see her quite regularly. How can I get her to see how she affects people around her?'

This type of person is part of a group of chronic gripers who grumble about everything - publicly and privately. They're cry babies who voice protracted protests over the unimportant. Driven by childish insecurity, they complain when everything's actually going well. They love to exaggerate unfair conditions - whatever they can blame on somebody else. When whiners warn you of trouble ahead, their intent is to establish an excuse in advance of a feared failure. Here are the steps you can take the next time she whines.

1. Get her permission to let you help her find solutions to her problems. *'I've heard you talking about these problems several times and you don't seem to have found solutions for them. Do you want me to see what I can do to help you solve these problems?'* If she refuses to let you help her solve her problems state, *'Well, if you won't let me help you, I don't want to discuss this issue again.'* If she agrees to let you help her, have her:
2. Write down the problem including all necessary details. Make a separate list for each problem (there will probably be several). Deal with only one problem at a time.
3. Write down all the possible solutions to the problem. At this point *you* can suggest additional solutions.
4. Write the pros (benefits) and cons (disadvantages) under each solution. Encourage her to be unemotional. Have her pretend the situation is happening to someone else and she's helping them determine the benefits and disadvantages of each solution.
5. Have her choose the best solution. This is the stage where she'll likely ask you, *'What do you think I should do?'* If you *do* suggest a solution and it doesn't work, she'll probably say, *'I told you it wouldn't work!'* (This type of person loves to pass-the-buck to someone else for their problems.) So *she* must choose the best solution - not you!
6. Help her set some concrete goals that will make the solution happen. Include deadlines for their completion. This will keep

Dealing with Difficult Situations

her from procrastinating. After step 6 she's on her own. If she complains to you again about the problem:

7. Say, *'Why are we discussing this again? You know exactly what you have to do to solve this problem and you've chosen to do nothing about it. I don't want to hear another word about this situation except to hear that you've resolved the problem.'*

This process stops whiners, complainers and bellyachers from going on and on about the same problem. It also forces them to solve their problems - not just beef about them. If you find yourself complaining too much, try this process for yourself. It will help you have a more positive attitude towards your ability to handle life's problems.

Role Reversal

'My father died recently and my ailing mother now lives with us causing lots of problems. My husband and I have no privacy and no time for ourselves.'

Often those in their forties who are still responsible for growing children, find they have the added responsibility of caring for aging parents as well. These aging parents might have married late in life and find that their own children are still seeing their fledglings leave the nest. These middle children might feel pulled at both ends by the needs of both their children and their parents. They may wonder when they'll have time to spend on activities they want to do themselves. In other families, by the time the grandchildren have grown, the parents can spend more time, energy and effort on not only their own needs, but those of their parents.

The change in roles - children looking after parents and parents becoming dependent on children, is a transition for all involved. Suddenly the parental support the grown children had expected and had counted on to last throughout their lifetime has disappeared. Some feel as if life has cheated them; they feel adrift without this support system.

As one woman put it, *'I knew in my heart that having my widowed father come to live with us a year ago wouldn't work out. This is because with non-family members, he always appears happy, but with his immediate family he's always been a difficult person to deal with.'*

From the beginning, she felt pulled four ways by the needs of her children and husband, her job and the extra demands of her father, who expected her to wait on him hand and foot. Though he could help, the only contribution he made to the smooth-running of their home was a small portion of his pension cheque - but never his time and effort. Why should he? He'd never lifted a hand to help around the home during his marriage - so why should he start now? His daughter had talked to him often about his lack of co-operation, but he refused to listen. Because of his stubborn attitude, it's no wonder she finally had to make alternate arrangements for his care.

Women do most of the looking-after of elderly parents regardless of whether these are her own parents or her spouses' parents. Most have full-time jobs and children of their own. As the demands increase, the part of their life that suffers most is their fun time with friends, their children and their spouses. It also can have a heavy financial toll on the family if the woman has to give up her full- or part-time job to become a parent's full-time caregiver. Even when the burden of the 'hands-on care' is over and the parent is in a nursing home, she remains the parent's watchdog. She's the defender of their rights and protector of their well-being.

Some caregivers of elderly parents find the pressures so intense that they're driven to abusive practices such as:

- Cheating them financially;
- Mistreating them emotionally or physically; and
- Cutting them off from seeing their friends.

For many caregivers the only respite they may have, is taking their parents to adult day care centres or have Meals on Wheels provide some of their meals. Caregivers must monitor their own actions and ask for professional help if the pressures cause any of the above serious complications.

Fortunately, many companies have begun to explore the types of help they can offer to employees who must look after elderly parents. Some consider flexible work schedules or sabbatical leave for employees who need time off to care for elderly relatives.

Dealing with Difficult Situations

I won't fight, but I won't give in either!

'My mother-in-law has got manipulation down to a science. I've had it up to here ... with her antics. Why can't she be more direct with us?'

Helen (a manipulator) lives in the household of her son Bob and daughter-in-law Emily.

Emily wants to re-decorate their family room by purchasing woven basket chairs with big pillows. They could use the pillows for sitting on the floor in front of the fireplace. Helen (the mother-in-law) prefers a comfortable lounge suite.

The following conversation takes place.

Emily: *'Some of those fabrics on the pillows I saw yesterday are beautiful.'*

Helen: *'Are they made of cotton?'*

Emily: *'Yes they are.'*

Helen: *'They'll soon show the dirt and they'll probably shrink when you wash them.'*

Emily: *'Well, maybe we could look for other kinds of fabric and cover them ourselves?'*

Helen: *'You should have that done professionally. Besides, anything that sits around on the floor will start looking terrible soon. (Wearily) But, if that's what you want, get them.'*

Emily: *'Well, I like big pillows. Is there anything you particularly want?'* (Leaving the door open for Helen to say what she really wants.)

Helen: *'Not exactly. Furniture should be sensible and made to last. But it's your house - do what you like, I can always sit in the lounge room.'* (Poor me!)

Later Helen reported to a friend that she was not the kind of mother-in-law who bothered her children with her opinions. Yet, Helen didn't support anyone else's ideas, unless they happened to be the same as hers.

Dealing with Difficult Situations

Emily needs to talk to Helen about her manipulation and encourage her to be more direct when she's asked if she wants something done a particular way. When Helen tried to throw the guilt-trip on her, *'It's your house. Do what you like; I can always sit in the lounge room.'*

Emily should have replied with, *'You're trying to make me feel responsible for how you feel. Why do you feel you would want to sit in the lounge room?'*

Deal with this type of person by identifying that she *is* trying to manipulate you and call her on her behaviour. Explain what happens to you when she acts this way and ensure her that you *will* listen to what she has to say.

The sufferer - or 'After all I've done for you!'

'My wife Jill gives in to our children when they ask her to do things for her. I know she doesn't want to do these things, but she does them anyway. However, her sighs and martyred expressions drive me around the bend! If she doesn't want to do the favours - why doesn't she say so?'

The sufferer gets what she wants by sending indirect messages. This is a form of passive resistance. These passive people are trying to be more assertive in their behaviour – but don't quite know how. So they may play the martyr, act overworked, persecuted or totally dependent. They sigh a lot and utter indirect complaints. They're trying to say, *'If you appreciated me or even noticed everything I do for you, you'd want to do more for me.'*

For example: Jill's daughter Susan phoned her at eight o'clock in the morning to say that the entire family had slept in and she needed her to drive her son to school that morning. Susan knew that her mother lived only a couple of blocks away and would have time to do this for them.

Jill replied, *'Susan, I've driven Joey to school twice this month already.'*

Susan, *'Oh Mum! Please?'*

Jill (letting out a big sigh), *'Oh, all right!'*

Her tone of voice and speech insinuates, *'Just look at the sacrifices I make for you. If you loved me more, you'd appreciate me more!?'*

Dealing with Difficult Situations

If you have to deal with this type of person, remember that you have a choice as to whether you do or do not accept the guilt they're trying to give to you. Describe what you see her doing and ask that she be more direct when she communicates with you. Say, *'Your comments show me that you're trying to make me feel guilty about .... Is that true?'* If there's some truth to their statements, try to rectify the situation.

Explain what your wife's body language tells others. Encourage her to attend an assertiveness training course so she'll be able to stand up for herself. However, be prepared to have her stand up to you as well, if you ask her to do something she doesn't want to do!

Can't Wake Up

'My wife just can't wake herself up in the morning and is constantly wasting half her day by spending it in bed. She admits that this is a serious problem for her. How can I help her get motivated to get up in the morning?'

Research shows that millions of people have serious difficulty waking up in the morning; some because they have nothing to get up for and others because they are 'owls.' The first problem occurs in far too many seniors who feel that life is over for them. They literally put in time until they die. These seniors must get the spark back into their lives so they have something to get up for. For some, this can simply be helping others more unfortunate than they or simply keeping themselves busy with projects.

In the case of owls (as sleep experts call them) they're no lazier than anyone else, but they *are* different. They need more or better quality sleep than they're getting. The most common reason for not being able to get up is that they haven't finished sleeping yet.

The 'night-owl syndrome' is one of the commonest causes of poor morning functioning. Its frustrated victims don't need more sleep than other people, but they need it at times (normally from about 3 am to 11 am) that aren't compatible with the workaday world. For most individuals, body temperature is at its lowest during sleep, begins rising around dawn, peaks in the afternoon, then subsides. By 11 pm or midnight, drowsiness sets in. Night owls, on the other hand, usually don't achieve peak temperature and performance levels until evening; thus, this low sleep-inducing body temperature doesn't arrive until the wee hours of the morning.

Dealing with Difficult Situations

Night-owls can escalate bedtime on a progressive schedule where they go to bed one hour earlier than the previous night for seven successive nights and get up one hour earlier than usual in the morning until they finally work around to going to bed at eleven or so. Once they've re-set their internal clock this way, they must stick to it.

Pinpointing other sleeping problems can be difficult. For instance, take the following case. We'll call her Marge. For years she'd been waking up exhausted no matter how much sleep she had logged during the night. Her doctor could find nothing wrong, nor did tests at a sleep research centre turn up any clues to her fatigue. Finally, one doctor asked if her husband snored. *'Yes,'* she replied, *'I have to poke him once or twice a night.'*

Here at last was the key. Marge only remembered waking up once or twice, but her brain was aroused from its normal sleep pattern every time her husband snored. She was, in effect, 'waking up' 300 to 400 times a night. She solved her problem by insisting that her husband obtain laser treatments to combat his snoring problem.

Some sleep researchers believe that sleeping in a room that's too dark also may cause difficulties. Normally, the change from night to daytime brightness acts as nature's alarm clock. That's why it can be so hard to get up on those black winter mornings.

Many of the factors that leave us tired after a night's sleep are just that minor. For instance, a hot, stuffy room ensures restlessness, while a cold one makes it hard to emerge from the covers and face the day. The most comfortable bedtime temperature ranges from 18 - 20°C. Experts say that sleeping in a room that's too bright can confuse the brain, which wants to sleep yet is given the cue to wake up. Continued night after night, these mixed signals can result in morning exhaustion.

Noise is another culprit and it doesn't have to be very loud. One slow-starting friend of mine used to fall asleep to music. She learned that she was aroused many times during the night by changes in the volume of sound from her radio. Then she began switching off the radio the moment she felt drowsy and within a few days she was hopping out of bed without a backward glance.

Although regular physical activity promotes better sleeping and easier awakening, exercise immediately before bed is a stimulant.

Dealing with Difficult Situations

The exception to this rule is lovemaking, thought to be the best nightcap of all.

Not all wake-up problems are so easily dealt with. Stress of almost any kind, including dieting, may increase sleep requirements. The break-up of a relationship or any circumstance causing grief, anger or depression may cause a greater craving for sleep. If you can sleep in such instances, experts advise trying to get the extra hours but urge patients not to use sleep as a means of ignoring problems.

Always phoning

'My elderly mother calls me every night and I find myself on the phone for half an hour. This interferes with what my wife and I have planned for the evening. I hate to be rude to her, because I think I'm the only one she talks to all day.'

I've found that when people don't have something to get up for every morning, they're lethargic and depend on others to amuse them and keep them company. Please help this woman channel her nurturing impulses in other directions by:

- Helping an older neighbour who can't leave home to do her shopping.
- Introducing her to another single person who is lonely.
- Suggesting that she visit seniors in a retirement home who have no visitors.
- Getting a pet to keep her company and giving her something to get up for every day.
- Giving help to a young mother with 2 to 3 children who has to take her children shopping.
- Helping the young family who can't afford a babysitter to have some private social time for themselves.
- Getting her involved in community club activities.
- Helping newly arrived citizens find their way around your monetary system, how to get around in our city, agencies that can help them adjust, courses to help them speak our language better.
- Having her join a seniors' group.

Allergies

'I'm allergic to cats, but my parents have them. I can tolerate being in their home for short visits, but when their cat comes near me, I have a terrible time breathing. Is it proper for me to ask that they keep their pet in another room while I visit?'

This is something you should discuss with them in detail before you decide to visit them. Explain your problem and ask for their co-operation. You're likely allergic to the cat's dandruff that would be throughout your parent's home. The only alternatives might be to have them visit you in your environment, meet them in a neutral place such as a restaurant or they get rid of the cat. Give them the alternatives and let them decide which one they wish to take.

CONCLUSION

You now have many tools, techniques and ideas on how to handle difficult situations both at work and at home. These tools can empower you to deal with irate, rude, impatient, emotional, upset, persistent and aggressive people. These crucial people skills allow you to deal with all types of difficult people and circumstances. Learn these skills and you can't help but enhance your relationships with others.

Your proficiency in people skills will help you control your moods and keep you cool under fire. You'll start on the road to understanding why people interpret situations differently.

These techniques do work! But like any new skill, you'll have to use them unfailingly until they become spontaneous and automatic. If you do, you can look forward to being able to control how you deal with and react to others.

No longer will you allow others manipulate you or decide what kind of day you'll have by:

- Making you lose your cool;
- Forcing you to do things you don't want to do;
- Preventing you from doing what you want or need to do;
- Using coercion, manipulation or other underhanded methods to get their way;
- Making you feel guilty if you don't go along with their wishes;
- Making you feel anxious, upset, frustrated, angry, depressed, jealous, inferior, defeated, sad or any other negative feeling;
- Making you do their share of the work.

Because you've gained this control, your self-esteem level will raise accordingly. The more self-assured you are, the less stress and apprehension you'll feel, which will give you more stamina and enthusiasm. The rest is up to you. Use these skills and brace yourself for the success that will inevitably follow.

You'll find more techniques and ideas in my first book that has been an international best-seller since 1990:

Dealing with Difficult People – How to deal with nasty customers, demanding bosses and uncooperative colleagues

And other sequels:

Dealing with Difficult Spouses and Children;

Dealing with Difficult Relatives and In-Laws.

You might also be interested in my bullying sequels entitled:

Dealing with Workplace Bullies - Society's Corporate Disgrace!

Dealing with School Bullies – Society's Educational Disgrace! and

Dealing with Domestic Violence and Child Abuse – Society's Judicial Disgrace!

BIBLIOGRAPHY

Cava, Roberta, *Dealing with Difficult People: How to deal with nasty customers, demanding bosses and uncooperative colleagues* (22 publishers - 16 languages)

Dealing with difficult Relatives and In-laws; Dealing with Difficult Spouses & Children; Dealing with Workplace Bullying; Dealing with School Bullying; and *Dealing with Domestic Violence and Child Abuse.*

Eckman, Paul, *Why kids die;* Penguin Books, 1989.

Fleming, Don, *How to stop battling with your child;* Prentice Hall, 1989; and *How to stop battling with your teenager:* Prentice Hall, 1989.

Gray, Dr. John, *Mars & Venus: Starting Over;* Pan Macmillan, Australia, 1998.

Killinger, Barbara, *Workaholics -* **The Respectable Addicts;** Key Porter Books, Toronto, 1990

Rapoport, Judith, *The boy who couldn't stop washing;* Dutton, 1980.

Tannen, Deborah, *You just don't understand; Women and Men in Conversation;* Morrow, 1990.

Uly, William, *Getting past No;* **Negotiating with Difficult People;** NY, Toronto, Bantom Books, 1991.

Woititz, Dr. Janet G. *The Intimacy Struggle;* Health Communications, 1993.

www.ingramcontent.com/pod-product-compliance
Lightning Source LLC
Chambersburg PA
CBHW071307110426
42743CB00042B/1202